BLOOM'S

HOW TO WRITE ABOUT

Shakespeare's Tragedies

PAUL GLEED

Introduction by Harold Bloom

BLOOM'S
LITERARY CRITICISM
An imprint of Infobase Publishing

Bloom's How to Write about Shakespeare's Tragedies

Bloom's Literary Criticism
An imprint of Infobase Publishing
132 West 31st Street
New York NY 10001

Library of Congress Cataloging-in-Publication Data

Gleed, Paul.
  Bloom's how to write about Shakespeare's tragedies / Paul Gleed ; introduction by Harold Bloom.
       p. cm. — (Bloom's how to write about literature)
  Includes bibliographical references and index.
  ISBN 978-1-60413-704-0
  1. Shakespeare, William, 1564–1616—Tragedies. 2. English drama (Comedy)—History and criticism. 3. Criticism—Authorship. 4. Tragedy—History and criticism. I. Bloom, Harold. II. Title.
  PR2983.G57 2010
  822.3'3—dc22   2010018554

Bloom's Literary Criticism books are available at special discounts when purchased in bulk quantities for businesses, associations, institutions, or sales promotions. Please call our Special Sales Department in New York at (212)967-8800 or (800)322-8755.

You can find Bloom's Literary Criticism on the World Wide Web at
http://www.chelseahouse.com

Text design by Annie O'Donnell
Cover design by Ben Peterson
Composition by Mary Susan Ryan-Flynn
Cover printed by Art Print Company, Taylor, PA
Book printed and bound by Maple Press, York, PA
Date printed: November 2010
Printed in the United States of America

10 9 8 7 6 5 4 3 2 1

All links and Web addresses were checked and verified to be correct at the time of publication. Because of the dynamic nature of the Web, some addresses and links may have changed since publication and may no longer be valid.

CONTENTS

SERIES INTRODUCTION

BLOOM's How to Write about Literature series is designed to inspire students to write fine essays on great writers and their works. Each volume in the series begins with an introduction by Harold Bloom, meditating on the challenges and rewards of writing about the volume's subject author. The first chapter then provides detailed instructions on how to write a good essay, including how to find a thesis; how to develop an outline; how to write a good introduction, body text, and conclusions; how to cite sources; and more. The second chapter provides a brief overview of the issues involved in writing about the subject author and then a number of suggestions for paper topics, with accompanying strategies for addressing each topic. Succeeding chapters cover the author's major works.

The paper topics suggested in this book are open ended, and the brief strategies provided are designed to give students a push forward on the writing process rather than a road map to success. The aim of the book is to pose questions, not answer them. Many different kinds of papers could result from each topic. As always, the success of each paper will depend completely on the writer's skill and imagination.

HOW TO WRITE ABOUT SHAKESPEARE'S TRAGEDIES: INTRODUCTION

by Harold Bloom

TRAGEDY, which flourished in ancient Athens, achieved its apotheosis in eight plays by Shakespeare: *Romeo and Juliet, Julius Caesar, Hamlet, Othello, King Lear, Macbeth, Antony and Cleopatra, Coriolanus.* The dramas of Aeschylus, Sophocles, and Euripides and Shakespeare's grandest works set a standard for tragedy that only Racine and Kleist later were able to attain.

There is a labyrinth of ways to write about Shakespeare's tragedies of blood: *Hamlet, Othello, King Lear, Macbeth.* Trying to be helpful, I will isolate a single strand: the development of the hero-villain persona from Christopher Marlowe's pioneering ventures on to Shakespeare's astonishing triumphs: Iago, Edmund in *King Lear,* Macbeth.

The Marlovian hero-villain begins with Tamburlaine the Great and culminates with Barabas in *The Jew of Malta.* Shakespeare served a kind of apprenticeship to Marlowe with Aaron the Moor in *Titus Andronicus* and with *Richard III,* both clearly indebted to *The Jew of Malta.*

You can argue that the counter-Machiavel Hamlet has elements in him of the hero-villain, though they are transfigured into a virtually transcendental form. It is with Iago, Edmund, and Macbeth that Shakespeare achieved an extraordinary triumph over Marlowe and such other contemporaries as Thomas Kyd and Thomas Middleton.

After Shakespeare, there are other great hero-villains in the language, all dependent on him: Milton's Satan in *Paradise Lost,* Melville's Captain Ahab in *Moby-Dick,* Chillingworth in Hawthorne's *The Scarlet Letter,* Shrike in Nathanael West's *Miss Lonelyhearts,* Judge Holden in Cormac McCarthy's *Blood Meridian,* Roy Cohn in Tony Kushner's *Angels in America.*

The hero-villain practices the art of Marlovian "pathetical persuasion," a rhetoric that carries "the argument of arms" into overwhelming stage eloquence. Iago and Edmund derive from Hamlet's sinuous analytic dexterity, carried by Iago to an astonishing negation:

> IAGO: And what's he then that says I play the villain,
> When this advice is free I give, and honest,
> Probal to thinking, and indeed the course
> To win the Moor again? For 'tis most easy
> Th' inclining Desdemona to subdue
> In any honest suit; she's fram'd as fruitful
> As the free elements. And then for her
> To win the Moor, were['t] to renounce his baptism.
> All seals and symbols of redeemed sin,
> His soul is so enfetter'd to her love,
> That she may make, unmake, do what she list,
> Even as her appetite shall play the god
> With his weak function. How am I then a villain,
> To counsel Cassio to this parallel course,
> Directly to his good? Divinity of hell!
> When devils will the blackest sins put on,
> They do suggest at first with heavenly shows,
> As I do now; for while this honest fool
> Plies Desdemona to repair his fortune,
> And she for him pleads strongly to the Moor,
> I'll pour this pestilence into his ear—

> That she repeals him for her body's lust,
> And by how much she strives to do him good,
> She shall undo her credit with the Moor.
> So will I turn her virtue into pitch,
> And out of her own goodness make the net
> That shall enmesh them all.

This is so persuasive that it all but burns away context, the consequence being that even Iago loses perspective. Compared to Iago, Edmund in *King Lear* is the most attractive of Jacobean hero-villains and yet is just as deadly. His freedom from hypocrisy charms us, but his aura is fatal, for others and for himself.

Macbeth is the perfection of the hero-villain in Shakespeare and so in all of imaginative literature. The Shakespearean tragic imagination attains its sublime in Macbeth's language:

>   Present fears
> Are less than horrible imaginings.
> My thought, whose murder yet is but fantastical,
> Shakes so my single state of man that function
> Is smothered in surmise, and nothing is
> But what is not.

The pathos of the hero-villain can never surpass that controlled phantasmagoria.

HOW TO WRITE
A GOOD ESSAY

by Laurie A. Sterling and Paul Gleed

WHILE THERE are many ways to write about literature, most assignments for high school and college English classes call for analytical papers. In these assignments, you are presenting your interpretation of a text to your reader. Your objective is to interpret the text's meaning in order to enhance your reader's understanding and enjoyment of the work. Without exception, strong papers about the meaning of a literary work are built upon a careful, close reading of the text or texts. Careful, analytical reading should always be the first step in your writing process. This volume provides models of such close, analytical reading, and these should help you develop your own skills as a reader and as a writer. As the examples throughout this book demonstrate, attentive reading entails thinking about and evaluating the formal (textual) aspects of the author's works: theme, character, form, and language. In addition, when writing about a work, many readers choose to move beyond the text itself to consider the work's cultural context. In these instances, writers might explore the historical circumstances of the time period in which the work was written. Alternatively, they might examine the philosophies and ideas that a work addresses. Even in cases where writers explore a work's cultural context, though, papers must still address the more formal aspects of the work itself. A good interpretative essay that evaluates Charles Dickens's use of the philosophy of utilitarianism in his novel

1

Hard Times, for example, cannot adequately address the author's treatment of the philosophy without firmly grounding this discussion in the book itself. In other words, any analytical paper about a text, even one that seeks to evaluate the work's cultural context, must also have a firm handle on the work's themes, characters, and language. You must look for and evaluate these aspects of a work, then, as you read a text and as you prepare to write about it.

WRITING ABOUT THEMES

Literary themes are more than just topics or subjects treated in a work; they are attitudes or points about these topics that often serve to structure other elements in a work. Writing about theme, then, requires not just that you identify a topic that a literary work addresses, but that you discuss what that work says about that topic. For example, if you were writing about the culture of the American South in William Faulkner's famous story "A Rose for Emily," you would need to discuss what Faulkner says, argues, or implies about that culture and its passing.

When you prepare to write about thematic concerns in a work of literature, you will probably discover that, like most works of literature, your text touches upon other themes in addition to its central theme. These secondary themes also provide rich ground for paper topics. A thematic paper on "A Rose for Emily" might consider gender or race in the story. While neither of these could be said to be the central theme of the story, they are clearly related to the passing of the "old South," and could provide plenty of material for good papers.

As you prepare to write about themes in literature, you might find a number of strategies helpful. After you identify a theme or themes in the story, you should begin by evaluating how other elements of the story—like character, point of view, imagery, and symbolism—help to develop the theme. You might ask yourself what your own responses are to the author's treatment of the subject matter. Do not neglect the obvious, either: what expectations does the title set up? How does the title help develop thematic concerns? Clearly, the title of "A Rose for Emily" says something about the narrator's attitude toward the title character, Emily Grierson, and all she represents.

WRITING ABOUT CHARACTERS

Generally, characters represent essential components of fiction and drama. (This is not always the case, though; Ray Bradbury's "August 2026: There Will Come Soft Rains" is technically a story without characters, at least any human characters). Often, you can discuss character in poetry. (T. S. Eliot's "The Love Song of J. Alfred Prufrock," comes to mind, as does Robert Browning's "My Last Duchess.") Many writers find that analyzing character is one of the most interesting and engaging ways to work with a piece of literature and to shape a paper. After all, generally characters are human, and we all know something about being human and living in the world. While it is always important to remember that these figures are not real people but creations of the writer's imagination, it can be fruitful to begin evaluating them as you might evaluate a real person. Often you can start with your own response to a character. Did you like or dislike the character? Did you sympathize with the character? Why or why not?

Keep in mind, though, that emotional responses like these are just starting places. In order to truly explore and evaluate literary characters, you need to return to the formal aspects of the text and evaluate how the author has drawn these characters. The twentieth-century writer E. M. Forster coined the terms "flat" characters and "round" characters. Flat characters are static, one-dimensional characters who frequently represent a particular concept or idea. In contrast, "round" characters, who are fully drawn and much more realistic, frequently change and develop over the course of a work. Are the characters you are studying flat or round? What elements of the characters lead you to this conclusion? Why might the author have drawn characters like this? How does their development affect the meaning of the work? Similarly, you should explore the techniques the author uses to develop characters. Do we hear a character's own words, or do we hear only other characters' assessments of him/her? Or, does the author use an omniscient or limited omniscient narrator to allow us access to the workings of the character's minds? If so, how does that help to develop the characterization? Often you can even evaluate the narrator as a character. How trustworthy are the opinions and assessments of the narrator? You should also think about characters' names. Do they mean anything? If you encounter a heroine named Sophia or Sophie, you should probably think about her wisdom (or lack thereof) since "Sophia" means wisdom in Greek. Similarly, since the name Sylvia is derived from the word "Sylvan," meaning "of the wood," you might want to evaluate that character's relationship with nature. Once again, you might look to the title of the work. Does Herman Melville's "Bartleby, the Scrivener" signal anything about Bartleby himself? Is Bartleby adequately defined by his job as scrivener? Is this part of Melville's point? Pursuing questions like these can help you develop thorough papers about characters from psychological, sociological, or more formalistic perspectives.

WRITING ABOUT FORM AND GENRE

Genre, a word derived from French, means "type" or "class." Literary genres are distinctive classes or categories of literary composition. On the most general level, literary works can be divided into the genres of drama, poetry, fiction, and essays. Yet, within those genres there are classifications that are also referred to as genres. Tragedy and comedy, for example, are genres of drama. Epic, lyric, and pastoral are genres of poetry. Form, on the other hand, generally refers to the shape or structure of a work. There are many clearly defined forms of poetry that follow specific patterns of meter, rhyme, and stanza. Sonnets, for example, are poems that follow a fixed form of fourteen lines. Sonnets generally follow one of two basic sonnet forms, each with its own distinct rhyme scheme. Haiku is another example of poetic form, traditionally consisting of three unrhymed lines of five, seven, and five syllables.

While you might think that writing about form or genre might leave little room for argument, many of these forms and genres are fluid. Remember that literature is evolving and ever changing and so are its forms. As you study poetry you may find that poets, especially more modern poets, play with traditional poetic forms, resulting in new effects. Similarly, dramatic tragedy was once quite narrowly defined, but over the centuries playwrights have broadened and challenged traditional definitions, changing the shape of tragedy. When Arthur Miller wrote Death of a Salesman, many critics challenged the idea that tragic drama could encompass a common man like Willy Loman.

Evaluating how a work of literature fits into or challenges the boundaries of its form or genre can provide you with fruitful avenues of investigation. Once again, you might find it helpful to ask why the work does or does not fit into traditional categories. Why might Miller have thought it fitting to write a tragedy of the common man? Similarly, you might compare the content or theme of a work with its form. How well do they work together? Many of Emily Dickinson's poems, for instance, follow the meter of traditional hymns. While some of her poems seem to express traditional religious doctrines, many seem to challenge or strain against traditional conceptions of God and theology. What is the effect, then, of her use of traditional hymn meter?

WRITING ABOUT LANGUAGE, SYMBOLS, AND IMAGERY

No matter what the genre, writers use words as their most basic tool. Language is the most fundamental building block of literature. It is essential, then, that you pay careful attention to the author's language and word choice as you read, reread, and analyze a text. Imagery is language that appeals to the senses. Most commonly, imagery appeals to our sense of vision, creating a mental picture, but authors also use language that appeals to our other senses. Images can be literal or figurative. Literal images use sensory language to describe some actual, real thing. In the broadest terms, figurative language uses one thing to speak about something else. For example, if I call my boss a snake, I am not saying that he is literally a reptile. Instead, I am using figurative language to communicate my opinions about him. Since we think of snakes as sneaky, slimy, and sinister, I am using the concrete image, snake, to communicate these abstract opinions and impressions.

The two most common figures of speech are similes and metaphors. Both are comparisons between two apparently dissimilar things. Similes are explicit comparisons using "like" or "as," and metaphors are implicit comparisons. To return to the previous example, if I say, "My boss, Bob, was waiting for me when I showed up to work five minutes late today—the snake!" I have constructed a metaphor.

Writing about his experiences fighting in World War I, Wilfred Owen begins his poem "Dulce Et Decorum Est" with a string of similes: "Bent double, like old beggars under sacks, / Knock-kneed, coughing like hags, we cursed through sludge." Owen's goal was to undercut clichéd notions that war and dying in battle were glorious. Certainly comparing soldiers to coughing hags and to beggars underscores his point.

"Fog," a short poem by Carl Sandburg provides clear example of a metaphor. Sandburg's poem reads:

> The fog comes
> on little cat feet.
>
>
> It sits looking
> over harbor and city
> on silent haunches
> and then moves on.

Notice how effectively Sandburg conveys surprising impressions of the fog by comparing two seemingly disparate things—the fog and a cat.

Symbols, by contrast, are things that stand for, or represent, other things. Often they represent something intangible, like concepts or ideas. In our everyday life we use and understand symbols easily. Babies at christenings and brides at weddings wear white to represent purity. Think, too, of a dollar bill. The paper itself has no value in and of itself. Instead, that paper bill is a symbol of something else, the precious metal in a nation's coffers. Symbols in literature work similarly. Authors use symbols to evoke more than a simple, straightforward literal meaning. Characters, objects, and places can all function as symbols. Famous literary examples of symbols include Moby Dick, the white whale of Herman Melville's novel, and the scarlet *A* of Nathaniel Hawthorne's *The Scarlet Letter*. As both of these symbols suggest, a literary symbol cannot be adequately defined or explained by any one meaning. Her Puritan community clearly intends Hester's *A* as a symbol of her adultery, but as the novel progresses, even her own community reads the letter as representing not just *adultery*, but *able, angel,* and a host of other meanings.

Writing about imagery and symbols requires close attention to the author's language. To prepare a paper on symbol or imagery in a work, try to identify and trace the images and symbols and then try to draw some conclusions about how they function. Ask yourself how any symbols or images help contribute to the themes or meanings of the work. What connotations do they carry? How do they affect your reception of the work?

Do they shed light on characters or settings? A strong paper on imagery or symbolism will thoroughly consider the use of figures in the text and will try to reach some conclusions about how or why the author uses them.

WRITING ABOUT HISTORY AND CONTEXT

As the opening paragraph noted, it is possible to write an analytical paper that also considers the work's context. After all, the text was not created in a vacuum. The author lived and wrote in a specific time period and in a specific cultural context, and like all of us, was shaped by his or her environment. Learning more about the historical and cultural circumstances that surround the author and the work can help illuminate a text and provide you with productive material for a paper. Remember, though, that when you write analytical papers, you should use the context to illuminate the text. Do not lose sight of your goal: to interpret the meaning of the literary work. Use historical or philosophical research as a tool to develop your textual evaluation.

Thoughtful readers often consider how history and culture affected the author's choice and treatment of his or her subject matter. Investigations into the history and context of a work could examine the work's relation to specific historical events like the Salem Witch Trials in 17th-century Salem, Massachusetts, or the restoration of Charles to the British throne in 1660. Bear in mind that historical context is not limited to politics and world events. While knowing about the Vietnam War is certainly helpful in interpreting much of Tim O'Brien's fiction, and some knowledge of the French Revolution clearly illuminates the dynamics of Charles Dickens's *A Tale of Two Cities,* historical context also entails the fabric of daily life. Examining a text in light of gender roles, race relations, class boundaries, or working conditions can give rise to thoughtful and compelling papers. Exploring the conditions of the working class in 19th-century England, for example, can provide a particularly effective avenue to write about Charles Dickens's *Hard Times.*

You can begin thinking about these issues by asking broad questions at first. What do you know about the time period and about the author? What does the editorial apparatus in your text tell you? These might be starting places. Similarly, when specific historical events or dynamics are particularly important to understanding a work but might be somewhat obscure to modern readers, textbooks usually provide notes to explain historical background. These are a good place to start. With this information, ask yourself how these historical facts and circumstances might have affected the author, the presentation of theme, or the presentation of character. How does knowing more about the work's specific historical context illuminate the work? To take a well-known example, understanding the complex attitudes toward slavery during the time Mark Twain wrote *Adventures of Huckleberry Finn* should help you begin to examine issues of race in the text. Additionally, you might compare these attitudes to those of the time in which the novel was set. How might this comparison affect your interpretation of a work written after the abolition of slavery, but set before the Civil War?

WRITING ABOUT PHILOSOPHY AND IDEAS

Philosophical concerns are closely related to both historical context and thematic issues. Like historical investigation, philosophical research can provide a useful tool as you analyze a text. For example, an investigation into the working class in Dickens's England might lead you to a topic on the philosophical doctrine of utilitarianism in *Hard Times*. Many other works explore philosophies and ideas quite explicitly. Mary Shelley's famous novel *Frankenstein*, for example, explores John Locke's *tabula rasa* theory of human knowledge as she portrays the intellectual and emotional development of Victor Frankenstein's creature. As this example indicates, philosophical issues are somewhat more abstract than investigations of theme or historical context. Some other examples of philosophical issues include human free will, the formation of human identity, and the nature of sin, or questions of ethics.

While writing about philosophy and ideas might require some outside research, usually the notes or other material in your text will provide you with basic information, and often footnotes and bibliographies suggest places you can go to read further about the subject. If you have identified a philosophical theme that runs through a text, you might ask yourself how the author develops this theme. Look at character development and the interactions of characters for example. Similarly, in fiction you might examine whether the narrative voice addresses the philosophical concerns of the text.

WRITING COMPARISON AND CONTRAST ESSAYS

Finally, you might find that comparing and contrasting the works or techniques of an author provides a useful tool for literary analysis. A comparison and contrast essay might compare two different characters or themes in a single work, or it might compare the author's treatment of a theme in two works. It might also contrast methods of character development or analyze an author's differing treatment of a philosophical concern in two works. Writing comparison and contrast essays, though, requires some special consideration. While they generally provide you with plenty of material to use, they also come with a built in trap: the laundry list. These papers often become mere lists of connections between the works. As this chapter will discuss, a strong thesis must make an assertion that you want to prove or validate. A strong comparison/contrast thesis, then, needs to comment on the *significance* of the similarities and/or the differences you observe. It is not enough to merely assert that the works contain similarities and/or differences. You might, for example, assert why the similarities and/or differences are important and explain how they illuminate the works' treatment of theme. Remember, too, that a thesis should not be a statement of the obvious. A comparison/contrast paper that focuses only on obvious similarities or differences does little to illuminate the connections between the works. Often, an effective method of shaping a strong thesis and argument is to begin your paper by noting the similarities between the works, but then to develop a thesis that asserts how these apparently similar elements are different. If, for example, you observe that Emily Dickinson wrote a number of poems about spiders, you might analyze how she uses spider imagery differently in two poems. Similarly, many scholars have noted that Hawthorne created many "mad scientist" characters, men who are so devoted to their science or their art that they lose perspective on all else. A good thesis comparing two of these characters—Aylmer of "The Birth-mark" and Dr. Rappaccini of "Rappaccini's Daughter," for example—might initially identify both characters as examples of Hawthorne's mad scientist type but then argue that their motivations for scientific experimentation differ. If you strive to analyze the similarities or differences, discuss significances, and move beyond the obvious, your paper should move beyond the laundry list trap.

PREPARING TO WRITE

Armed with a clear sense of your task—illuminating the text—and with an understanding of theme, character, language, history, and philosophy, you are ready to approach the writing process. Remember, that good writing is grounded in good reading, and that close reading takes time, attention, and more than one reading of your text. Read for comprehension first. As you go back and review the work, mark the text to chart the details of the work as well as your reactions. Highlight important passages, repeated words and image patterns. "Converse" with the text through marginal notes. Mark turns in the plot, ask questions, and make observations about characters, themes, and language. If you are reading from a book that does not belong to you, keep a record of your reactions in a journal or notebook. If you have read a work of literature carefully, with attention to both the text and the context of the work, you have a leg up on the writing process. Admittedly, at this point, your ideas are probably broad and undefined, but you have taken an important first step toward writing a strong paper.

Your next step is to focus, to take a broad, perhaps fuzzy, topic and define it more clearly. Even a topic provided by your instructor will need to be focused appropriately. Remember that good writers make the topic their own. There are a number of strategies—often called invention—that you can use to develop your own focus. One such strategy is called *freewriting*. In freewriting you spend ten minutes or so just writing about your topic without referring back to your text or your notes. Write whatever comes to mind; the important thing is that you just keep writing. Often this process allows you to develop new, fresh ideas or approaches to your subject matter. You could also try *brainstorming*. Write down your topic and then list all the related points or ideas you can think of. Include questions, comments, words, important passages or events, and anything else that comes to mind. Let one idea lead to another. In the related technique of *clustering*, or *mapping*, write your topic on a sheet of paper and write related ideas around it. Then list related subpoints under each of these main ideas. Many people then draw arrows to show connections between points. This technique helps narrow your topic and can also help you organize your ideas. Similarly, asking journalistic questions—Who?, What?, Where?, When?, Why?, and How?—can develop ideas for topic development.

Thesis Statements

Once you have developed a focused topic, you can begin to think about your thesis statement, the main point or purpose of your paper. It is absolutely imperative that you craft a strong thesis; otherwise your paper will likely be little more than random, disorganized observations about the text. Think of your thesis statement as a kind of road map of your paper. It tells your reader where you are going and how you are going to get there.

In order to craft a good thesis, you must keep a number of things in mind. First of all, as the title of this subsection indicates, your paper's thesis should be a statement, an assertion about the text that you want to prove or validate. Often beginning writers formulate a question that they attempt to use as a thesis. For example, a writer exploring the character of Shylock in *The Merchant of Venice* might ask, Although the Venetian Christians tell us that Shylock is a villain, does Shakespeare himself appear to agree? While a question like this is a good strategy to use in the invention process to help narrow your topic and find your thesis, it cannot serve as the thesis statement because it does not tell your reader what you want to assert about Shylock. A writer might shape this question into a thesis by instead proposing an answer to that question: Although the Venetian Christians tell us that Shylock is a villain, there is enough evidence in the play to suggest that Shakespeare has a much more complex, even sympathetic view of his character. We can see this not only in Shylock's statements of vulnerability and weakness, but also in the dubious, hypocritical conduct of the play's Christians. Notice that this thesis provides an initial plan or structure for the rest of the paper—I will spend some time establishing how the Venetian community perceives Shylock, then move into a discussion of scenes where Shylock's words reveal him to be a victim in his own right, and then finally into a section treating the portrait of the apparently "good" Christians of Venice who are really no better than Shylock. Notice, too, that the thesis statement does not necessarily have to fit into one sentence.

Secondly, remember that a good thesis makes an assertion that you need to support. In other words, a good thesis does not state the obvious. If you tried to formulate a thesis about *The Taming of the Shrew* by saying, The play is about gender relations, you have done nothing but state the obvious. This example gives the reader merely a theme, and a thesis is much more than a theme or subject. The thesis is what you have to say about your theme, of course. In other words, while your essay certainly can be about gender in *Shrew*, it must make a precise point about witchcraft. And, of course, the theme of gender in *Shrew* is a rich one that might stimulate many good thesis statements. For example: While many modern productions of *The Taming of the Shrew* set out to present a feminist interpretation of the play, one in which Kate winks knowingly as she ironically speaks her closing lines, there seems little evidence in the text for this modern reinvention of the play. Instead, it seems most likely that the play's comic resolution is intended as a celebratory return to the patriarchal order that Kate has threatened throughout the play.

As the comparison with the road map also suggests, your thesis should appear near the beginning of the paper. In relatively short papers (three to six papers) the thesis almost always appears in the first paragraph. Some writers fall into the trap of saving their thesis for the end, trying to provide a surprise or a big moment of revelation, as if to say, "TA DA!!! I've just proved that Shylock is a sympathetic figure!" While surprise endings may be thrilling in a murder mystery novel, they are utterly self-destructive in an academic essay. Placing a thesis at the end of an essay can seriously mar the paper's effectiveness. If you fail to clearly define your essay's point and purpose at the beginning, it makes it difficult for your reader to assess the clarity of your argument and understand the points you are making. Your argument should not come as a surprise to the reader at the end. When you do this, you have forced your reader to re-read your essay in order to assess its logic and effectiveness.

Finally, you should avoid using the first person ("I") as you present your thesis. Though it is not strictly wrong to write in the first person, it is difficult to do so gracefully. While writing in the first person, beginning writers often fall into the trap of writing self-reflexive prose (writing *about* their paper *in* their paper). Often this leads to the most dreaded of opening lines: "In this paper I am going to discuss. . . ." Not only does this self-reflexive voice make for awkward prose, it frequently allows writers to boldly announce a topic while completely avoiding a thesis statement.

Outlines

As with most things in life, essay writing is made easier by some advance planning. Many students avoid making plans because they feel it wastes time or that "it's just not my style." While there certainly is something to be said for spontaneity—a great deal, in fact—making a plan will not prevent you from having "eureka" moments as you write. Nor will making an outline mean that you spend an extra hour or so in the company of *that* essay you would so dearly love to see the back of. In fact, it is almost certain that making an outline will allow you and your essay to bid each other good night significantly sooner than you otherwise might have. Think of it this way. If somebody asked you to get in a car and drive from Carlisle, Pennsylvania, to Washington, D.C., wouldn't you want a map and detailed directions? You would certainly get to Washington quicker—and with far less stress—than if all you knew was that you wanted to get to the capital. Think of all the wrong turns you would make without your map and directions. Writing an essay is exactly the same. Making an outline not only means that you will get to your desired destination sooner, but also that you will probably steer clear of the single-lane, standstill traffic jam known as writer's block.

However, not all outlines are created equal. While some planning is better than none when it comes to essay writing, better planning is best. One useful method is based on an adaptation of the brainstorming technique mentioned in the preceding "Preparing to Write" section. Let us say that we will be writing an essay on gender in *Macbeth*. All you have right now is a theme, something that interested you enough while you read to make you pick it as a topic. Take a sheet of paper and brainstorm on gender in the play, not editing or ordering your thoughts in any way. This should take a while, and ideally should be done with *Macbeth* in hand, thumbing through the pages and looking at your margin notes and underlining. Write down everything that might go into an essay on gender in *Macbeth*. The result should be a page of brief notes, with lots of points, details, and thoughts. Study the list carefully, thinking about possible arguments that could be developed from your material. After some reflection, let us say you decide on the following thesis: In *Macbeth*, gender distortions become associated with other facets of the "unnatural," becoming central to the play's thematic movement of natural versus unnatural and a vital part of the play's tragedy. In this way, the play connects the distorted gender identities of the Weird Sisters and Lady Macbeth with their influence over Macbeth, assigning equally to both the status of sin and "evil." Here is what your brainstormed notes may look like:

The way Lady Macbeth constantly berates Macbeth with emasculating insults

Lady Macbeth's "unsex me" speech

The hypermasculine report of Macbeth we hear in 1.2

The way the play seems to marshal up the forces of nature through Birnam Woods

Macbeth's comment that his wife could only have male children

By the end, Macbeth becomes a disorderly version of the bloody warrior

Banquo observes the witches have beards

Lady Macbeth dies silently, offstage

Lady Macbeth's image of the breastfeeding mother killing her child

Count up the number of points you have and then take a clean piece of paper. Write down numbers for each of your points, plus two more.

For example, there are 10 points above so write 12 numbers on my second piece of paper. If you have 30 points, write 32 numbers, and so on. For the preceding example, my paper would look like this:

1)
2)
3)
4)
5)
6)
7)
8)
9)
10)
11)

The next step is the most important—and most difficult—one. Alongside number one, write a heading, something like "Introduction/ clear statement of thesis," while next to the final number you write "conclusion." In this case, as we know, the argument centers on the observation that Gender ambiguities and distortions are a central part of the tragedy of Macbeth. We need to pick a strong first point now to follow from this thesis statement. What is our most compelling piece of evidence for this essay? Well, this would differ from writer to writer, of course, so there is no single "correct" answer. The important point is that you have a clear order and a precise logic for the progression from one point to another. It may be helpful to think, also, in terms of "moves" or groups of points. For example, a strong first move could be to initially connect the Weird Sisters and Lady Macbeth in order to begin talking in terms of gender about the characters as intimately related elements of the same tragedy. As there is more to say on Lady Macbeth in terms of gender ambiguities, you could start with the witches and transition into Lady Macbeth to show how both parties are related by several strong links, the most prominent of which is broadly a rejection of early modern gender norms.

The aim is to produce a list of points moving from idea to idea logically and seamlessly. Think of it as a bit of a puzzle. Here is one solution that works:

1) Introduction and thesis: Gender ambiguities and distortions are a central part of the tragedy of *Macbeth* (see earlier in this section for a fuller articulation of the thesis statement for this paper)
2) Banquo observes the witches have beards
3) Lady Macbeth's "unsex me" speech
4) Lady Macbeth's image of the breastfeeding mother killing her child
5) Macbeth's comment that his wife could have only male children
6) The way Lady Macbeth constantly berates Macbeth with emasculating insults
7) The hypermasculine report of Macbeth we hear in 1.2
8) By the end, Macbeth becomes a disorderly, lawless version of the hypermasculine
9) Lady Macbeth dies silently offstage
10) The way the play seems to marshal up the forces of nature through Birnam Woods
11) Conclusion

The essay has now been mapped out with the transitional links between each of the main arguments established. Each point moves logically to the next. Here, for example, points 2, 3, 4, and 5 are grouped together as one "move"—the establishment of the connection between the Weird Sisters and Lady Macbeth and then a quick development of the essay's central concept of gender distortion. This will be anchored by a detailed reading of Lady Macbeth's "unsex me" soliloquy. Points 6 and 7 function together as a "move" focused on Macbeth and the ambiguities of his gender; the tension between Lady Macbeth's insults and the report we hear of Macbeth in 1.2 will be a nice way of framing this. The remaining points all become part of a final "move" toward understanding this gender confusion in the context of the play's anxieties about the "unnatural." While, in a sense, the gender norms return in grotesque and exaggerated forms, the seeming free play of gender, emblematically seen first in Banquo's confusion over the witches beards, still needs to be corrected and "punished" by the final action of the play.

Some students may wish to develop an outline even more, attaching to it more detail and specificity. For example, it can be beneficial to know which textual quotations you will be using and when, so make sure the outline includes a list of act, scene, and line numbers to refer to as you write. A more elaborate version of an outline for the same essay could look something like this:

1. Introduction and thesis
   - The complexity of gender politics in the play, but, equally, the observation that all of these complexities are rooted in the relatively simple notion of distorted gender norms.
   - The incorporation of these ambiguous gender roles into the play's theme of the natural versus the unnatural, including the assertion that these gender distortions are symbolically linked to the murder of Duncan.
   - Thus, gender issues are central to the play's tragedy.

2. Connecting the Weird Sisters and Lady Macbeth.
   - Banquo's remark about witches' beards.
   - Introduce the idea that this literal example of gender ambiguity sets up the more symbolic but even more striking gender distortions to come with Lady Macbeth's character.

3. Close read Lady Macbeth's soliloquy in 1.5.

- Suggest the incantation-like quality of the passage first to provide a hook to the preceding conversation about the witches.
- Draw out the images of gender distortion, focusing particularly on the eradication of the feminine in lines like "take my milk for gall."

4. Additional textual evidence to illuminate the play's early and sustained treatment of Lady Macbeth's play with gender.
   - The terrifying image of the breastfeeding mother killing her baby.
   - Macbeth's observation that his wife could only have male children.

5. The way in which Lady Macbeth emasculates Macbeth.
   - A sampling of the many emasculating insults she throws at Macbeth, with a particular emphasis on 3.4.
   - The way in which this emasculation is powerfully at odds with the hypermasculine report of Macbeth we hear in 1.2.

6. The relationship between Macbeth, Lady Macbeth, and the Witches.
   - Explore the implications of the interaction between this trio for the play's tragedy.
   - Suggest the connection between these gender distortions and other "unnatural" actions in the play, including the murder of Duncan.

7. Conclusion
   - A discussion of how the gender distortions of the central pair fade or are even reversed by the end of the play, but the effect of

```
them still looms large over the play as a
whole.
```

At the end of the chapter is a sample essay based on this outline, so you can see one version of how this paper might look. The most important thing for now, however, is to know that this road map will save you time and produce a better essay, one that flows well and builds its argument logically and carefully.

Body Paragraphs

Once your outline is complete, you can begin drafting your paper. Paragraphs, units of related sentences, are the building blocks of a good paper, and as you draft you should keep in mind both the function and the qualities of good paragraphs. Paragraphs help you chart and control the shape and content of your essay, and they help the reader to see your organization and your logic. You should begin a new paragraph whenever you move from one major point to another. In longer, more complex essays you might use a group of related paragraphs to help support major points. Remember that in addition to being adequately developed, a good paragraph is both unified and coherent.

Unified Paragraphs:

Each paragraph must be centralized around one idea or point, and a unified paragraph carefully focuses on and develops this central idea without including extraneous ideas or tangents. For beginning writers, the best way to be assured that you are constructing unified paragraphs is to include a topic sentence in each paragraph. This topic sentence should convey the main point of the paragraph, and every sentence in the paragraph should relate back to that topic sentence. Any sentence that strays from the central topic does not belong in the paragraph and needs to be revised or deleted. Consider the following paragraph about love in *As You Like It.*

```
It seems, then, that Shakespeare cannot rightly be
called a cynic when it comes to love but rather a
realist. Rosalind's pragmatic advice to Orlando centers
```

> on realizing that the idealism and optimism of love's
> first bloom is unsustainable. Instead, she argues, it
> is vital to the health of a relationship to understand
> that frustrations and acrimony are inevitable in a
> partnership, and that there really is a thin line
> between love and hate, and that that line will likely
> be straddled often in the lifetime of a relationship.
> It is important, too, to see that Orlando is able
> to reestablish his brotherly love for Oliver by the
> play's close. This is only one part, of course, but an
> important part nonetheless, of the play's fairy tale
> push to a blissful comic resolution.

The paragraph begins well enough. Notice, though, the break that takes place with the sentence "It is important . . ." The shift from Rosalind and Orlando to Orlando and Oliver is jarring, and the final reference to the "fairy tale" push of the play's resolution seems to develop naturally but is actually a significant thematic departure. Monitor your own thinking and movement within each paragraph; just as the overall essay needs to flow and transition smoothly, so too does each paragraph.

Coherent Paragraphs:

In addition to shaping unified paragraphs, you must also craft coherent paragraphs, paragraphs that develop their points logically with sentences that flow smoothly into one another. Coherence depends on the order of your sentences, but it is not strictly the order of the sentences that is important to paragraph coherence. You also need to craft your prose to help to help the reader see the relationship between the sentences. Let us imagine that a writer revised the above paragraph to create a unified passage, but the text he settled on now highlights a different problem:

> It seems, then, that Shakespeare cannot rightly be
> called a cynic when it comes to love but rather a
> realist. Rosalind's pragmatic advice to Orlando centers
> on realizing that the idealism and optimism of love's
> first bloom is unsustainable. Instead, she argues, it

is vital to the health of a relationship to understand
that frustrations and acrimony are inevitable in a
partnership, and that there really is a thin line
between love and hate, and that that line will likely
be straddled often in the lifetime of a relationship.
Petrarchan love poetry creates impossible romantic
goals. Orsino, in *Twelfth Night*, shows that such people
are simply in love with being in love.

This paragraph demonstrates that unity alone does not guarantee paragraph effectiveness. The argument is hard to follow because the author fails both to show connections between the sentences and to indicate how they work to support the overall point.

A number of techniques are available to aid paragraph coherence. Careful use of transitional words and phrases is essential. You can use transitional flags to introduce an example or an illustration *(for example, for instance)*; to amplify a point or add another phase of the same idea *(additionally, furthermore, next, similarly, finally, then)*; to indicate a conclusion or result *(therefore, as a result, thus, in other words)*; to signal a contrast or a qualification *(on the other hand, nevertheless, despite this, on the contrary, still, however, conversely)*; to signal a comparison *(likewise, in comparison, similarly)*; and to indicate a movement in time *(afterwards, earlier, eventually, finally, later, subsequently, until)*.

In addition to transitional flags, careful use of pronouns aids coherence and flow. If you were writing about *The Wizard of Oz*, you would not want to keep repeating, the phrase "the witch" or the name "Dorothy." Careful substitution of the pronoun "she" in these instances can aid coherence. A word of warning, though: when you substitute pronouns for proper names, always be sure that your pronoun reference is clear. In a paragraph that discusses both Dorothy and the witch, substituting "she" could lead to confusion. Make sure that it is clear to whom the pronoun refers. Generally, the pronoun refers to the last proper noun you have used.

While repeating the same name over and over again can lead to awkward, boring prose, it is possible to use repetition to help your paragraph's coherence. Careful repetition of important words or phrases can lend coherence to your paragraph by helping remind readers of your key points. Admittedly, it takes some practice to use this technique effectively. You may find that reading your prose aloud can help you develop an ear for effective use of repetition.

To see how helpful transitional aids are, compare the paragraph below to the preceding paragraph about love in *As You Like It*. Notice how the author works with the same ideas but shapes them into a much more coherent paragraph whose point is clearer and easier to follow. The result is a paragraph that is both unified and coherent:

> It seems, then, that Shakespeare cannot rightly be called a cynic when it comes to love but rather a realist. Rosalind's pragmatic advice to Orlando centers on realizing that the idealism and optimism of love's first bloom is unsustainable. Instead, she argues, it is vital to the health of a relationship to understand that frustrations and acrimony are inevitable in a partnership, and that there really is a thin line between love and hate, and that that line will likely be straddled often in the lifetime of a relationship. This wisdom is a direct response to Orlando's embrace of the ideals of Petrarchan love poetry, including its commonplaces of the lover-poet's suffering and the mistresses' cruelty. Orlando becomes an example of a particular kind of male figure in Shakespearean comedy, twinned with Orsino of *Twelfth Night*. These men are simply in love with being in love.

Introductions

Introductions and conclusions present particular challenges for writers. Generally, your introduction should do two things: capture your reader's attention and explain the main point of your essay. In other words, while your introduction should contain your thesis, it needs to do a bit more work than that. You are likely to find that starting that first paragraph is one of the most difficult parts of the paper. It is hard to face that blank page or screen, and as a result, many beginning writers, in desperation to start somewhere, start with overly broad, general statements. For example, the mere sight of an opening line like Throughout history Shakespeare's plays have been considered the greatest ever written will likely create in the experienced reader a feeling of exasperation. Not only will she have seen this type of opening in scores and scores of essays before (perhaps even several times in the pile of essays she is currently working through), the phrase, frankly, is not exactly true. Few viewpoints or attitudes have applied throughout history or throughout time. While some instructors encourage students to start broadly and proceed to a more narrow focus—and this can work well—it is a risky strategy. Potentially, it creates what could be called the funnel effect: a substantial chunk of writing at the start of an essay that narrows into the desired focus of the paper; but why not just get right to the point? There is a great rule to remember: If you have a sentence, paragraph, or page of writing that could be erased entirely from the paper without anyone noticing it is missing, that portion of the essay probably should not be there in the first place. Academic writing is an economical genre of writing, and, generally speaking, every line and paragraph should be playing a part in supporting your thesis and developing your arguments—moving forward. So it makes sense to start an introduction with a powerful quotation from your text, precise questions that will then allow you to arrive at your thesis statement by answering them, or even the thesis itself. Each of these methods will draw the reader into a paper, enveloping them immediately in the issues and problems at hand. Basically, in whatever way you feel is best, get right to the principle text or texts of your essay. See how there is no extraneous thought or writing in the following introduction, and after initially establishing the key topic—components of two Shakespeare plays that are not actually "part" of the play that contains them—the introduction quickly poses questions and follows up with an answer that functions as the essays thesis statement:

The "induction" scene from *The Taming of the Shrew* and the play within the play in *A Midsummer Night's Dream* are both fascinating departures from the dramas they are part of. However, while the humiliation of Christopher Sly by an aristocratic hunting party brings forth many of the themes that will be central to the play, its relationship to the text as a whole is more questionable than Bottom's play in *Dream*. What effect does the "disappearance" of Sly from the play have on the action in Padua? What are the metaphysical implications of a framing device that does not frame? By comparing the Sly episodes with the play within a play from *Dream*, two distinct "types" of metatheatrical devices become clearly visible. While Bottom's play offers an alternate ending and threatens to darken the outcome of Shakespeare's play, the Sly action fundamentally calls into question the "reality" of the play it introduces.

Conclusions

If many writers struggle with introductions, the act of starting a paper, they frequently also struggle with conclusions, the appropriate wrapping up of the work. Both introductions and conclusions should receive special attention from the writer because they mark important moments of engagement with the reader. Just as the introduction is our opportunity to make a good first impression on the reader, to give her an early sense of the paper's quality—and teachers marking large stacks of papers unfortunately but almost inevitably have often learned to form early opinions about the essays they read—the conclusion is an opportunity to leave your reader with a pleasant aftertaste. If the reader was juggling between a B+ and an A-, for example, a rousing and skillful conclusion might be just enough to nudge him toward the higher grade (while, conversely, a confused, forgettable, or poorly substantiated conclusion could deflate his enthusiasm just enough for him award the lower grade). Conclusions can be difficult to write. Sometimes students simply give up and come to a sudden stop. It is as if they feel that they have said all they wanted to say, so any further writing would just be a waste of time. This tends to be one hallmark of an extremely weak paper. A safe but rather boring and mechanical solution to the conclusion problem is what could be called the "sports highlights" approach. While a soccer match might have lasted 90 minutes, for example, the highlights on the evening news may be just a few seconds. It will show the score and probably the goals. It may also show a near miss or two. A basic, competent conclusion does something similar. It restates the thesis (the score) and recalls the key pieces of evidence that helped you to support that argument (the most memorable action). More creative conclusions might also suggest related problems outside the essay's scope but potentially of interest to your reader (see the last few sentences of the following example). The braver souls among us might also see the conclusion as an opportunity to get a little lyrical or poetic in the final lines (again, see attempts at this in the following example), the verbal equivalent of fireworks at the end. What a good conclusion will not do is any of the three following things. First, it will not begin with the phrase In conclusion... The fact that it is the last one or two paragraphs of your essay should be enough to clue most readers into the fact that you are now concluding your essay. Second, do not introduce big new ideas in the conclusion—it is too late. If a good idea arrives late in the drafting of the essay, revise the paper and put the idea where it fits best in the work (sometimes students will even find that they have an idea good enough to become a new thesis statement. If this is the case, you must tweak the body of the essay so that it appears this argument was what you had in mind all along). Finally, do not feel the need to end with a moral. Students often channel memories of childhood stories by ending an essay along the lines of Thus, we see Kate as the victim of vicious suppression. But how many women, 400 years after this play was written, continue to suffer psychological and physical abuse at the hands of men no less savage and out of place in the modern world than Petruccio. While the final sentiments of this conclusion are noble, they have taken the essay away from *The Taming of the Shrew* and into the ethical world of the author's life and social concerns. This "moral swing" has been noted by a number of commentators on student work, and writers should guard against it.

Here, then, is a conclusion that serves its purpose quite well. Let us say the thesis for this essay is Although *As You Like It* appears to be a wholehearted comedy, ending in not one but four marriages, the play is nonetheless busy questioning, even undermining, the commonplaces of the comic genre:

As we have seen, then, *As You Like It* is a play that creates strong tensions between form and content. While it is finally a comedy, it is comedy in part about the very limits of comedy. It is clear that all four of the final pairings, to varying degrees, are faulty and, despite the nuptial ceremonies, do not necessarily promise "happy ever after." Moreover, the impossibility of Frederick's conversion, along with the exaggerated convenience of Rosalind's resolution of the play's otherwise intractable problems of romance, further add to the sense of Shakespeare writing a play that asks its audience not only to question the structure of the play but their own theatrical expectations and desires. The play, of course, represents just one stage in Shakespeare's examination of comedy, however. How will he develop the generic innovations of *As You Like It* in the comedies ahead of him? What traces of future plays can we find in this much-loved comedy? What is certainly evident here, however, is that Shakespeare was drawn to the idea of providing what the audience anticipated, while at the same time offering them plays that tested the boundaries of theatrical form.

Citations and Formatting

Using Primary Sources:

As the examples included in this chapter indicate, strong papers on literary texts incorporate quotations from the text in order to support their points. It is not enough for you to assert your interpretation without providing support or evidence from the text. Without well-chosen quotations to support your argument you are, in effect, just saying to the reader, "take my word for it." It is important to use quotations thoughtfully and selectively. Remember that the paper presents your argument, so choose quotations that support your assertions. Do not let the author's voice overwhelm your own. With that caution in mind, there are some guidelines you should follow to ensure that you use quotations clearly and effectively.

Integrate Quotations:

Quotations should always be integrated into your own prose. Do not just drop them into your paper without introduction or comment. Otherwise, it is unlikely that your reader will see their function. You can integrate textual support easily and clearly with identifying tags, short phrases that identify the speaker. For example:

```
According to Antonio, "In nature there's no blemish but
the mind."
```

While this tag appears before the quotation, you can also use tags after or in the middle of the quoted text, as the following examples demonstrate:

```
"In nature there's no blemish but the mind," suggests
Antonio.
```

You can also use a colon to formally introduce a quotation:

```
It is at this point that Antonio gives us one of the
most concise visions of tolerance found anywhere in
Shakespeare's work: "In nature there's no blemish but
the mind."
```

When you quote brief sections of poems (three lines or fewer), use slash marks to indicate the line breaks in the poem:

```
Antonio's frustration at what he believes to be
Sebastian's betrayal is the catalyst for a powerful
outburst against superficial beauty that masks moral
weakness: "But, O, how vile an idol proves this god!
/ Thou hast, Sebastian, done good feature shame. / In
nature there's no blemish but the mind."
```

Note: Not all of Shakespeare's dialogue is written in poetry. Sometimes his characters speak in prose too. Often the distinction is an important one, loaded with different implications. For example, lower-class characters are more likely to speak in prose rather than verse, or the use of prose may suggest a moment of intimacy when a character feels he or she can shed the niceties of poetic speech and talk more directly. Whatever the reason, prose is easily identified by the fact that each line does not begin with a capital letter. When quoting prose lines from Shakespeare's plays, there is no need for the slash marks. So, for example, a few lines after Antonio's moving outburst in *Twelfth Night*, Sir Toby (an aristocrat, but a drunk and waster too—hence the prose) has the following line, which serves to demonstrate how to quote small amounts of prose dialogue:

> Sir Toby then quips: "Come hither, Knight. Come hither, Fabian. We'll whisper o'er a couplet or two of most sage saws."

Longer quotations (more than four lines of prose or three lines of poetry) should be set off from the rest of your paper in a block quotation. Double space before you begin the passage, indent it ten spaces from your left-hand margin, and double space the passage itself. Because the indentation signals the inclusion of a quotation, do not use quotation marks around the cited passage. Use a colon to introduce the passage:

> Antonio's frustration at what he believes to be Sebastian's betrayal is the catalyst for a powerful outburst against superficial beauty that masks moral weakness:
>
> > But, O, how vile an idol proves this god!
> > Thou hast, Sebastian, done good feature shame.
> > In nature there's no blemish but the mind.
> > None can be called deformed but the unkind.
> > Virtue is beauty, but the beauteous evil
> > Are empty trunks o'er-flourished by the devil.
>
> For Antonio, it is fidelity and honesty that are the true markers of beauty, not the "empty" features of a handsome face.

It is also important to interpret quotations after you introduce them. Explain how they help to advance your point. You cannot assume that your reader would interpret the quotations the same way that you do. The last sentence discussing Antonio's fidelity and honesty marks an attempt to launch into immediate interpretation of the cited passage.

Quote Accurately:

Always quote accurately. Anything within quotations marks must be the author's exact words. There are, however, some rules to follow if you need to modify the quotation to fit into your prose.

1. Use brackets to indicate any material that might have been added to the author's exact wording. For example, if you need to add any words to the quotation or alter it grammatically to allow it to fit into your prose, indicate your changes in brackets:

   ```
   Viola confesses that "As [he] is a man, [his]
   state is desperate for [his] Master's love."
   ```

2. Conversely, if you choose to omit any words from the quotation, use ellipses (three spaced periods) to indicate missing words or phrases:

   ```
   Orsino announces that "When that is known . . .
   / A solemn combination shall be made / Of our
   dear souls."
   ```

3. If you delete a sentence or more, use the ellipses after a period:

   ```
   It is at this point that Antonio gives us one
   of the most concise visions of tolerance found
   anywhere in Shakespeare's work: "In nature
   there's no blemish but the mind. . . . Virtue
   is beauty, but the beauteous evil / Are empty
   trunks o'er-flourished by the devil."
   ```

Punctuate Properly:

Punctuation of quotations often causes more trouble than it should. Once again, you just need to keep these simple rules in mind.

1. Periods and commas should be placed inside quotation marks, even if they are not part of the original quotation:

   ```
   Shakespeare, in Kevin Webster's pithy phrase, was
   "rooted in his moment, not born of the eternal."
   ```

   The only exception to this rule is when the quotation is followed by a parenthetical reference. In this case, the period or comma goes after the citation (more on these later in this chapter):

   ```
   Shakespeare, in Kevin Webster's pithy phrase,
   was "rooted in his moment, not born of the
   eternal" (135).
   ```

2. Other marks of punctuation—colons, semicolons, question marks, and exclamation points—go outside the quotation marks unless they are part of the original quotation:

   ```
   What does Webster mean when he writes that
   Shakespeare was "rooted in his moment, not born
   of the eternal"?
   ```

   ```
   The fastidious Webster asks, "Are you certain
   you have cited me properly?"
   ```

Documenting Primary Sources:

Unless you are instructed otherwise, you should provide sufficient information for your reader to locate material you quote. Generally, literature papers follow the rules set forth by the Modern Language Association. These can be found in the *MLA Handbook for Writers of Research Papers* (sixth edition). You should be able to find this book in the reference section of your library. Additionally, its rules for citing both primary and secondary sources are widely available from reputable online sources. One source is the Online Writing Lab [OWL] at Purdue University. OWL's guide to MLA style is available at http://owl.english.purdue.edu/owl/resource/747/01/. The Modern Language Association also includes answers to frequently asked questions about MLA style on this helpful Web page: http://www.mla.org/style_faq. Generally, when you are citing from literary works in papers, you should keep a few guidelines in mind.

Parenthetical Citations:

MLA asks for parenthetical references in your text after quotations. When you are working with prose (short stories, novels, or essays) include page numbers in the parentheses:

> Shakespeare, in Kevin Webster's pithy phrase, was "rooted in his moment, not born of the eternal" (135).

When you are quoting poetry, include line numbers:

> Shakespeare's Sonnet 18 has developed the reputation of a classic love poem. Many readers, then, are surprised to learn that the following oft-quoted lines are addressed to a man: "Shall I compare thee to a summer's day? / Thou art more lovely and more temperate" (1–2).

Shakespeare's plays—and early modern drama more generally—also have a specific format for citations. Included in the parenthetical reference, in this order, are the act, scene, and line numbers. The first of the two line numbers indicates where the quote begins, while the second tells the reader the number of the last line you quoted. It should look like this:

> The meaning of *The Taming of the Shrew* can be changed by an ironic reading of Kate's last speech. Does she really mean it, for example, when she states that "Thy husband is thy lord, thy life, thy keeper, / Thy head, thy sovereign . . ." (5.2.150–51)?

Works Cited Page:

These parenthetical citations are then linked to a separate works cited page at the end of the paper. The works cited page lists works alphabetically by the authors' last names:

> Shakespeare, William. *The Taming of the Shrew*. *The Norton Shakespeare*. Ed. Stephen Greenblatt, et al. New York: Norton, 1997: 133–203.

The *MLA Handbook* includes a full listing of sample entries, as do many of the online explanations of MLA style.

Documenting Secondary Sources:

In order to assure that your paper is built entirely upon your own ideas and analysis, instructors often ask that you write interpretative papers without any outside research. If, on the other hand, your paper requires research, you must document any secondary sources you use. You need to document direct quotations, summaries or paraphrases of other's ideas, and factual information that is not common knowledge. Follow the guidelines above for quoting primary sources when you use direct quotations from secondary sources. Keep in mind that MLA style also includes specific guidelines for citing electronic sources. OWL's Web site provides a nice summary: http://owl.english.purdue.edu/owl/resource/747/08/.

Parenthetical Citations:

As with the documentation of primary sources, described above, MLA guidelines require in-text parenthetical references to your secondary sources. Unlike the research papers you might write for a history class, literary research papers following MLA style do not use footnotes as a means of documenting sources. Instead, after a quotation, you should cite the author's last name and the page number:

> According to one recent biography of Shakespeare, "the dramatist borrowed heavily from a variety of sources, but the originality of each and every play is still without doubt" (Kazinski 216).

If you include the name of the author in your prose, then you would include only the page number in your citation. For example:

> As Robert Kazinski observes of Shakespeare, "the dramatist borrowed heavily from a variety of sources, but the originality of each and every play is still without doubt" (216).

If you are including more than one work by the same author, the parenthetical citation should include an identifiable word or words from the title in order to indicate which of the author's works you cite. For example:

> As Mary Rudolph puts it, "the final notes of A *Midsummer Night's Dream*, with Puck's evocation of dead men and ominous owls, mar the comic resolution of the play and encourage us to reconsider the preceding events from the play in this new, dark light—the dream becomes a faintly awkward and uncomfortable nightmare" (*Midnight* 134).

Similarly, if you summarize the particular ideas of your source, you must provide documentation:

> It has been observed that Puck's somber speech at the close of the play is potent enough to challenge the comic character of the play (Rudolph 134).

Works Cited Page:

As with the primary sources discussed above, the parenthetical references are keyed to a separate works cited page at the end of the your paper. Here is an example of what the text of a works cited page that uses the examples cited above. You can find a complete list of sample entries in the *MLA Handbook* or from a reputable online summary of MLA style.

WORKS CITED

Kazinski, Robert. *Shakespeare From Afar.* New York: NY Press, 2006.

Rudolph, Mary. *Another Book About Shakespeare.* London: Cockney Press, 1993.

——. *Shakespeare at Midnight.* New York: NY Press, 2005.

Plagiarism

Failure to document carefully and thoroughly can leave you open to charges of stealing the ideas of others, which is known as plagiarism, and this is a serious matter. Remember that it is important to use quotation marks when you use distinct language used by your source, even if you use just one or two words. With the preceding quotation from Mary Rudolph in mind, it would be plagiarism if you wrote the following: Because of Puck's dark, ominous speech at the play's close, the comic ending of the play is marred and the dream of the play becomes an uncomfortable nightmare. See how the words and ideas of Rudolph plainly make up the core of this sentence. Instead, you should write in such a way as to acknowledge the source of the thoughts and language in your writing. Something like the following would be fine: Critics have observed that Puck's lines about shadowy night creatures might even make the play something other than a comedy. But what does it become? Is there enough in the play, perhaps, to transform it into "a faintly awkward and uncomfortable nightmare" (Rudolph 134)?

Some cases of plagiarism are the result of students simply not understanding how to quote from secondary sources. This can be avoided simply by having a non-negotiable bottom line: if the words are not yours, put them in quotation marks and tell the reader who wrote them. Paraphrasing the arguments of others is fine, but again you must acknowledge the source. Something like this: Mary Rudolph has written convincingly about the distorting effect of Puck's speech about lions, corpses, and owls, suggesting that the play at this point is transformed from dream to nightmare.

Closely related to all of this is the question of how to use secondary sources. A lot of accidental plagiarism is the result of students wanting to use outside opinions and ideas, but not knowing what to do with them. The two most effective ways of using outside sources—both of which have built in guards against accidental plagiarism—are either as evidence to support your argument or as a challenge to your ideas that you must defeat. In the first case, you are basically saying, Here is someone who thinks the same as I do: Mary Rudolph makes a fine point when she argues that *A Midsummer Night's Dream* finally may be seen as more nightmare than dream (134). In the second, you challenge the author: While Mary Rudolph has suggested that the play is more nightmare than dream (134), this seems like an exaggeration. . . . The first strategy can become a little static if used too often, but the second can really generate a lot of energy in your paper.

However, many cases of plagiarism are simply the result of dishonesty and laziness. Be aware that plagiarism can haunt a student years after the event, perhaps even preventing him or her from getting into certain schools or programs down the road. While it has become all too easy to plagiarize using the Internet, Web-based methods for catching plagiarists are developing quickly as well. Perhaps the greatest weapon instructors have against plagiarism, however, is a well-trained eye; many instructors will have read hundreds if not thousands of student essays and will have become adept at noticing the signs of plagiarism. It is certainly possible that you may know people who have plagiarized and gotten away with it, but their luck is sure to run out sooner rather than later.

Finally, while it is not necessary to document well-known facts, often referred to as "common knowledge," any ideas or language that you take from someone else must be properly documented. Common knowledge generally includes the birth and death dates of authors or other well-documented facts of their lives. An often cited guideline is: if you can find the information in three sources, it is common knowledge. Despite this guideline, it is, admittedly, often difficult to know if the facts you uncover are common knowledge or not. When in doubt, document your source.

Sample Essay

Richard Kline
English 210
Professor Gleed

"YOU SHOULD BE WOMEN . . .":
GENDER CONFUSION IN *MACBETH*

The gender politics of *Macbeth* are complicated but rooted nonetheless in the simple idea that deviating from normal gender roles and conventions is bad and unnatural. In no small way, this anxiety is located at the core of the play's tragedy; when gender norms are breached, nature itself is offended and the imbalance must be righted. Such a highly conservative ideology seems at odds with the mind of the playwright behind the comedies *As You Like It* or *Twelfth Night*. However, in *Macbeth*, gender "abnormalities" are viewed with such fear that they are symbolically interwoven with and morally likened to the murder of Duncan itself.

The first part of this essay will attempt to link the Weird Sisters and Lady Macbeth through ideas of gender "deformity." This relationship begins in the third scene of act 1. When Banquo first sees the witches, he is struck by the visual dualities and paradoxes of the trio. The sisters "look not like th' inhabitants o' th' earth / And yet are on't" (1.3.39–40), but Banquo quickly refines the incongruities into the more precise language of gender: "You should be women, / And yet your beards forbid me to interpret / That you are so" (1.3.43–45). As Michael Long puts it, in this scene the witches "flout and threaten all the definitions and demarcations which constitute the order of the cultural world" (56). The beards become an important symbol of this distortion and a key clue to view it through the lens of gender. This apparently slight reference to gender ambiguity is actually an important foreshadowing of Lady Macbeth's soliloquy two scenes later and the unfolding gender politics of the play.

This soliloquy from act 1, scene 5 deserves to be quoted in its entirety:

The raven himself is hoarse
That croaks the fatal entrance of Duncan
Under my battlements. Come, you spirits
That tend on mortal thoughts, unsex me here,
And fill me from the crown to the toe top-full
Of direst cruelty! Make thick my blood;
Stop up the access and passage to remorse,
That no compunctious visitings of nature
Shake my fell purpose, nor keep peace between
The effect and it! Come to my woman's breasts,
And take my milk for gall, you murd'ring
   ministers,
Wherever in your sightless substances
You wait on nature's mischief! Come, thick night,
And pall thee in the dunnest smoke of hell,
That my keen knife see not the wound it makes,
Nor heaven peep through the blanket of the dark,
To cry 'Hold, hold!' (1.5.37–52)

Carolyn Asp argues that "Lady Macbeth consciously attempts to reject her feminine sensibility and adopt a male mentality because she perceives that her society equates feminine qualities with weakness" (378). While this is true, there is much more to her desires here. It appears to be more complicated than a straight exchange of feminine qualities for masculine ones. From Lady Macbeth's "Come, you spirits," Shakespeare is encouraging us to see this speech as nothing less than an incantation, an anticipation of the Weird Sisters and their spells and enchantments in act 4, scene 1. Yet it is the desired ends of the "spell" here that are most telling. Just as the witches are briefly but strikingly characterized in transgendered terms, Lady Macbeth here courts internal "deformities" that mirror the sister's beards. Seeking to remove all traces of her inward femininity, she asks the spirits to "take my milk for gall"; she desires her breast milk, an archetypal image of virtuous maternity, be replaced by bitter, poisonous "gall." This murderous gall will drown out the "passage to remorse" and all "compunctious visitings of nature," symbolically killing of the "natural" woman within her and replacing it, not so much with masculinity exactly but with an ambiguous new creature that is neither man nor woman (what Viola of *Twelfth Night*, in much lighter circumstances, nonetheless calls a "monster").

As if Lady Macbeth's soliloquy has not made this point soundly enough, the playwright gives us two further images of her distorted gender identity. The terrifying image of a mother killing her suckling babe (1.7.48–59), something Lady Macbeth says she would rather do than go back on a plan to kill Duncan, and Macbeth's observation that his wife could "Bring forth men-children only" (1.7.73) further emphasize Lady Macbeth's movement away from womanhood and femininity. Thus we see that the relationship between the witches and Lady Macbeth emerges clearly in the first movements of the play. As Marjorie Garber puts it:

> I think we can say with justice that those unisex witches, with their women's forms and their confusingly masculine beards, are, among other things, dream images, metaphors for Lady Macbeth herself: physically a woman, but, as she claims, mentally and spiritually a man. (713)

If, then, these early scenes of the play establish a bond between the Weird Sisters and Lady Macbeth through ideas of gender abnormalities, it is important to further note that Lady Macbeth repeatedly attempts to compel Macbeth to action by emasculating him. This strategy adds yet another layer to the play's discourse on gender. As late in the play as act 3, scene 4, Lady Macbeth asks of her husband, "Are you a man?" (3.4.58), likens him to a woman listening to an old woman's story (3.4.64–65), and quips "What, quite unmanned in folly?" (3.4.72). These emasculating slurs provide a sharp contrast with the hypermasculine report heard of Macbeth's valor in battle heard in act 1, scene 2. But the sum of the two competing versions of Macbeth's gender identity echoes the indeterminacy we have already witnessed in the women that surround him.

It is this relationship between Macbeth, the Weird Sisters, and Lady Macbeth that cuts to the heart of the play's tragedy. The ideology of *Macbeth* seems to be that when these "monstrous" women, women with beards and gall-filled bodies, exert an influence over Macbeth that they are not politically or culturally entitled to, and when Macbeth permits such influence to be asserted and to win out, the gender norms that underpin society (and even the play's mythology of the natural world itself) are being challenged and deconstructed. The gender identities of all three parties are fatally undermined by this process, and the consequences of this destabilization are severe. It seems that the play, by finally falling back on the language of nature versus the unnatural, by setting Macbeth against a vengeful forest of trees, so to speak, encourages us to see all of the central couple's sins and errors as part of the same unnatural set of actions.

Although by the end of the play Macbeth is no longer associated with the feminine but rather a lawless and distorted version of the brutal warrior we heard of in act 1, scene 2, and Lady Macbeth has retreated into a chilling version of ideal Renaissance womanhood (she is finally silent and invisible, dying offstage as if without importance), the consistent play with gender norms in the first half of the drama creates a set of tragic problems that cannot be redeemed. It is only by the advance of Birnam Woods and the restoration of Duncan's line to the throne, two powerful emblems of natural order correcting unnatural disorder, that the symbolic specter of women and men who cannot be easily categorized and identified is banished.

WORKS CITED

Asp, Carolyn. "'Be bloody, bold and resolute': Tragic Action and Stereotyping in Macbeth." *Macbeth: Critical Essays*. Ed. S. Schoenbaum. New York: Garland Publishing, 1991: 377–97.

Garber, Marjorie. *Shakespeare After All*. New York: Anchor Books, 2004.

Long, Michael. *Macbeth: Twayne's New Critical Introductions to Shakespeare*. Boston: Twayne Publishers, 1989.

Shakespeare, William. *Macbeth*. *The Norton Collected Works of Shakespeare*. Stephen Greenblatt, et al, eds. New York: W. W. Norton, 2008.

HOW TO WRITE
ABOUT SHAKESPEARE:
AN OVERVIEW

FOR MANY students, the greatest obstacle to writing about Shakespeare is the process of reading Shakespeare. The root of the problem for many, not surprisingly, is Shakespeare's language, which is unfamiliar at times and can seem difficult to read. Like everything else, practice, patience, and a little effort will help. In the meantime, there are some things you can do that will make Shakespeare much more accessible to you. First, do not overestimate or make too much of the role Shakespeare's language should play in your encounter with his work. For many dedicated readers of Shakespeare, it is precisely the language, its poetic power and verbal creativity, that separates Shakespeare from the ordinary. Yet a fuller understanding or appreciation of the Shakespearean idiom is not something that needs to come immediately. Rather, at the core of the plays are themes, questions, and ideas that pulse with the energy of humanity, and these are open and accessible to all. Do not let the language get in the way or become an obstacle to an appreciation of Shakespeare as a storyteller, as a representer and presenter of lives. Thus, read to understand the play not to understand the line. If you allow yourself to get bogged down in each and every word, each and every line, the task of reading Shakespeare will become onerous. Here are some considerations to bear in mind:

1. **Before you read, know the plot:** Shakespeare's language causes most problems for the student who does not already know the play's plot. If a reader does not know what is going on in the narrative, he or she will feel lost and confused trying to piece it all together. Conversely, if the student has a sense of the plot, of roughly what will be happening at each point in the play, it is easy to push through unfamiliar language and still understand, in broader terms, what you have read. Plot summaries of the plays are widely available on the Web and in print. Ask your instructor, too, if he or she would not mind giving an overview of the whole plot for you before you read.

2. **Watch a movie:** As most people will not have the opportunity to see a Shakespeare play performed onstage at the same time they begin reading it in class, a film adaptation can be an excellent alternative option. There is an important caution to be offered here, though. All film versions of Shakespeare's plays change the text in some way. Whether it is a faithful adaptation that merely chops off a few minor scenes or offers interesting and original interpretations of a character or scene, or a film that radically overhauls its Shakespearean source, a movie should never be used as a substitute for the play. Good film versions of a play, however, allow students to see a version of the play acted out, to hear the language spoken, and to witness the passion and drama of the text made real. A subsequent reading of the play is made easier and smoother by watching the movie (again, be careful to keep play and film separate in your thinking, as there will be differences. Also, do not accept the film's interpretation of the play as your own or as the only one available).

   Shakespeare on film is actually a large and active area of study for contemporary scholars. There are many versions of the major plays (*Hamlet, Othello,* and *Macbeth,* for example), and these vary in quality and purpose. Watch as many as you can find of your chosen play before reading it. Often, unless the movie is newly released or has attained classic status, Shakespeare films can be difficult to track down. An Internet DVD rental membership, offering access to a huge catalog of titles, is probably the best way to find many of the films. Often you can find inexpensive used copies on Internet auction sites too. Alternately, for productions that stick closely to the original text, during the early 1980s, the British Broadcasting Corporation (BBC) set about filming the bulk of Shakespeare's canon, shooting most of the text scene for scene and adding little in the way of radical interpretation. Arguably the creative team involved aimed to interpret the plays as closely to the Renaissance mentality as possible. While the films offer little in terms of gloss or production values, they give an accurate account of the text, thereby making excellent tools for reading support.

3. **Use glosses but not obsessively:** Good editions of Shakespeare's plays come with glosses printed on the page. They are used when the editor of the play believes a word will be particularly unfamiliar to modern audiences, so a "translation" is provided either in the margins of the text or at the bottom of the page. Of course, glosses are helpful inclusions, and even advanced or experienced Shakespearean readers use them frequently. However, do not check every word; do not look at every gloss. Checking the glosses too frequently drastically slows your reading pace and may prove to be unnecessary. If you read a speech and its overall sense is initially elusive, check the glossed words, phrases, and lines to see if they offer any help or insight. If you have an overall sense of the speech, it might be better to keep reading and become absorbed in the rhythm and flow of the text.

4. **Talk to teachers and participate in discussions:** Perhaps the greatest resource you have at hand will be your instructor. If you have questions about any aspect of the play, ask. Become involved, too, in class discussions about the plays—just as Shakespeare's language is clearest when spoken, so are his themes most accessible when debated. Classroom discussion is often the best place to elicit and define a special and important aspect of Shakespeare's drama: its contemporary relevance.

While some instructors might not encourage it in a paper, a fascinating discussion could be started, for example, by asking what life might be like for Othello and Desdemona today. What has changed over the centuries for interracial couples? Starting or playing a part in these conversations can make Shakespeare seem alive. If no such opportunities arise in class, chat about it elsewhere with other students in the class. It is fascinating to reflect on how much we are alike and different from the lives of those who came long before us.

Certainly, Shakespeare—like all artists—is of his moment, writing for his contemporaries about his own world. But equally, as we have seen, Shakespeare's contemporaries were not as far removed from us, from our troubles and fears, our hopes and joys, as the archaic language and footnote-laden lines of a Shakespeare volume suggest. Readers of the future will most likely need glosses to explain the references and allusions that populate contemporary literature. Cultures are based on a "language" of their own, a system of shared knowledge, assumptions, and beliefs that distinguish them from others. There are also the more superficial codes such as manners and fashion that serve as an expression and embodiment of those cultural codes and precepts. Yet, just as a trip to a foreign country can offer uncertainties and a great many more thrills, so, too, does a journey to Shakespeare's England. It is a remarkable journey, rewarding us with many unfamiliar sights and sounds.

TOPICS AND STRATEGIES

Knowledge of important historical movements and backdrops will provide the writer with a valuable reservoir to draw from in virtually any essay on Shakespeare's drama. The chapters on individual plays point out specific historical contexts and suggest how research into those contexts could provide the backbone of an excellent essay. While specific knowledge of different events or trends will help, depending on the play, essays generally become more authoritative and impressive when they demonstrate sensitivity to the broad strokes of Shakespeare's world. Shakespeare's writings reflected the reality and concerns, historically and socially, of his era. Familiarity with this contextual currents can serve to strengthen and broaden the scope of your essay:

1. **The Elizabethan and Jacobean stage:** Some understanding of the theatrical world of Shakespeare's time, its conventions and how it was perceived, will assuredly help the writer as she assesses texts written to be performed there. However, though the stage was unquestionably important to English Renaissance culture, it meant different things to different people. Critics today, like Shakespeare's contemporaries, hold a variety of opinions about how exactly the theater worked, who controlled it, and what effect it had on the wider society. For example, modern critics are divided on the important issue of whether the Renaissance stage served to support state authority or challenge it. In other words, was the theater a radical or a conservative institution? (The answer probably varies from play to play, author to author, of course). Certainly it was heavily policed and censored by the authorities and frequently defended by the government (which suggests the latter of the above scenarios), but a great many things still found their way onto the stage that implicitly called into question the role and function of the English state. As she works, the writer can also usefully consider the question of political and social ideology, especially if the Shakespeare play in question is an overtly political one (and many of the tragedies and all of the histories are explicitly political).

   The central opponents of the stage, however, tended not to be government officials but religious radicals who saw the theater as a devilish hotbed of sin and deception. These critics objected to such things as the practice of boy actors playing women's roles, suggesting that such conventions toyed with moral and physical convention. Shakespeare, however, seems to have found this aspect of Elizabethan stagecraft great fun. In many of his plays, writers can find and make use of Shakespeare's playful exploration of a boy playing a woman (with the "woman" then further disguising "herself" as a man in a number of cases).

The locations of the playhouses did little to discourage the notion of theater as a seedy business. After all, the stages were largely located south of the River Thames, away from the city and nestled among brothels, taverns, and the many other pastimes of London's least fortunate. Many of the stages doubled as arenas for bloodthirsty entertainments such as cockfighting or bearbaiting (a "sport" in which a chained bear fought off the attacks of savage dogs for the pleasure of a paying audience). It should come as no surprise, then, that actors, writers, and others associated with the world of the theater were by no means the "thespians" of our time but had the reputation of vagabonds and "masterless" men who were loosely protected and supported by royal or aristocratic patronage. They were seen largely as wasters and borderline criminals, and many of them at one point or another came to violent blows.

What might the reader and essay writer take from this? Broadly, it should be clear that the Elizabethan and Jacobean stage was a contested area, one whose politics and influence were as uncertain to contemporaries as they are to modern scholars. These plays were often much more than entertainment, and consciously or not, exerted a powerful force on English political and social life. The task of the writer, then, is to judge the direction of any given play's "social energy," whether it be in matters of sexuality or statehood, and begin to unravel the complex and potentially explosive mix of intention and consequence.

2. **The New World and the ancient world:** Only a small number of Shakespeare's plays explicitly treat the discovery of the Americas or life beyond the borders of Europe (see the chapter on *Othello* in this volume), but it is impossible to overestimate the effect of the New World on Renaissance consciousness. As a reader, be aware that exploration of the New World forced Europeans to reflect on their own identities as well as the identities of the indigenous peoples they were newly encountering. Certainly, the tragic tale of European expansion into the Americas is well known, and most students will be familiar with the enormous suffering that resulted from the colonialist agenda.

Less familiar, perhaps, are the philosophical debates that circulated in Europe, thousands of miles away from the front lines of colonialism and exploitation. At the loftiest level, the "discovery" of the New World forced thoughtful people to ask exactly what it was that separated European civilization from the perceived wildness and disorder of indigenous life. Most entered into this debate, however, from the starting point of European superiority, unwilling to consider that there might be something to learn about human existence from these hitherto unknown populations and cultures. Invariably the encounter merely confirmed and cemented the righteousness of a European, Christian model of life. A few sympathetic souls, however, most notably the French essayist Michel de Montaigne, rejected the preconception of European superiority. Montaigne argued that the savagery of Europeans in the New World meant that the colonizers had little right to consider themselves more civilized than the native peoples they butchered, enslaved, and abused.

On a more pragmatic level, much of the intellectual energy invested in the New World took the form of economic calculation. Shakespeare's England, along with Spain, led the way in trying to establish profitable and powerful outposts in the New World. Certainly, as a result of the New World encounter, the economies of the Old World expanded and an age of consumerism and mercantilism was rapidly accelerated. So the energy of the New World infuses many aspects of life in Shakespeare's world, and the drama of the colonial encounter becomes an engine for powerful forces of social transformation.

For the student composing an essay on one of Shakespeare's tragedies, it is important to keep in mind the broad and far-reaching nature of change during the Renaissance, an important part of which was stimulated by the colonialist encounters with foreign and previously unknown peoples. It might also be helpful to touch on some recent changes in the way scholars talk and think about the Renaissance. Historians, in fact, now tend to prefer the term *early modern* to describe the century or so before and after Shakespeare's death. In part, this change of terminology comes out of a gathering consensus that the term *Renaissance,* or rather the image of wholesale rebirth and reinvention it conjures up, is misleading. These historians caution that not everyone experienced a renaissance and that the medieval world did not disappear instantly in a brilliant burst of collective genius. The truth is much more complex and muddled. Certainly there was an enormous outpouring of artistic, scientific, and intellectual innovation, and elites across Europe (especially in Italy) sought to reconnect with the great achievements and spirit of the ancient world. It is also true, however, that this creativity had significant geographic and class-based limitations. For many people, life continued as it had for centuries, as agrarian peoples remained rooted to the earth, the cyclical seasons, and the mysteries of the supernatural. The term *early modern* captures this duality nicely, especially with the addition of the qualifying adjective. The concept of the Renaissance encourages us to see the period in which Shakespeare lived as the birth of *our* contemporary world, a time that ushered in the world we now inhabit. *Early modern* is more judicious, however, pointing out that while it *was* in many ways the period that generated so many of the systems and ideas we continue to use, it was merely a stage of development rather than an explosion of civilization and culture.

This duality is important to remember as you write on any aspect of the period, particularly the plays of Shakespeare, which so beautifully crystallize this coexistence of change and continuity. Shakespeare himself, a country-born man who found success in the exploding metropolis of London, might even serve as a metaphor for his age. As you read and write, think about this twofold nature and look for ways in which Shakespeare—who clearly knew the court and the latest ideas well—represents the forces of change but also remembers his simpler, country origins in reflecting on the "old ways." Like his world, though, all Shakespeare's plays retain traces of continuing, long-established ways of life alongside glimpses of and insight into new ways of thinking and behaving. The writer would do well to look for the harmonies and tensions between these two modes of life as she examines the themes, characters, and ideas contained in each play.

3. **Queen Elizabeth I and King James I:** Arguably, no dynasty of English monarchs left a greater mark on Britain than the Tudors. Beginning with the crowning of Henry VII in 1485 and ending with the death of Elizabeth I in 1603, the Tudor monarchs reigned over a period of epochal change for the English nation. Shakespeare lived during the final, tense years of Tudor England and continued his career into the reign of the first Stuart king, James I. Elizabeth and James, then, must be understood as key figures at the center of Shakespeare's world. However, while Shakespeare certainly sought to earn the approval of his monarch through writing, he also used his stage to participate in conversations about the nature of monarchical power and the latest affairs at court. The writer must first and foremost remember that the theater was not merely an art form that responded to events from a distance but a part of the Tudor and Stuart political system.

It is not really clear that we have an equivalent today. Perhaps film and television come closest, but the parallel is not a particularly strong one. These mediums (especially film) can be political, and they can mount powerful critiques of government and policies, though this is rare given the enormous budgets involved and the need for broad audience support. The key difference, perhaps, is the closeness of early modern theater to the seat of power. If the film industry today was based in Washington, D.C., and those involved in the production of movies were themselves watchful hangers-on around powerful people, and the government meddled directly and openly with the content of film, then the parallel might be an apt one. As it is, though, early modern theater differs markedly from anything in our time. The theater was policed by the government, but the theater, in delicate and subtle ways, in turn policed the government by offering a lively forum for veiled but serious political debate often leavened with the use of jokes or humor. The most powerful Elizabethans and Jacobeans may have watched theatrical performances, but the theater as an institution also watched them and frequently, though always discretely, mindful of the terrible consequences of speaking too plainly or boldly, made those same individuals the subject of its drama. Most powerful of all, the monarch was a magnetic subject for many playwrights, not least of all Shakespeare.

Shakespeare and Elizabeth I are bound together in our historical imagination, twin symbols of the mythological greatness of their age. In his film *Shakespeare in Love,* Tom Stoppard depicts the sovereign as a powerful devotee of the playwright, even playing a hand in orchestrating his love life. This is a fantasy, no doubt, but the stage did link the two figures tightly, and Elizabeth would have enjoyed Shakespeare's plays at private performances and Shakespeare's livelihood was boosted by the continuance of that pleasure. In the final years of Elizabeth's reign, there is evidence that Shakespeare's plays were significant components of an increasingly vexed conversation about the aging, fading queen.

Elizabeth had come to power in less than ideal circumstances. While she was daughter of Henry VIII, a still-much-loved king a decade after his death, her mother was Henry's disgraced and executed second wife, Anne Boleyn. Moreover, Elizabeth inherited a weakened state, one destabilized by two brief and unsuccessful reigns. The boy king, Edward VI, Henry's sickly son, had ruled between 1547 and 1553, during which time his handlers enacted a vigorously Protestant agenda. After his death, Henry's first daughter, Mary, began her short and destructive time in power. She married a Spaniard, King Philip, and in the process annoyed a great many Englishmen; Mary's subjects balked at the prospect of their country's great enemy inheriting the reigns of power. More harmful still, Mary aggressively reversed the Protestant policies of Edward and set about a bloody and murderous defense of Roman Catholicism against heretics. She executed large numbers of Protestant reformers, many of whom quickly became martyrs to the cause of the English Reformation. We can only imagine what effect this theological back and forth had on the populace of England, but Elizabeth learned a great deal from it.

One of her great triumphs as monarch was to nimbly walk the tightrope of religious difference in England, never adopting the extremes of her predecessors. Elizabeth was a Protestant queen, but her reign is characterized by a mood of relative religious tolerance, even while some around her pushed hard for a more hawkish model of reform. Still, for all her effective ambiguity in religious matters, the Catholic Church saw her as an enemy and the pope made vocal protests to encourage Catholic assassins against England's Protestant queen. Such attempts were, of course, never successful, though they became increasingly frequent in the final years of her reign.

Those final years were generally unstable and fraught with danger and intrigue. Her decision to never marry had been contested vigorously by England's political elites, but Elizabeth never wavered on this vital matter. During her childbearing years, there was no shortage of suitors, foreign and domestic, suitable and undesirable. She encouraged some, but accepted none; her rhetoric was as powerful as it was consistent: She saw herself as married to the people and viewed England as her spouse. Speculations never ceased, of course, and it appears that Elizabeth, never a wife, was several times a woman in love. Approaching the end of her reign, however, these strategies that once strengthened Elizabeth's position were working against her. A general unease appears to have infused English life at the close of the 16th century: Who would rule when Elizabeth died?

The answer to that question—as a result of furtive negotiations carried on behind Elizabeth's back—was Scotland's King James VI, who became James I of England upon the queen's death. James does not cut as recognizable a figure as Elizabeth for us today, but for Shakespeare's fellow citizens, James, as a male monarch with an existing heir, was a welcome presence. The long-nagging problems of succession had been resolved without great pain, and James's monarchy, though not necessarily as remarkable as Elizabeth's, was marked by relative stability. James was an intellectual who wrote on numerous subjects but was particularly interested in political philosophy and theories of monarchy. His reign, however, was stained by a number of sexual and moral scandals, all of which, historians tend to agree, circumscribed the effectiveness of his rule. If the Tudors appear now to have been the most successful of English dynasties, the Stuarts, James's heirs, arguably suffered the greatest ill luck and misery in English royal history. Nonetheless, James was the last king Shakespeare knew.

Whether it is in passing allusions to Elizabeth (such as we find in *A Midsummer Night's Dream*), engagements with James's intellectual interests (the use of witchcraft in *Macbeth*, for example), or displaced and buried consideration of contemporary royal politics (as many have found in *Julius Caesar*), Shakespeare's plays are infused more with the presence of the monarchs of his lifetime, about which he could not openly write, than with those of English kings of history. The essay writer can find in the narratives of Richard II or Henry IV, for example, a great deal of conversation about Elizabeth I. Late in life, she identified herself with the embattled and deposed Richard II of Shakespeare's stage, yet another example of the degree to which the plays are alive with an energy drawn from the political, cultural, and social life of the author's time. No matter to what extent the student wishes to penetrate the historical and political context of the day, it is useful to be aware of Shakespeare's role as a chronicler of his time. Our task as writers is not so much to reconstruct Shakespeare's world through our essays but to respect and conduct into our own work the energy with which he wrote and observed the life around him.

4. **Shakespeare and anonymity:** After considerable discussion of Shakespeare's world and times, what about the man himself? What about his possible beliefs, opinions, dreams, fears, and personality traits? Such information could help the writer greatly; however, surprisingly, given Shakespeare's near monolithic status in our culture, we actually know little about the man behind the plays. This fact is made even more difficult to believe by the countless biographies of Shakespeare that have been published

through the years, but it has undoubtedly added to the awe and power of Shakespeare's work, existing as it seems to, independent of a human author. As we have seen, Shakespeare's dialogic method, staging in his plays philosophical conversations that are not satisfactorily resolved by a single answer, means that Shakespeare as author fundamentally "disappears" into his plays, and there is little in our knowledge of the man to help us recover him intact. The bare facts, mostly collected from mundane legal documents, take us more or less only this far: Shakespeare was born into a middle-class family in the country town of Stratford upon Avon. As a young man he married a somewhat older woman who, as a crosschecking of parish records reveals, was already pregnant. Shakespeare left behind his family in Stratford to seek—successfully—his fortune in London, first as an actor, then writer, then shareholder in a theatrical company. We do not know how often he returned to his wife and children while he was in London, nor very much of how he lived when in the city. By the time he retired, Shakespeare was wealthy enough to purchase one of the finest houses in his hometown of Stratford, where, coming full circle, he spent the final years of his life. As you can see, there is little in this silhouette of a man's life to illuminate the great works of literature he produced. It is ironic, poetically so, that we know his work so intimately but essentially know no more of his life than we could discover of any one of his countless, forgotten contemporaries. This speaks to the transience of human life and the longevity of art; it reminds us, too, that literature has a life of its own, independent of the author's intentions. Essay writers, therefore, may actually fare better in the playwright's absence, for there is no ultimate truth or real answer to uncover, rather endless possibilities.

It is thus left to each reader and writer to invent his or her own Shakespeare. As you do so, of course, you invent (and then reinvent) yourself as a Shakespeare scholar. The following chapters will offer a variety of approaches to the plays, some of which are traditional, some quite modern. For example, Shakespeare scholarship over the last few decades has been largely dominated by the desire to historicize the plays, to explore them in the historical context in which they were written. In many of the chapters, viable historical approaches to a given play are presented, to encourage writers to explore the interaction between Shakespeare's work and the material world that surrounded him. During the middle of the twentieth century, however, criticism tended to be more formalist in nature, examining the texts as self-contained worlds. Students, more or less free from the vagaries and fashions of the academy, can benefit from this view of the literary text as a world unto itself and can explore the psyches, motivations, and, personalities of Shakespeare's carefully crafted characters. Writers can engage in the seemingly academic matters of form and genre or make use of their twenty-first-century sensibilities and address about issues such as postcolonialism or homosexuality in Shakespeare's works. So much has been said and written about the plays already, but rest assured you will see, think, or say something that is fresh and original as you encounter Shakespeare. The challenge before you is then to help you put those ideas where they belong: on paper for someone to read, consider, and enjoy.

Bibliography

Bloom, Harold. *Shakespeare and the Invention of the Human*. New York: Penguin, 1999.

Fernie, Ewan, ed. *Reconceiving the Renaissance: A Critical Reader*. New York: Oxford University Press, 2005.

Guy, John. *The Tudors: A Very Short Introduction*. New York: Oxford University Press, 2000.

Hadfield, Andrew. *The English Renaissance: 1500–1620*. New York: Blackwell, 2001.

Hale, John. *The Civilization of Europe in the Renaissance*. New York: Simon and Schuster, 1993.

Greenblatt, Stephen. *Will in the World: How Shakespeare Became Shakespeare*. New York: W.W. Norton, 2004.

McDonald, Russ. *Shakespeare: An Anthology of Criticism and Theory, 1945–2000*. New York: Blackwell, 2004.

Morrill, John. *Stuart Britain: A Very Short Introduction*. New York: Oxford University Press, 2000.

Shapiro, James. *A Year in the Life of William Shakespeare: 1599*. New York: HarperCollins, 2006.

HOW TO WRITE ABOUT SHAKESPEARE'S TRAGEDIES

ON HEARING the news of his wife's death, with his own end nearing and the responsibility for so many atrocities squarely on his conscience, Macbeth speaks the following lines:

> She should have died hereafter;
> There would have been a time for such a word.
> To-morrow, and to-morrow, and to-morrow,
> Creeps in this petty pace from day to day
> To the last syllable of recorded time,
> And all our yesterdays have lighted fools
> The way to dusty death. Out, out, brief candle!
> Life's but a walking shadow, a poor player
> That struts and frets his hour upon the stage
> And then is heard no more: it is a tale
> Told by an idiot, full of sound and fury,
> Signifying nothing.   (5.6.17–28)

The images conjured here are terrifying, supremely disturbing. Life is simply the passage to death. A person is nothing more than a "poor player," an actor who "struts and frets" briefly before making an exit. Notice, too, that the image here is disorderly. When the melancholy

Jaques of *As You Like It* adopts the common metaphor of life as a stage, he is deliberate in noticing the orderly seven stages of a person's life, the carefully scripted nature of our lives. There is sadness in the image of returning, at the end, to a second infancy, but there is purpose, too, a sense of life's poetry and composition. Not so for Macbeth. The actors in his metaphor seem in the grip of a most painful stage fright, a panic seizing them as they face the stage with no lines ready and no meaningful part to play. All they can do is feebly posture and prance before they are called on to leave.

It is not just the actors that are wanting, though; the stage on which they tromp seems for Macbeth to deserve nothing more than this pitiful display. Is there something behind all of this? For Macbeth, there is nothing great or good but simply "an idiot" whose tale, though it can be loud and heated, means nothing.

This is surely one of the bleakest passages in all of Shakespeare, and it cuts to the heart of what tragedy might be. In ancient times, Aristotle had written of tragedy's ability to command pity and fear, and this formula still has surprising high currency today. The fear is easy to see in the preceding passage, Macbeth's fear and our fear. What if he is right? The pity may be a little harder to reach, but, as many critics have observed, though Macbeth has done unspeakable things, because we have watched him travel his path to ruin from the earliest moments of doubt and uncertainty, recognition of his plight may be provoked. It may not exactly be pity or even sympathy. Rather, perhaps, it is what the early twentieth-century critic A. C. Bradley, speaking of Shakespearean tragedy broadly, described as a sense of waste; we feel that things have gone wrong but that they could, instead, have gone well. Macbeth's life could have been great rather than villainous, benighted, and cut short.

When writing about Shakespeare's tragedies, then, one way of approaching the task is to start by understanding the precise nature of this gap, in the play or plays you are treating, between what could have been and what is. Then identify, in as much detail as you can, the reasons why the darker outcomes emerged, why the brighter possibilities were eclipsed. Sometimes this line of thinking will soon take you to a relatively easy or obvious first stop. For example, in *Timon of Athens* the two principal forces that drive Timon to exile and then death are a) his excessive generosity and b) the selfishness of his so-called friends. In *Coriolanus,* you might even suggest that the title character's exile and death are primarily propelled by one factor alone: the tragic hero's dedication to honesty at all costs. However, though this is a fine place to begin, it simply touches the surface of the play's tragedy, and as a writer of literary criticism it is your job to go beyond the surface and show your reader what they might not be able to see by themselves. So what does pushing beneath the surface look like in this case? First, it has been observed by many critics that Shakespeare's tragic heroes frequently are undone by an inability to function in a new or different environment. In this case, Coriolanus is an excellent warrior, but when he is called on to move into the world of politics, his bluntness and candor lead to his downfall. Even this observation, however, does not take us far enough into the play. Coriolanus's tragedy is fuller and more complete than this. After all, if it was simply a matter of poor decision making on the tragic hero's part, we might be more annoyed than we are moved by his plight. So, at this point in the drama, we turn to Coriolanus's mother, Volumnia, and the information Shakespeare deliberately and overtly gives us about her parenting of the young Coriolanus. We learn that she raised her son with a singularity of focus, methodically shaping and crafting him to be an outstanding warrior, a hero whose fiber is comprised of war and battle. To put it simply, then, it is not Coriolanus's fault that he is who he is. His individuality, something we think of optimistically as being at the command of the individual, has in fact been forged by others, by forces and pressures external to the individual. So Coriolanus's tragedy is not so much that he makes bad choices but rather that he is utterly incapable of making good ones—it is not in him, literally, to make the right moves at this pivotal time. As we then think beyond the play and consider the impact of this predicament for ourselves, we might begin to recognize the extent to which we ourselves have been conditioned and shaped by the external world rather than consciously self-fashioned (though, of course, by definition, our conditioning prevents us from fully comprehending the extent to which we are conditioned). So, from a relatively simple starting point—the man is just too honest for his own good—we have pushed our way to a much more complex set of ideas. The progression is a necessary one in a strong, well-defended essay and comes from answering simple questions about why this great hero-warrior ends up isolated and dead instead of being the toast of Rome.

Pushing beyond an obvious or easy first step in the interpretive process is one method for arriving at a strong thesis or topic. At other times, there is no simple or quick answer to grab hold of at the beginning. *Hamlet,* of course, for example, falls into this category, as arguably *Othello* does too. There have certainly been long-held interpretive readings of the plays that attempt to simplify the text and its characters in order to pursue a convenient and manageable argument. You should work hard to avoid simply following the pack and accepting a pat answer that, after further investigation, simply does not add up. Perhaps the stalest interpretive move with *Hamlet,* for example, is to suggest some variation of the critical mantra "Hamlet is a thinker not a doer," or, in a different form, "The play is a tragedy of inaction." As numerous frustrated critics have argued back, Hamlet does act—he kills Polonius thinking he is Claudius and with seeming ease dispatches Rosencrantz and Guildenstern to their doom, to name but two extremely decisive actions. So the writer's task, in this instance, is to embrace the difficulty of the play, perhaps by recognizing that a play as vast and multifaceted as *Hamlet* resists neat and tidy axioms. This process is likely to include acknowledging paradoxes and contradictions within the work, speaking more in the language of multiple possibilities and interpretations than in the confident but perhaps blinkered language of definitive answers.

Othello, too, has a number of easy answers circling at the surface of the text. It was long held, for example, that Othello is foolishly jealous and that the hero's all too explicit shortcomings and flaws lay at the core of the drama. Many questioned the power of the play because they could not view Othello as a credible tragic hero. However, with the application of a more socially aware critical lens, we can argue that *Othello* is one of Shakespeare's most brilliantly perceptive and intricate dramas. Again, we try to explore the gap between the positive "what could have been" and the tragic "what is" that prevails at the close of the play. To say that the gap results merely from Othello's foolishness is obviously inadequate. So, again, as literary critics do, we push harder and work for better, more compelling answers to our questions. The writer at this point asks herself what other factors are present in play. There is obviously Iago, but as vital as he is to the play's tragedy, he is merely the lit match to Othello's fuse, the facilitator of the Moor's rage; his presence may cause the explosion, but the conditions had to be in place for the match to amount to anything more than a tiny flame. The writer then persists, looking to identify the nature of these conditions and understand them better. It is not enough to say that Othello is a fool who willingly buys into Iago's schemes. Othello is easily revealed to be no dullard. His scenes in the early parts of the play reveal that he is quick minded and articulate, capable of turning difficult situations into successful outcomes. Pursuing this line of thinking, it will not take long, perhaps, for the write to identify one prominent aspect of Othello's character as a particularly promising avenue for investigation: his racial identity. After all, what is it that sets Othello apart from the other Venetians, what makes him vulnerable and subject to an unusual level of scrutiny and suspicion? Before we meet Othello, we have heard Iago and Roderigo's racist slurs and sensed the anxiety of Desdemona's father about the interracial marriage of his white daughter to a black man. Shakespeare foregrounds not only Othello's race but the vulnerable and marginalized position he inhabits in white-dominant Venice. We learn soon after that Othello is tolerated because he is useful to the state, and we feel certain, moreover, that his integration into Venetian society is based on nothing more substantial than this mere utility. It is entirely understandable, then, that Othello should be consciously and unconsciously aware of or anxious about his position both in the Venetian court and as husband to a noble white woman in Renaissance Europe. Iago prods and pokes repeatedly at these raw nerves of insecurity, telling Othello that it seems inevitable that Desdemona will desire the love of a white man over her black husband. So what appears to be simple foolishness ultimately reveals itself as a complex sociological condition, a pattern of behavior illuminated by psychological and multicultural readings of the tragic hero and the social forces acting on him.

What all of these reflections have in common, limited as they may be, is a desire to go deeper into the text, an unwillingness to accept easy and quick readings of the play. Some of this work will be done as you actively read the plays, but much of it will be done in the prewriting stage of your essay and beyond. As you read the plays, especially if you are encountering the play for the first time, there may be simply too much going on—the pull of the plot, the struggles with Shakespeare's language—for you at first to get much beyond "why can't Hamlet enact the revenge he seeks?" or "Why is Othello so ridiculously gullible?" It is often through the act of writing about the plays that our thinking moves to a new level or achieves nuance and greater complexity. By combining a determination to make complicated arguments with the willingness and need to work in detail with the text in quotation, the writing process compels us to rise to the demands of Shakespeare's tragedies.

TOPICS AND STRATEGIES
Themes

Sometimes in Shakespeare's drama, the themes override the characterization; other times, these components of thematic power and intricately crafted characterizations go hand in hand and have equal presence in the play. *Coriolanus* and *Titus Andronicus* provide examples of the first kind, along with many of the early comedies, while the major tragedies distinguish themselves with the most carefully and thoroughly crafted characters of the early modern stage. In each case, however, Shakespeare reveals a mind of incredible scope, drawn to ideas, themes, and avenues of thought more than even narrative force—*Hamlet* provides an example of this, of course. The title of A. D. Nutall's recent book, *Shakespeare the Thinker*, succinctly characterizes the nature of Shakespeare's work.

There is never a shortage of things to think, talk, or write about when you encounter a Shakespeare play. The plays are extraordinarily powerful works that have a seemingly limitless capacity to stimulate and reward the careful student. This is made vividly evident in Shakespeare's use of themes—everything from anti-Semitism to witchcraft crosses his mind and enters his work. However, while there are countless themes that flash brightly or subtly, it might be useful to begin by briefly examining a few themes that Shakespeare returns to frequently, often examining them from multiple perspectives during the course of his career.

Sample Topics:
  1. **Love:** Is Shakespeare a cynic about love in the tragedies?

> Even in his comedies, Shakespeare is reluctant to embrace an idealistic notion of love. He rather seems almost preoccupied with the arbitrariness of desire and affection. Romeo's power-

ful infatuation for the quickly forgotten Rosaline highlights the unstable nature of young love. However, every once in a while, Shakespeare imagines a kind of love that, while highly imperfect, works and binds two people together in a profoundly meaningful relationship. In the comedies we see the highest expression of this in Rosalind's advice to the lovesick Orlando in *As You Like It,* but do we see anything like this in the tragedies?

By definition, we would expect the tragedies to be even less optimistic about love than the comedies. Look for individual examples of love that flourishes despite obstacles present to prevent it. These may be quite isolated or outside of the heterosexual, romantic model of affection. Consider, for example, the death of dutiful servant Eros for the sake of Antony or the devotion of Kent to Lear.

Pay close attention to more traditional couplings in the play, particularly in the so-called "love tragedies" of *Antony and Cleopatra, Othello,* and *Romeo and Juliet.* Try to identify the nature of the relationship. What impedes it? Would it flower under more fortuitous circumstances? Many historically minded critics have suggested that, for example, the love between Romeo and Juliet is intended to be seen as not only immature but unwise. Others, of course, have found it beautiful and compelling, an ode to youth and passion. Equally, the seemingly more dubious and ambiguous relationship between Antony and Cleopatra has often been talked about as, in the end, singularly moving and intense as Cleopatra imagines an eternity with her husband after death. Others still have seen in the pair's death nothing more than mere political expediency, a need to be in charge and to avoid humiliation at the hands of Octavius. Be aware that all of the major relationships in the tragedies are open to a variety of (often quite oppositional) readings. Look for clues from the couple themselves, but also references to them scattered throughout the text.

2. **Otherness:** Does Shakespeare tend to express sympathy for marginalized figures in the tragedies?

Marginalized characters, sometimes referred to by literary critics as "the other," in order to emphasize the radical isolation such figures can experience from "mainstream" society, appear frequently in Shakespeare's plays. He seems to have been greatly interested in what we would today call sociology and even, more precisely, multicultural theory. In the comedies and romances, we see his extended treatment of Shylock in *The Merchant of Venice* as well as the indigenous islander Caliban in *The Tempest.* Though both portraits are highly problematic to modern readers (Shylock possesses many of the stereotypical traits of the stock Renaissance Jew, including a murderous streak, and Caliban is a would-be rapist and revolutionary), they are far more nuanced than Shakespeare's contemporaries would have expected or even, perhaps, desired.

When looking at Shakespeare's treatments of marginalized figures, look carefully at the balance struck between commonplace, negative characteristics and the humanizing or sympathetic traits that complicate the picture. If they are given redeeming features, what are they and how do we respond to them? As for their negative traits, does Shakespeare seem to encourage us to recognize that they emerge at least in part from the isolation and ill-treatment the characters may experience? Othello provides perhaps the most complex example of this kind of character, but you may also explore characters such as Cleopatra, or Aaron the Moor from *Titus Andronicus.* The latter represents Shakespeare's least sophisticated foray into the subject of race, relying almost solely on crude and poisonous stereotypes. Even in this instance, however, as critics have noted, Shakespeare incongruously makes Aaron, the man who gets people to chop off their hands simply for laughs, a passionately devoted father.

Moreover, when considering a rigid patriarchy like early modern England, you can also extend the idea of otherness to include women. While this notion of marginality can be broadly applied to Renaissance women, it seems even more fitting for those who resisted the early modern stereotype of womanhood. It is often said that the most prized virtues for women were chastity, obedience, and silence; those that challenged these norms faced significant difficulties and even punishments. You can obviously write an almost infinite number of essays on Shakespeare's treatment of women and "radical women" in particular. Moreover, you can reasonably argue that Shakespeare was a protofeminist or highly sexist. These are, of course, clumsily anachronistic terms, but they work as entryways into the drama. Take, for example, the tragic figure of Lavinia in *Titus Andronicus*. She is treated with nauseating cruelty by family and strangers alike. Her treatment is so horrifying that we have to believe Shakespeare intends to convey a strongly cast message about the politics of gender. But what? Does Shakespeare, through his play's lurid stagecraft, essentially join the gang of men who abuse and so disgustingly mistreat Lavinia? Or, does he set up a figure so beaten and tormented that she becomes an emblem of women's suffering, a figure of goodness who plays by the rules of early modern gender norms but is nonetheless victimized and tortured. Of course, you might choose to take Shakespeare out of the equation entirely and say that it does not matter what he intended, the play is so grotesque in its treatment of an innocent woman that it has no place in our culture, or that the play has a valid place precisely because it tells a story vivid and painful enough to talk about the history of gender injustice.

Lavinia is "other" because of her sex, but Shakespeare is drawn, too, to female characters that mark themselves as radically different by breaking social conventions. These figures make compelling topics and can be found in a variety of plays including *Titus Andronicus, Macbeth, Antony and Cleopatra,* and (in a somewhat different context) *Othello.*

3. **Politics:** Do the tragedies as a whole reveal a certain political sensibility? Do political tensions exist between the plays? Might we describe Shakespeare's politics as conservative or progressive?

Of course, all texts are in some way political, but among the tragedies *Julius Caesar, Coriolanus, Macbeth, Antony and Cleopatra,* and *Hamlet* seem to meditate most intensely on power and statecraft. It seems, too, that you can explore these plays in part through a tension between old ways and new ways of practicing politics. Shakespeare often depicts an older order being threatened and then replaced by the new one. The characteristics of the old order seem to be rooted in a kind of idealized nobility, often appealing but ultimately doomed to extinction, while the new order is characterized by a kind of shallowness and artifice—the traits that many people often associate with politicians today. This transitional state seems to center on the birth of modern political life in the age of Shakespeare. *Hamlet* provides a good example as the likes of Old Hamlet and Old Fortinbras make way or are forced aside by the calculating and politically savvy Claudius, Young Fortinbras, and Hamlet himself. While the older kings would fight in chivalric duels to settles old scores, Fortinbras marches an army to squabble and die over a worthless plot of land and Claudius murders his brother for the crown. You can identify and explore this pattern in a number of different places throughout the tragedies. Nonetheless, it remains difficult perhaps to pin down Shakespeare's sympathies. It seems likely that, because he returns many times to this political dynamic, it weighed on his mind, seemingly in wistful and nostalgic ways. At the same time, change makes good drama, and you should be wary of jumping to too many conclusions about the politics of any given play or the tragedies as a whole. Coriolanus, for example, resembles Old Hamlet and Old Fortinbras, but if we pity him at all we are also deeply frustrated by him and feel that his time is indeed finished. Moreover, we may not like what replaces this old order, but it is nonetheless clear that people like Young Fortinbras, Aufidius, or, in an unusually positive depiction of this new breed of political animal, *Macbeth*'s Malcolm, are destined to succeed and that the political future belongs to their kind.

An important companion text for so many political essays on Shakespeare will be Machiavelli's *The Prince*. In this early sixteenth-century text, Machiavelli outlines his understanding of how politics works and what a prince needs to do in order to maintain power. Machiavelli's advice has always been controversial and upsetting, but it offers classic insight into political life and the workings of power. Members of the new political order in Shakespeare's tragedies have been thoroughly schooled in Machiavelli, and we will understand them better and write about them more effectively if we become familiar with their teacher. Fortunately, *The Prince* is an accessible book, loaded with gruesome stories and devilish characters. The work addresses such questions as "Is it better for a prince to be loved or feared?" with a candor that earned its author enduring infamy.

Characters

In her recent book *Shakespeare and Modern Culture,* Marjorie Garber suggests that Shakespeare's plays have been instrumental in the shaping of our culture and that they were an important source of inspiration for thinkers as integral to the construction of modernity as Freud and Marx. Garber's book follows from Harold Bloom's *Shakespeare: The Invention of the Human* in its efforts to reveal the almost unimaginable consequences of Shakespeare's writing. Bloom writes of Shakespeare as a turning point, a kind of one-man Renaissance, while Garber more scientifically traces the threads of Shakespeare's afterlife right into the fabric of our daily lives. For both, however, it is Shakespeare's ability to create complex, nuanced, and multifaceted characters that lies at the center of his genius. Although the claims of these authors may be more substantial that of previous generations of critics, the obsession with Shakespeare's characters reaches back as far as Shakespearean criticism itself. Perhaps the most influential critic of Shakespeare's characters is A. C. Bradley, an early twentieth-century scholar who wrote on the figures populating the tragedies. It is often said that, for Bradley and his critical descendents, Shakespeare's characters function as if real people, virtual human beings capable of an interior existence hitherto seen only in living, breathing, thinking men and women.

Although it remains somewhat unfashionable to talk of Shakespeare's characters in this way at the upper levels of academia, it seems undeniable that such thinking will aid students in their writing. Simply put, try imagining Shakespeare's fullest and richest characters as "real" people in the way that Bradley and others have done. You do not need to state it this way in your essay, of course, but if you approach a character alive to the fact that he or she, like all us, will be imbued with inconsistencies, contradictions, insecurities, and desires, you will have gained the flexibility you need for your essay to succeed.

With Shakespeare's tragedies in mind, then, let us begin to sketch out some of this remarkable terrain as we look at a variety of character "types" and groups. Naturally not all of Shakespeare's creations will fit this celebrated formula of complexity and psychological sophistication, but promising directions can present themselves to the writer even when the characters are more thinly sketched.

Sample Topics:

1. **The obviously flawed tragic figure:** How might we respond to tragic figures that seem to glaringly "bring it on themselves"? Can these figures still stir enough feeling in us to make their tragedies great?

It is a commonplace of tragic theory to suggest that tragic heroes possess an inherent flaw that finally ensures their fall. Antony's love for Cleopatra, for example, might be seen as a particularly endearing example, while Titus's bloody adherence to the conventions of Roman virtue is another. As a writer, however, one of your tasks will be to assess the nature of such flaws, to ask, in a sense, how accountable the tragic hero is for his failings and to what extent his tragedy is impacted and defined by the tragic flaw. If the flaw is too obvious, perhaps, unchecked at the surface of the character, then perhaps you may begin to suggest that the value of the tragedy is weakened. However, in even identifying a character as a tragic hero too obvious in his or her flaws, you are making a key interpretive decision. Certainly not everyone will agree with you. For example, over the centuries various critics have bemoaned what they identified as naïve gullibility or unthinking jealousy in Othello, though one could argue just as effectively that his unique and unstable position in Venetian society provides an important sociological explanation for his stunningly bad choices.

King Lear similarly could be seen as a self-destructive figure or a victim of circumstance and environment. Timon and Coriolanus are perhaps less debatable, more obvious candidates for inclusion in a list of tragically flawed characters. Irrespective of the viewpoint you adopt and argue, the key is to attempt to understand the choices that a character makes, assessing the psychological pressures and social forces behind a character's action. Coriolanus may at first look like an irresponsible fool, but the further we delve into his upbringing and formative experiences, the more we see that he may not possess the ability to act any differently than he does. Once you have assessed these nature versus nurture considerations, it is then time to question the impact of character flaws on the tragic spirit of the play. To continue with the example of *Coriolanus*, the play's tragedy is far less effective and compelling if we perceive the titular hero as something of a moron than if we understand him to have been shaped and constructed by external forces that deny him the imagination to be truly free.

2. **The genuinely sympathetic tragic figure:** How does "pity" or justified sympathy influence our responses to certain figures in Shakespeare's tragedies?

In a sense, this character "type" is the opposite of the overly flawed character discussed in the preceding section. While it is hard to muster much sympathy for the too-green, self-indulgent Timon, a modern audience is likely to have nothing but compassion and sympathy for Romeo and Juliet. Although far less innocent, we may also have powerful feelings of sympathy for Antony, Cleopatra, and Hamlet too. Equally, Othello has shifted from foolish gull to sympathetic victim as our understanding of psychology and racial identity has developed.

For the writer, then, the task with such figures is essentially the reverse of the approach to discussing the tragically flawed protagonists. Rather than assessing how a potential lack of sympathy might shape our response to a play, the job at hand is to reflect on what happens when the "pity" that Aristotle spoke so memorably of is heightened and intensified. You may obviously conclude that the impact of tragedy is fuller, more keenly felt, more nuanced if feelings of pity are stirred (though it is not this simple, of course. *Macbeth* is still an incredibly powerful tragedy, though as many have suggested we do not ever really feel pity for Macbeth). With pity, perhaps, we arrive at identification, sadness, and maybe even the first stirrings of a vague empathy rather than mere sympathy. It may be the rare person who can recognize in herself the failings of Timon (though we all arguably possess something of Timon's brand of foolishness), but we can all quickly embrace the parts of Hamlet that are confused, uncertain, self-doubting, and seemingly somewhat frightened by life.

3. **The villain:** What philosophical or psychological questions are raised by Shakespeare's villains? Are there any patterns or common threads between many of them?

One aspect of Shakespeare's villains that has attracted critical attention is the degree to which they appeal to us and, to a certain extent, mirror us. For example, many have argued that Iago represents our desires to see entertainment unfold in the play—without him, there would be none. His predilection for sharing his thoughts and stratagems with us automatically forces a degree of collusion. This playful aspect of the villain is taken to its most lurid extreme in Aaron from *Titus Andronicus*, a figure who forces us to interrogate our desires to see spectacle on the stage. *King Lear*'s Edmund is a somewhat more complicated version of the same figure. If you choose to work with the relationship of a villain to the reader/audience, you should obviously pay close attention to soliloquies and asides, moments where we are being taken into the character's confidence—becoming part of his plot—whether we like it or not.

These same figures will also give you the opportunity to reflect on the nature of evil more broadly. Once again, Iago is the quintessential example here. Why does Shakespeare seem so fascinated by figures that are unambiguously monstrous emblems of vice and evil? Be careful not to fall into the trap of thinking that a figure of concentrated evil is by nature a thin or two-dimensional sketch. Rather, look to discover how Shakespeare actually seems to see pure evil as anything but simple. For example, Iago really is open to all kinds of psychological questioning and probing, even though Othello, close to the end, feels surprised he does not see devil's hooves on such a monster. While Othello may believe that Iago's evil is simplistic and straightforward, we as writers can discern otherwise.

Philosophy and Ideas

The comedies are rich in philosophy, but it is often playful and lightly worn. Amid the comedy of crossdressing or the pastoral delights of the forest of Ardenne in *As You Like It,* for example, it can be easy to lose sight of the philosophical discourses underpinning the play. It takes a moment, like Jaques's musings on the "seven ages of man," to pull us down from the airier pleasures of the text and focus us more coolly on the intellectual content of the work. In the tragedies, of course, the nature of the drama keeps the intellectual character of the plays ever in the mind's eye. With the possible exception of *Titus Andronicus,* a play that aspires to entertain more than edify, to stimulate emotional responses more frequently and sharply than intellectual ones, the tragedies are inclined to philosophy to the extent that we may label a work such as *Hamlet* or *King Lear* among the great philosophical writings of Western civilization.

Shakespeare's tragedies may have all the philosophical clout of a treatise by René Descartes, Georg Wilhelm Friedrich Hegel, or some other enduring philosopher, but the framework is infinitely more accessible—there are stories and characters. Shakespeare wants to be accessible and available in a way that traditional philosophers often are not.

Another important difference between Shakespeare and these great thinkers, however, can appear at first to be a difficulty. While the great philosophical thinkers may shift or radically change perspectives over their careers, there is typically a coherent and cogent "argument" being made. Often it is one that can be clearly associated with or directly attributed to a particular thinker (Freud and the power of the unconscious, for example). There is no such consistency or clarity of purpose in Shakespeare, however. You may feel you can make a claim about some aspect of Shakespeare's thinking based on one character or play, only to find that even another closely related play does not help you support your argument or directly contradicts it. When writing about Shakespeare's philosophy, then, you can often speak and think in terms of snapshots, of moments in which a certain idea or thought emerges, forms, and crystallizes in isolation.

Sample Topics:

1. **Fate:** What kinds of forces appear to operating in the lives of Shakespeare's tragic heroes? More broadly, can we say that Shakespeare seems to favor a version of human action that rests on free will, or does he instead more frequently ascribe events to something like predetermination?

   As so often when writing about Shakespeare, steering a middle course seems best. Once again, we find multiple possibilities and a variety of ideas expressed, even within a single play. For example, *Macbeth* turns on the dilemma of free will. Do the predictions of the Weird Sisters hold real power to determine Macbeth's future, or is it his own greed and ambition that drive him forward (and, therefore, his freedom to choose his own actions)? Can both be true at the same time? *Julius Caesar*, of course, explores similar philosophical territory. Look for social and psychological alternatives to fate, other pressures that can resist and curtail a character's potential to exercise free will. For example, Timon makes astonishingly bad choices and appears to bring ruin directly on himself. While this is undeniably true, his end would not be half so disastrous were it not for the fickleness of his friends and the vagaries of the economic system in which he cannot choose to live. The construction of Coriolanus's character from an early age, likewise, ensures that if he has free will, it must be understood as incomplete because he is not aware of or capable of making all the choices that are theoretically available to him.

2. **Metatheater:** How does Shakespeare stage his own medium, the theater, for philosophical purposes in his plays? When he incorporates a "play within a play," what are some of the possible metaphysical consequences?

We call something metatheatrical if a playwright stages some kind of dramatic practice or discourse within a play. This can be a fleeting moment akin to an "in joke" (such as a quip in *Julius Caesar* about future theatrical productions of the events being staged), or fully developed and carefully crafted productions of a play within a play. The most celebrated example of this in Shakespeare's tragedies is, of course, the play performed in *Hamlet.* However, like many of his contemporary playwrights, Shakespeare seems to have been particularly attracted to this self-referential practice. We see a particularly complex episode in *A Midsummer Night's Dream* in which a tragedy, much like *Romeo and Juliet,* is staged incongruously and jarringly at a wedding feast.

As a writer you should be aware of and utilize both the general philosophical quality of such moments and the particular implications of a specific instance of metatheatricality. For the former, the effect of metatheatricality is always to interrupt the illusion of reality on the stage; the audience is forced to be aware that they are watching a play, their attention consciously drawn to the fact that they are in an audience watching actors perform. The effect of this is to invite questions about the nature of reality, the difference (or similarity) between action onstage and off. If some of the characters onstage form an audience watching a play, the "real" audience in the theater might reflect on their own role as spectators as opposed to participants.

In addition to these general characteristics of metatheatricality, consider the particular context of the play within a play. How does it comment on the larger play overall? Is the relation between the plays one of harmony or tension? What is the purpose of the production for the characters performing the play with a play? What is the effect on the characters spectating and portraying members of the audience onstage?

Compare and Contrast Essays

One previously discussed approach to discussing Shakespeare's thinking is capturing a snapshot that might be isolated in his work (isolated in that it may not have broad or far-reaching implications and may not be used to support or substantiate any contention about Shakespeare's work as a whole). This approach can be adapted to include more than one play, teasing out the implications of a tightly defined element or aspect of each of the works. The more limited scope of the inquiry may not allow the writer to make solid claims about Shakespeare's drama as a whole. The picture is bigger, but the element being analyzed remains a snapshot. Alternatively, as another approach to a compare or contrast essay, analysis of tensions and differences can be as revealing and vital to our understanding of Shakespeare as ambitious attempts to uncover continuities. A thesis that sets out to explore the implications of subtle or radical differences among Shakespeare's play may raise useful questions and encourage detailed exploration of the texts. In analyzing and breaking down a literary work, raising questions is as rewarding as suggesting answers.

Sample Topics:

1. **Comparing tragedies with tragedies:** What are some key strategies for handling connections within Shakespeare's tragic canon?

   Of course, all of the material in this chapter lends itself to the development of compare and contrast essays. For example, King Lear and Timon can be included among the flawed characters Shakespeare's tragedies have given life to. If Timon and Lear are both flawed characters, can we say they are equally flawed? Are they flawed in different ways, or does similarity dominate? Do we feel their tragedies with equal force? A good rule when writing a compare and contrast essay is to ask, "Is similarity more obvious than difference here, or vice versa?" If you are working with two texts, characters, or themes that appear immediately more alike than different, perhaps the exploration of difference becomes the most rewarding path to take (and, of course, if differences appear to dominate, then push the idea of similarity). In the example of Timon and King Lear, the two figures initially appear somewhat similar. Their actions to begin with, and the nature of their flaws, too, are closely related. Yet *King Lear* is one of Shakespeare's most admired plays, while *Timon* is one of his least. Lear may initially frustrate us, but we passionately pity him by the end of his play (and probably long before the end too). Timon potentially just annoys us. Given our initial idea of similarity, explanations for these vastly different theatrical outcomes will clearly be meaningful and important, helping us to understand both plays better.

A second consideration when approaching compare and contrast essays: The comparison of the two (or more) texts should allow the reader of the essay to discover something that looking at one text alone would not. The analysis of one play will either reinforce the interpretation of an aspect of another work, or the drawing of differences will illuminate absence or lack, what is prominently featured in one drama while not in another.

2. **Comparing tragedies to comedies:** Are Shakespeare's comedies and tragedies to be treated as different terrain by the writer? Can it be productive to compare comedies and tragedies?

You should feel at liberty to view comedies and tragedies alongside one another and to encourage and explore interactions between them. While there seems to be a theoretical division between the formal aspects of comedy and tragedy, and the tones can sometimes appear to be different enough to discourage comparison, close reading will often dispel such self-imposed limitations. As has long been said of Shakespeare's plays, the playwright himself seems to have minimized the distance between comedy and tragedy to the point where the border can seem porous, fluid, or altogether nonexistent. The *Bloom's How to Write about Shakespeare's Comedies* volume in this series will provide you with more material on each respective comedy, but a general rule for Shakespeare's comedies is that the dramatist never allows for a simple and entirely happy ending. There are always loose ends or shadows cast that compromise or subvert the notion of a positive resolution.

One way of approaching essays exploring connections between comedies and tragedies, of course, is through theme. You might feel, for example, that the unrelenting bleakness of *Macbeth* cannot be addressed in the same essay as the farcical early comedy *The Taming of the Shrew*. Nonetheless, thematically, the plays feature significant area of overlaps. Both explore the consequences of a woman (or women) with too much power, women who attempt to control men, and the inevitable outcome of such "unnatural" behavior. Both plays "punish" the principle woman involved (Kate and Lady Macbeth) and symbolically or literally silence them (Lady Macbeth's suicide off stage and Kate's submissive gesture of placing her hand on the floor for Petruccio to step on if he please) as the patriarchal order is once again restored at the close of each play. Depending on how this approach is handled and developed, of course, the discussion could just as easily become a character-based compare and contrast essay focusing on Kate and Lady Macbeth more specifically than an essay on the general overlap of themes would require.

Bibliography

Dillon, Janette. *The Cambridge Introduction to Shakespeare's Tragedies*. Cambridge, England: Cambridge UP, 2007.

Dobson, Michael, ed. *Performing Shakespeare's Tragedies Today: The Actor's Perspective*. Cambridge, England: Cambridge UP, 2006.

Garner, Shirley Nelson and Madelon Sprengnether, eds. *Shakespearean Tragedy and Gender.* Bloomington, IN: Indiana UP, 1996.

Leggatt, Alexander. *Shakespeare's Tragedies: Violation and Identity.* Cambridge, England: Cambridge UP, 2005.

McEachern, Claire, ed. *The Cambridge Companion to Shakespearean Tragedy.* Cambridge, England: Cambridge UP, 2002.

Zimmerman, Susan, ed. *Shakespeare's Tragedies.* New York: St. Martin's, 1998.

ANTONY AND CLEOPATRA

READING TO WRITE

CRITICS HAVE long identified the play's lack of narrative explanation or character motivation at vital moments in the drama. If you feel you do not know the reason for something in this play, there is a good chance it because the text has kept it from you, not that your reading was flawed. There are numerous moments in the text that are frustratingly blurred. Critics have cited, among more common and important examples, the decision of Cleopatra to take flight in the naval battle (3.11) or the troubling uncertainties of the final betrayal of Antony at sea in 4.13. Readers may potentially feel they missed some subtle or complicated explanation for these narrative turning points, but, in fact, no explanations are given. Janet Adelman, in a widely anthologized essay on this play, explores the consequences of these indeterminacies (see "Further Reading"). Equally, critics commonly note the fact that we get little insight into the major characters through the standard technique of soliloquy. A question as fundamentally significant as whether or not Cleopatra actually loves Antony remains unanswered and unanswerable. Does she betray Antony several times and then finally take her life to avoid the humiliation of defeat rather than a life without Antony? Or does Cleopatra remain true to her lover to the point that she takes her own life in order to be "reunited" with him? Or, in some complex and human way, could both of these contradictory possibilities be simultaneously true? Critics have long wrestled with this crux and other such questions in the play. As a writer you, too, should embrace the uncertainties of the play, offering potential solutions but remaining aware that in work on this play, even more so than most of Shakespeare's canon, singular "truths" are unlikely to present themselves.

To unpack some of this motivational uncertainty as well as to establish a few key themes and ideas of the text, here is Caesar's reaction to the news of Mark Antony's death:

> O Antony!
> I have follow'd thee to this; but we do lance
> Diseases in our bodies: I must perforce
> Have shown to thee such a declining day,
> Or look on thine; we could not stall together
> In the whole world: but yet let me lament,
> With tears as sovereign as the blood of hearts,
> That thou, my brother, my competitor
> In top of all design, my mate in empire,
> Friend and companion in the front of war,
> The arm of mine own body, and the heart
> Where mine his thoughts did kindle,—that our stars,
> Unreconciliable, should divide
> Our equalness to this. Hear me, good friends—
> But I will tell you at some meeter season. (5.1.35–49)

This passage could feature in a variety of essays. Obviously it would find room in a character essay on Caesar but also in a compare and contrast essay exploring the relationship between Antony and Caesar. An essay on the abstract notion of fate ("our stars, / Unreconciliable") in the play could treat this passage alongside other moments, not least the Soothsayer's scene (2.3) in which the moment of Antony's "defeat" to Caesar is foreshadowed, in which these great leaders of the world appear to be at the mercy of preordained destinies. Certainly Caesar possesses a vivid, almost messianic sense of the power he will wield.

The implications of the passage also encourage us to think about Antony's death and to ask what exactly led him to his suicide. With characteristic self-importance, Caesar claims that "I have follow'd thee to this," but it seems clear that there is much more to Antony's final choice than the military pressures of Caesar. While Caesar interprets his rival's downfall in strictly political terms here, Antony clearly couches his death in the terms and mythology of tragic romance: "I will o'ertake thee, Cleopatra, and / Weep for my pardon . . . Dido and Aeneas shall want troops, / And all the haunt be ours" (4.14.44–54).

Still, the relationship between Antony and Caesar exists at the core of the passage's imagery. After his claim of success, so to speak, at the beginning of the passage, Caesar imagines Antony as a disease in his body, something to be lanced and removed. However, as critics note, by the end of the passage the body imagery has shifted. Antony is no longer a foreign presence to be resisted by Caesar's body politic, but nothing less than part of the same body: "The arm of mine own body, and the heart / Where mine his thoughts did kindle." Writers have used this passage, then, to talk not merely about the pairing of the two men, or even of their mirroring, but of the fundamental, organic cohesion of the two rulers. So, while the passage begins with images of separation (Antony is foreign to Caesar; Antony must die if Caesar is to live—"I must perforce / Have shown you such a declining day, / Or look on thine."), it has been observed by some that the final images build toward unity not division. These writers have naturally sought to show how the connection between these two men is as important to the tragic movement of the play as the coupling of Antony and Cleopatra. Additional material and strategies for such an essay is included in the "Compare and Contrast" section.

TOPICS AND STRATEGIES

Every essay requires a focus; you cannot write about everything in the play at once. In the section on how to write an essay, you will be presented with a number of ways of turning a focus into a thesis, observations into arguments. However, the starting point is nearly always finding an initial point of departure, making first observations. You can then seize on and develop the budding ideas you will have as you make your way through the play. By no means should you feel limited to these topics, however. Instead they can be viewed as triggering suggestions encouraging you to break out into your own critical directions.

Themes

As with many other elements of the play, the themes of *Antony and Cleopatra* are often slippery and uncertain. As we have seen, however, by creating an abundance of ambiguity and free play, the fuel that drives interpretive essay writing, Shakespeare has gifted the essay writer with the raw materials for a rich and novel argument. Equally, the writer should be encouraged by the play's much discussed scale and ambition; *Antony and Cleopatra* encompasses a wide embrace; intellectually, geographically, and aesthetically it reaches for the kind of plenitude we hear of at the Egyptian feasts. There is, simply put, a wealth of material included in the play, and often what is at its margins is as interesting and resonant as what is to be found at the apparent backbone of the text. These marginal elements are often at once distinct from and integrated with the central action, so there are many, many available topics for the writer. The theme of suicide, something in the text explored by a number of critics, proves the point here well. The suicides of Antony and Cleopatra present grand puzzles in the play, but it seems an incomplete analysis if we consider the deaths separately from the suicides of Enobarbus and Eros. Both these apparently peripheral actions contribute to an important thematic pattern in the work and can be used by the writer to inform the more central suicides later in the play or to create a broader conceptual framework that weighs all four episodes more equally as parts of a whole. With this in mind, look for material to be used in these essays in the "Characters" section as well.

Sample Topics:

1. **Love:** What different kinds of love can be said to emerge in the play? Can we broadly say that *Antony and Cleopatra* is cynical or finally optimistic about love?

Perhaps you may want to work with a broad definition of love in the play, or perhaps you might want to limit your analysis to the central pair of lovers. However, even if you select the latter option, you may want to acknowledge that, once again, the scope of the play is broad and events at the apparent margins of the play matter. Take for example the suicide of Eros at 4.14. This act seemingly of pure devotion appears to set a high standard for the lovers to meet in the following scenes, and critics have given much time to understanding this figure whose name is obviously of importance. Among other figures that may be included in an essay of this kind are Fulvia and Octavia, the first wife who appears so inconsequential to Antony (despite some all-too-late claims he makes to the contrary) that the play does not take the trouble to introduce her in person, and the expedient second wife who apparently never earns Antony's affection. What does Cleopatra represent, however? Certainly she is made sensual to the point of fantasy (2.2.240–45) and is often associated by others with Antony purely in terms of his lust. Equally, even toward the close of the play, as critics note, Antony seems uncertain of Cleopatra's motives and feelings for him. How would you characterize the clearly complex love that Cleopatra and Antony share?

Another important aspect of the play's meditation on love is the conflict between politics and love. These two realms seem to be at odds, as the politically motivated but ultimately disastrous marriage of Octavia and Antony demonstrates. Others have even applied the terms of love to the relationship between Antony and Caesar, and the previously cited passage from the play should provide some initial clues as to how this avenue might be approached. Critics have suggested that perhaps both final suicides can be at least partly characterized as politically motivated acts instead of or as well as acts of desperate love.

Obviously with so much related material here, substantial work at the prewriting stage is required. As always, look to get focus and clarity upfront with a well-crafted thesis statement that guides the rest of your essay. When you are done, ask of each paragraph in the essay if it helps to support your thesis claim. If a section of your essay does not, revise to make sure it does or remove the passage. When handling a topic on which there is much to say, the danger of losing coherence is considerable.

2. **Betrayal:** Can anyone in the play be trusted?

At the heart of the play's dramatic action is betrayal. So many of the decisive narrative turns rely on it, and we see it so often that, as with a theme such as suicide, we can catalog the instances and derive a larger meaning from the pattern. It certainly seems that almost everyone in the play is capable of betrayal, from the most prominent instances between Antony and Cleopatra to the seemingly peripheral infidelities of Decretas (4.14). Again, other characters to think about in this essay include Fulvia, Lepidus, Octavia, Enobarbus, and Seleucus. The latter character has been productively considered by critics, and his odd and brief appearance has been put to good use in arguments about the play's broader concerns with betrayal and fidelity. Again, Eros seems to be a figure used for contrast and to add another hue to the moral palette of *Antony and Cleopatra.* Yet critics have also asked whether all of the betrayals turn out to be as simple as they seem. For example, Enobarbus passionately comes to regret and fatally repent his betrayal of Antony. As you write, then, it may be the best strategy to keep in mind Shakespeare's celebrated moral complexity, even more diffusive in this play than can be typically seen elsewhere in his work.

3. **Gender:** How does *Antony and Cleopatra* contributes to Shakespeare's continuing preoccupation with porous gender identities? How is Antony associated with femininity and Cleopatra with masculinity? What are the potential consequences of any shifting we may observe between these gendered terms?

In both his comedies and tragedies, Shakespeare seems fascinated by the dramatic possibilities of shifting gender roles and identities. Often, in the comedies at least, this blurring of gender can be liberating and leads to a state of free play (*As You Like It* and *Twelfth Night* arguably provide the best examples of this "positive" interpretation of fragmented genders). At other times, however, Shakespeare seems anxious about the possibilities of confusion between masculine and feminine norms. In particular, the extended elevation of a woman into a position of power over a man seems to be a serious source of concern in his drama (even in the problem comedy *All's Well That*

Ends Well, where Helen pursues the hapless Bertram with the authority and determination associated with masculine dominance in the period). Perhaps nowhere in Shakespeare is this situation exploited more than in *Macbeth* (see the "Compare and Contrast Essays" section), though we see it also lead to terrible consequences in another Roman tragedy, *Coriolanus.*

Look for moments where Antony is feminized and Cleopatra made masculine. Often-noted examples of the latter include Cleopatra's use of Antony's sword (2.5.23) or her desire to fight in battle (3.7), while of the former we are given immediate illustration in the opening lines of the play. There are numerous other moments that a writer could usefully incorporate, however. For example, consider Antony's tactically weak decision to fight at sea, and the role other characters assign to Cleopatra in this decision, or Cleopatra's bullying treatment of the messenger in 2.5. Again, nothing should be oversimplified when it comes to this play. For example, you might want to illuminate moments where Cleopatra is depicted as exceedingly feminine or moments where Antony, perhaps self-consciously overcompensating, as some have argued, asserts his manhood. Where it does occur, however, try to identify what role these ambiguities and paradoxes play in the vision of the play as a whole.

Characters

If unexplained pivotal plot points lead to narrative and thematic ambiguities, these same moments of uncertainty also have an impact on our ability to discuss and write about the characters of the play. It has also long been observed that there are relatively few soliloquies in *Antony and Cleopatra,* few moments in which the central characters can share directly with the audience their thoughts and feelings in the way we routinely see in *Hamlet* or *Macbeth,* for example. Many critics have argued, then, the net result of all this is that we do not understand these characters as well as we would like or expect to in a Shakespearean tragedy. Again, *Coriolanus* arises as another play also lacking a protagonist with the desire to speak directly to us and explain himself. The titular character of *Timon of Athens,* though he does deliver soliloquies, is a strangely thin sketch of a tragic hero, so although he does not resist our attempts to understand him, the dimensions of his character do not invite deep psychological analysis. So *Antony and Cleopatra* is not alone in distancing or alienating its tragic characters from the audience, but the lovers of this play are far more substantial characters than Timon or Coriolanus. The result, then, is that there is much to write about the characters of *Antony and Cleopatra*, but, to use a detective analogy, no one is confessing to anything, and we have a lot of deduction to perform. You have to listen to the witness statements, so to speak, of the minor characters who frequently offer insights (though not always reliable ones, of course) into the motives and actions of the principal characters. The writer, then, needs to "fill in the blanks" and account for those things the play and its characters do not tell us.

Finally, thinking about how the writer can use the voices of minor characters in the play, another often-cited facet of this play is the prominence of figures supposedly at the margins of the work. There are a number of minor characters substantial enough to support an essay, though you should by no means treat them in isolation from the rest of the play. The key to working with the minor characters in most works of literature (and certainly in *Antony and Cleopatra*) is to demonstrate how these personages become part of the dialogue (through what they say and what they do) illuminating the major characters and themes of the play.

As the lack of individual insight leads to a particularly high degree of interconnectedness between the characters, review all of the following character discussions before writing about any one figure. You may find helpful material in each section as you explore how one character is partially shaped by a relationship with another.

Sample Topics:

1. **Antony:** Is Antony responsible for his own tragedy? If so, what are his tragic flaws?

Obviously you will craft and direct this essay as you see fit, but you may want to incorporate a number of the following moments in your analysis. Think about the depiction of Antony we are given by others in the play's first scene and then the early indication of his character emerging from the death of Fulvia

(1.2). Caesar's report of Antony at the beginning of 1.4 and the Soothsayer's scene (2.3) forge an early dynamic between the two leaders that may be worth elaborating on depending on the context of your essay on Antony. The third act offers a number of moments that seem to encourage a problematic or even negative reading of Antony. For example, you may want to look at the apparent military failures on Antony's part in 3.7 and 3.11. Antony's treatment of Thidias in 3.13 has been interpreted by critics as an attempt to reassert the former's injured sense of masculinity. If you agree, how do you use this cruel swagger in your essay? The ambiguously mournful tone of 4.2 is also important to understanding Antony as the play approaches its resolution, while you will of course want to pay attention to his argument for suicide and his initially flawed attempt on his own life (4.14). Some critics have suggested this scene is intended to embarrass Antony and that it adds yet another failure to his growing list of mistakes, an interpretation that is certainly open to debate. Do you agree? How do you finally feel the play wants us to view Antony? Do you sympathize with him more than you condemn him? How do you understand and organize your treatment of the three engines driving Antony's tragedy: Cleopatra, Caesar and Roman politics, and Antony himself?

2. **Cleopatra:** Critics often say that Shakespeare has made his portrait of Cleopatra much more sympathetic and complex than she is in the classical source by Plutarch. Certainly even Antony finds her difficult to comprehend. What exactly are the uncertainties that surround Cleopatra, and how might we begin to offer potential resolutions?

We are often told that in Shakespeare's source for the story of *Antony and Cleopatra*, Plutarch gives us an Antony straightforwardly seduced and corrupted by Cleopatra. Her influence over him is lamentable and his weakness for Cleopatra tragic. It is far from clear, in Shakespeare's play, however, that we are supposed to see the relationship, or the pair's tragedy, with such simple clarity. You may want to chart in your essay a course between the potentially untrustworthy aspects of Cleopatra's character and the almost juvenile girlishness that smacks of innocence at heart. A convenient framework for this discussion may be the language of gender discussed in the preceding "Themes" section: Cleopatra's beguiling femininity and her aggressive masculinity.

As with an essay on Antony, take care during the prewriting stage to organize the ample material available. Think about incorporating a number of the following moments. First, look at the earlier portions of the play in which we see Cleopatra missing Antony (1.5) and the sensual, erotically powerful descriptions we are given of her by Enobarbus (2.2.197–211; 2.2.239–45). These feminine strands of Cleopatra may be interesting juxtaposed with the image of Cleopatra as an angler catching Antony (2.5.8) and her almost comically abrasive hectoring of the messenger in 2.5. This pattern of stereotypically feminine behavior (3.3) and martial manliness (3.7) can be witnessed again soon after in the buildup to the key question of how influential Cleopatra can be said to be in the decision to fight by sea rather than land (3.11). These gender ambiguities are paralleled by what might be called moral ambiguities surrounding Cleopatra's trustworthiness. Scenes such as 3.13, 4.13, and 4.14 each offer potential examples of dishonesty or even betrayal on Cleopatra's part (see the preceding "Themes" section). Of course, the contemplation of suicide and the execution of the act in 5.2 will likely play a significant role in your essay. Things to pay close attention to in this important scene include issues of motivation (what exactly is it that pushes Cleopatra to her suicide? It may be more than one particular hope or fear, though, so look for complexity in your analysis) and, given the ongoing gender ambiguities throughout the play, you may want to also reflect on the distinctly gendered imagery surrounding Cleopatra's final moments.

3. **Caesar:** Are we supposed to think of Caesar as the "villain," or, in less simplistic terms, the principal obstacle to happiness in the play?

Like other characters in this play, Caesar is ambiguous and prone to contradiction and paradox. A particularly interesting strand of argument to follow in an essay on Caesar is his interconnectedness with Antony. Once again, the Soothsayer scene (2.3) will be vital for this topic as will Caesar's lament for Antony in 5.1. Yet while Caesar appears to be aware of the bond he shares with Antony, the indivisible nature of their fates, Caesar is a stronger and more skilled politician than Antony is. While fate for Antony seems to be a movement toward tragedy, you may want to explore Caesar's confidence that, for him, fate is the wind carrying him toward greatness. Do you interpret his political vision at 4.6 and his interpretation of the play's action as being a movement toward his own "glory" (5.2.152) as confidence or arrogance? In an important sense, is he right in this claim? In other words, how much influence does he have over the tragic action at the end of the play and the deaths of the two lovers?

Form and Genre

Antony and Cleopatra's formal elements have attracted the attention of numerous readers and critics. For example, some writers have handled the play's rapid movements over vast geographic spaces. Other critics have written eloquently on the importance of minor characters in the play and the way in which Shakespeare incorporates so many voices into his text. The play, thus, is often said to feel enormous in its scale and reach, and you may want to participate in the project of trying to understand Shakespeare's use of breadth as a device to underpin his dramatic form.

Moreover, critics often suggest that *Antony and Cleopatra* is something of a generic hybrid; an unclear tragic vision and traces of the comic combine to make the play difficult to define or categorize. Nonetheless, perhaps the most accessible essay to write on form and genre is one rooted in an attempt to clarify the nature of the play's tragedy. To do this, naturally, you will draw on much of the material in the preceding sections, but formulate it as a broader, more holistic approach to the play.

Sample Topic:

1. **Tragedy:** Do the formal peculiarities of the play mitigate the effectiveness of the tragedy? If we are not left with the kind of intense tragic "vision" that might be expected from one of Shakespeare's major tragedies, how might we describe the kind of insights and emotions that remain with us at the end of *Antony and Cleopatra*?

A useful strategy for approaching this topic might be to think about the ending of the play. How do you feel about the ending of the play? Where do your sympathies lie? Where or on whom do you place "blame" for what has happened to the two lovers? This task is a difficult one precisely because, as is true throughout the work, the characters and the narrative structure do not give you all the information you need to make up your mind. With this in mind, then, a good strategy might be to foreground the tentative nature of your conclusion, articulating alternative possibilities and interpretations at some point within the essay (though to avoid the essay collapsing in a mire of uncertainty, you should probably offer a particular reading—your thesis and central argument—as somewhat more compelling, of course. Unless, that is, your argument is precisely that the nature of the play's tragedy is simply too hard to characterize with any precision, in which case you will likely consider a variety of possibilities with roughly equal priority). The play seems to desire elusiveness, so it is entirely appropriate to respect this in your paper. To help you in this task, review this chapter thoroughly. Your material will likely be drawn from various aspects of the play once you have defined your initial parameters.

Compare and Contrast Essays

The lack of certainty or clear definition surrounding the characters means that, even more than usual, we evaluate one figure in the context of another, reaching for more insight than the individual character alone seems willing to provide for us. A great example here, of course, would be Antony and Caesar, with Caesar himself suggesting that the two were as one (though after the death of Antony, of course, a time when such claims are easy and convenient). You may also look for interesting compare and contrast options elsewhere among the characters. For example, you may want to think about Cleopatra alongside the fundamentally different Octavia. If you add Antony's first wife, Fulvia, to this framework, the dynamics become more complicated but potentially more interesting. While Octavia functions seemingly as a model of early modern womanhood against which to contrast Cleopatra, Fulvia seems to have much more in common with her rival in Egypt. Eros, too, is a useful figure for compare and contrast essays because he seems understandable and readable in comparison to the other characters. He seems to have been placed in the drama for no other reason than to provoke comparison, so it seems fitting to have him become the subject of a compare and contrast essay. It might be interesting, for example, to compare this faithful lover of Antony with Cleopatra. Alternatively, Eros's suicide could be compared with one of the other suicides in the play, particularly the more ambiguous deaths of Antony and Cleopatra. Of course, the classic division of the play appears to be between Egyptian and Roman sensibilities. While the play certainly exploits this binary, probably the most successful essays of this kind will at least partly try to complicate the binary of decadent Egypt against officious Rome. One way of doing this might be to explore the potential comparison between Cleopatra and Caesar, suggesting that Cleopatra's political skill is significant and driven by a desire for power and the upper hand in matters of state and empire.

Sample Topic:

1. **Comparing Cleopatra to Lady Macbeth:** To what extent can these powerful women be said to resemble each other? Can we use Shakespeare's more obvious feelings toward Lady Macbeth as a way of interpreting Cleopatra?

   A natural relationship can be established between Cleopatra and Lady Macbeth. Each of the plays seems to hinge on an anxiety created by the female control of men. Do you think *Macbeth* demonstrates a different kind of anxiety and even comes to a different conclusion than *Antony and Cleopatra*?

It may be a useful starting point to suggest that the two characters are variations on a theme, rather than similar models. It seems likely that the character of Cleopatra contains the possibilities of Lady Macbeth, though they are in competition with other elements that seem suppressed in or absent from Lady Macbeth. What might these other elements be?

You will certainly want to foreground each character's play with gender too. Again, you may find that, while there are important similarities, differences of degrees can certainly be established. Think, for example, about Lady Macbeth's desire to be "unsexed," to be made wholly unfeminine. Issues of motherhood and images of maternity could also be important here. While Lady Macbeth imagines herself killing the nursing child, it is the "nursing" snakes that kill Cleopatra in her play. These potent and powerful images need unpacking and could provide an excellent central crux for your essay. You may also naturally find your conversation extends to reflection on Antony and Macbeth.

Bibliography for *"Antony and Cleopatra"*

Daileader, Celia R. "The Cleopatra Complex: White Actresses on the Interracial 'Classic' Stage." *Colorblind Shakespeare: New Perspectives on Race and Performance.* Thompson, Ayanna, ed. New York: Routledge, 2006: 205–20.

Deats, Sara Munson, ed. *Antony and Cleopatra: New Critical Essays.* New York: Routledge, 2005.

Del Sapio Garbero, ed. *Identity, Otherness and Empire in Shakespeare's Rome.* Surrey, England: Ashgate; 2009.

Drakakis, John, ed. *Antony and Cleopatra.* New York: St. Martins, 1994.

Schalkwyk, David. *Shakespeare, Love and Service.* Cambridge, England: Cambridge UP, 2008.

Wofford, Susanne. *Shakespeare's Late Tragedies: A Collection of Critical Essays.* Upper Saddle River, N.J.: Prentice Hall, 1996.

CORIOLANUS

READING TO WRITE

*C*ORIOLANUS MAY not be Shakespeare's breeziest play to read, but it is nonetheless a manageable play for the student essay writer. It has several fascinating (though equally frustrating) characters, prominent gender and class concerns, and strong potential connections with Shakespeare's more frequently studied plays. Moreover, like many of Shakespeare's tragedies, of course, the play has a rich political vein, but such discourses here are more accessible and readily unpacked than, say, the knotty politics in another of Shakespeare's Roman plays, *Julius Caesar*.

To get a taste of some of these issues, closely examine a passage from the play. Here, Volumnia chastises her son, Coriolanus, after he has bungled an attempt to mollify the tribunes and the citizens of Rome. She is frustrated that Coriolanus seems to be incapable of showing enough humility to win the support he requires from the people to become consul.

> Because that now it lies you on to speak
> To th' people; not by your own instruction,
> Nor by th' matter which your heart prompts you,
> But with such words that are but roted in
> Your tongue, though but bastards and syllables
> Of no allowance to your bosom's truth.
> Now, this no more dishonors you at all
> Than to take in a town with gentle words,
> Which else would put you to your fortune and
> The hazard of much blood.

I would dissemble with my nature where
My fortunes and my friends at stake required
I should do so in honour: I am in this,
Your wife, your son, these senators, the nobles;
And you will rather show our general louts
How you can frown than spend a fawn upon 'em,
For the inheritance of their loves and safeguard
Of what that want might ruin. (3.2.55–69)

A number of themes and issues emerge in this paragraph that are meat and drink to the essayist. First, there are the gender concerns inherent in the passage and its speaker. Here we see Volumnia asserting political authority over her son by playing the role of what might today be called a spin doctor or political consultant. Volumnia has a gifted political mind, as we will see later in this chapter, and her skills are all the more striking in the play because they belong to a woman. Throughout the play, as she is in this passage, Volumnia is outspoken and forceful, chastising and coercing in order to secure her political ambitions through her son.

Moreover, understanding the exact nature of what she is advocating in this passage is vital for establishing both Volumnia's political vision and her son's converse unyielding lack of political acumen. Coriolanus prizes above all else a transparent notion of virtue, one in which a man's ways and actions should be as blunt as his sword is sharp. As critics of the play have noted, after all, there is little need for words in battles of the ancient world, and his brute power communicates effectively in that arena. Here, however, Volumnia councils against such forthrightness, telling her son not to speak "th' matter / Which your heart prompts you," but rather words that demonstrate "no allowance / To your bosom's truth." Such speech can be memorized, "roted in your tongue," and spoken as well rehearsed lines of artifice (again, critics have noted the presence of theatricality and performance in the political discourses of the play). To communicate this to her martial son, she skillfully uses a military metaphor, suggesting that to deal in politic speech with the Tribunes and the people would be no more shameful than trying to use words to subdue a besieged town. However, such duplicity is nonetheless against Coriolanus's nature, a nature that Volumnia boasts elsewhere to have engineered with precision and care. This, then, is what is often offered as the tragedy of Coriolanus: he is a man out of tune with the world he finds himself in, someone who does not belong and cannot function. Just as Hamlet cannot easily bring himself to act and kill a man in revenge, as his situation calls him to, Coriolanus lacks the ability to conceal his thoughts and words as his new political role demands of him.

Finally, at the close of the paragraph, we see the class tensions that fracture throughout the play. These divisions are witnessed in the opening lines of the angry, hungry Roman citizens through to the final moments of Coriolanus's life, surrounded by a bloodthirsty mob in Corioles. Volumnia naturally aligns herself with the noble Patricians of Rome, alluding contemptuously to the "general louts" who must be falsely "fawn[ed] upon . . . For the inheritance of their love." We will explore this topic more fully in the "Themes" section below, but its seems that, broadly speaking, the play seems to share Volumnia's disdain for the lowly citizens of Rome, depicting them frequently as gullible dupes easily blown this way and that by the winds of flattery and empty rhetoric.

The writer can see, then, that the play deals with binary absolutes, oppositions between such dichotomies as upper class and lower class or truth and deception. Though these binaries are always more complicated than they look, this structural pattern within the play offers useful material for the writer to explore and exploit.

TOPICS AND STRATEGIES

Every essay requires a focus; you cannot write about everything in the play at once. In the section on how to write an essay, you will be presented with a number of ways of turning a focus into a thesis, observations into arguments. However, the starting point is nearly always finding an initial point of departure, making first observations. You can then seize on and develop the budding ideas you will have as you make your way through the play. By no means should you feel limited to these topics, however. Instead they can be viewed as triggering suggestions encouraging you to break out into your own critical directions.

Themes

Having seen how several themes emerge from Volumnia's previously cited speech, let us develop some of them further. Obviously, *Coriola-*

nus is a political play, but the political discourses of the play take the shape of a familiar narrative: old ways versus new. As critics suggest, Coriolanus represents an older order, one apparently rooted in ancient ideals of honor and virtue. Set against this is the "emergence" of a new political spirit. This new breed of politics is characterized in *Coriolanus* by power plays and deception, the use of strategy to maintain and consolidate individual political authority. Critics observe a similar political climate in *Hamlet.* Where Old Hamlet and Old Fortinbras settled disagreements in chivalric one-on-one combat, acolytes of the new political model, including Young Fortinbras and Claudius, make their moves secretly and without regard for what they see as obsolete ideals of honor and virtue. In Shakespeare's time, this political model would likely have been associated with the writings of the early sixteenth-century Italian philosopher Machiavelli. His best-known work, *The Prince,* outlined a new way of understanding political ethics, one tied to pragmatism rather than idealism. In a sense, it does not matter too much that Machiavelli's writings were actually more subtle and morally nuanced than was popularly understood (Machiavelli believed that the stability of the state was the ruler's first and only responsibility, and therefore, almost any tactics that might be used to secure this security should be "on the table"), the commonly held understanding of Machiavelli in early modern England was that he indiscriminately advocated "evil" means to achieve often "evil" ends. It turns out that in his play, Coriolanus is essentially the only remnant of this older, transparent approach to politics (though did such a time of transparency ever exist? We can be certain that Machiavelli did not create the beast, but merely named it). Even Aufidius, a man we believe is Old Fortinbras to Coriolanus's Old Hamlet, turns out to be nothing less than the most adroit political schemer in the play, a Claudius apparently gifted enough to get away with it. The political tragedy of this play, then, turns out to be one of alienation and isolation—a man rooted in the past and incapable of understanding or functioning in the present; a stranger in an ugly new place.

Sample Topics:

1. **The new political order:** Why, exactly, is Coriolanus so out of place in this new political order? What skills does he lack? Does

the play sympathize with him, or dispassionately see his extinction in more Darwinian terms?

The "new" political order values concealment and maneuvering, while Coriolanus is the model of bluntness and transparency. To build your argument about the political world of the play, then, you will need to isolate and treat some of the many relevant passages and episodes in the text. There is so much in here, however, that carefully selecting and limiting passages will be necessary if you are working with a smaller page count for your essay. For example, during act 3 we see Coriolanus struggling repeatedly with the task of pretending to be respectful and humble. Part of the frustration experienced by his supporters (as well as by the readers) is, simply, that he keeps making the same mistake over and over again. Some view these scenes as grimly comic, especially as those around him repeatedly counsel mildness and meekness while apparently sensing that their man cannot pull it off. There is a sad, almost slapstick quality to this. If you do not have many pages to fill, you may want to select a passage or two from this movement and let your reader know that there is more where that came from, so to speak, and that the total political failure of Coriolanus in 3.3 is steadily stored up in the preceding scenes. After all, there are many examples of Coriolanus's lack of political savvy to be found throughout the play, and it does seem well worth emphasizing that this is a constant problem for Coriolanus, from beginning to end. Arguably, he is absolutely unchanged by the end of the play, making the same mistakes in the final scenes as he does in the opening ones. For example, note the arrogance of his entrance into the play at 1.9, his reluctance to speak in 2.2 and Menenius's mounting frustration with his ally in 2.3. Equally, at the close of the play, Coriolanus seems to be profoundly and naively unaware of political intrigue and competition, despite having suffered so greatly for the same flaw earlier in the play. He has no sense of Aufidius's growing jealousy or that he might needs to move cautiously through the settlement of the truce between Rome and the Volscians.

Importantly, though, this essay should not simply be an examination of how Coriolanus fails but why. To help you with this, look for attempts by his friends and allies to explain and justify their candidate's behavior. Look for several occasions where Menenius does this, but other characters give powerful insights into Coriolanus too. Volumnia does, of course, but an exchange such as the one between two nameless officers in the opening lines of 2.2 is also extremely useful.

In addition, also, you will want to show models of the new political order in action. Brutus and Sicinius, of course, provide the most visible examples through most of the play, but as suggested above, it is Aufidius who is finally the most successful practitioner of Machiavellian politics.

2. **Class tensions:** To what degree is class warfare central to the play's action, and to Coriolanus's personal tragedy?

Discord between the classes and the emergence of an attempt (no matter how shallow and symbolic only) to enfranchise the people is an important part of the shifting political environment of *Coriolanus*. Although partially distinct from the Machiavellian politics addressed above, the two areas overlap significantly as the central political challenge that Coriolanus cannot accomplish is representing himself to the people. Moreover, it seems as though a key feature of political scheming in the play is an ability to manipulate public sentiment. Brutus and Sicinius accomplish this skillfully, until events overwhelm them, of course. However, again, it is Aufidius who can finally be seen managing the people and staging Coriolanus's murder with terrifying political professionalism.

So, class tensions could appear as part of an essay on the general politics depicted in the play—with the plebeians as a political tool to be handled by the successful politician—or can be treated individually in an essay that literary critics might broadly term a Marxist study of the text. Such approaches to literature are interested in the divide between the rich and poor, the elite and the commoners in the text, and evaluate power relations between the two groups, how authority is used to suppress lower social classes and/or how resistance can be witnessed in the political struggles of ordinary folk. Part of your essay, then, may be devoted to understanding the role played by the ordinary citizens of the text. Can you identify Shakespeare's opinion of them? Watch carefully how they respond to attempts to secure their favor and to the threats that emerge in the second half of the play (scenes such as 2.3 or the end of 4.6 will be particularly helpful here). How do the elites view the commoners—and this, most importantly, even includes the Tribunes who supposedly represent the people? You will be able to identify "big" moments of class tension, such as Coriolanus's awkward and obligated conversations with the people, or his frequent oath of "hang 'em," but the play also seems to go out of its way to present smaller moments of tension between the low and the high. Look at 4.5 and 5.2, for example. A key function of such an essay, then, might be to understand how the play itself views the plebeians, and to situate these ordinary folk within the political discourses of the play.

3. **Masculinity:** What is Coriolanus's ideal of masculinity? How does this ideal become another component of his tragedy?

Building on some of the issues previously discussed, Coriolanus's political failures could be reworked into an essay on masculinity in the play. His early displays of candor, coupled with the kind of exaggerated martial skill witnessed at the end of act 1, help to define Coriolanus's ideals of manly honor. You might also use lines from Volumnia in 1.3, for example, to help you articulate this idea of manhood even further.

However, having established this notion of masculinity, there are a number of ways to make the picture more complex. For example, Volumnia becomes an interesting site for writers interested in gender studies. How does she display the key masculine tropes she so admires in her son? The idea of male bonding, the privileging of male friendships over relationships with women, might also be incorporated. A close reading of Coriolanus's loving reunion with Aufidius in 4.5 will be especially useful. Another scene of particular interest for many essays on gender in the play will be 5.3, the moment when the women in Coriolanus's life successfully attempt to win him over and assuage his demand for revenge. Finally, can we equate Coriolanus's failures with a rejection, on the part of the play, of his brand of hypermasculinity?

Characters

Critics often remark that Coriolanus lacks the complexities and self-awareness of other great Shakespearean tragic figures. Certainly it is hard to think of another such figure whose flaws are so easily visible and frustrating. Othello's excess of jealousy may have drawn the ire of critics for centuries, but he is being dragged along by Shakespeare's most chilling villain. Perhaps King Lear comes closest to resembling Coriolanus when he foolishly divides up his kingdom and demands fawning declarations of love from his daughters. But Lear painfully arrives at an understanding of his arrogance, while Coriolanus appears to die apparently without acquiring such self-knowledge. In a sense, then, Coriolanus and others in the play resemble figures found in Shakespeare's earlier works where characters frequently exist as embodiments of certain ideologies or ideas. And it does feel as though in this play Shakespeare is more interested in the political ideas he is exploring rather than the characters he uses to bring life to those ideas. Nonetheless, Coriolanus remains compelling precisely because he is so stubbornly unrepentant. He represents that part of us that does not learn, that cannot change or better itself because it simply lacks the emotional and experiential resources to do so. To a greater or lesser extent, we all struggle to adapt and are all hamstrung by the fact that we only know what we know and think what we think. Given time—and often it needs lots of time—we can adjust, redefine ourselves in the face of new challenges and changes, but Coriolanus is not given such time and the pull of his conditioning is irresistible.

Sample Topics:

1. **Coriolanus:** Does this inability to learn, to understand what is happening to him and why, make Coriolanus's tragedy more painful or less?

An essay on Coriolanus will rightly draw on much of the material in the preceding "Themes" section, so review that material before continuing. Also, be aware that the formula that often works well for character studies (the character is x and the beginning and y at the end) will likely be difficult to incorporate here. As we have seen, Coriolanus's story does not really provide the writer with a narrative of internal change. To counter this, you may simply ask the question: "well, why doesn't he change?" The essay becomes then a study of his concreteness, his impenetrable and immovable sense of self and the personal history that has created this identity. Key moments will likely come from the introduction to Coriolanus's arrogance and martial skill in act 1, through the infuriating and protracted displays of political failure in act 3, to his continuing hotheaded behavior in the play's closing action. What difference, exactly, is there between the man who makes an unwise and self-destructive refrain of "hang 'em" at the beginning of the play and the portrait of an arrogant, blinkered fool witnessed in Cominius's report of Coriolanus at 5.1.63–73?

2. **Volumnia:** In what ways in Volumnia central to her son's failings and final demise?

The play clearly wants us to see that Coriolanus is physically, mentally, emotionally, and morally a product of his mother. Feminist critics have produced impressive work exploring the intricacies of maternal imagery in this play, and tracing the paradoxical connection between Coriolanus's harsh masculinity and his mother's body. To understand Volumnia's role in her son's life, evaluate the upbringing she forced on him and her delight in his valor and military honor seen in 1.2, for example. Many critics have probed successfully the troubling fantasies and pleasures of Volumnia reflecting on her son's fate in battle (2.1.111, for example), but you should also incorporate how she actively councils him to deceive and equivocate in act 3. Critics have rightly noted the irony of this as it is in no small part Volumnia's conditioning of Coriolanus that makes such flexibility seemingly impossible. Closely read 3.2 to explore this idea, as well as Volumnia's interesting reflections on her role as mother, further. Equally, give substantial consideration to 5.3 in which Volumnia looks to pacify her son and get him to retreat from battle. Finally, what do you make of Volumnia's disappearance from the play after she succeeds in this task and is welcomed triumphantly back into Rome?

3. **Aufidius:** Symbolically, what is Aufidius's function in the play?

An essay on Aufidius may inevitably have something of a compare and contrast feel to it, naturally incorporating the figure of Coriolanus too. If Aufidius is the principal topic of the paper, you may want to actively control Coriolanus's presence in the essay to make sure that you do not lose focus. He will remain, of course, but make sure that the statements you make are statements that reveal something about Aufidius and/or the larger play, unless you go with an argument along the lines of "a better understanding of Aufidius allows us to more clearly perceive Coriolanus's tragedy" (in other words, the thesis is framed as being about Coriolanus through the figure of Aufidius).

In almost any version of the essay, though, you will likely want to articulate the basic structure of Aufidius' presence. It seems likely that this will include two distinct phases. For the first phase, look for parallels between Aufidius and Coriolanus, a closeness and similarity that apparently transcends their rivalry. Particularly helpful will be the flattering portrait of Aufidius we see at 1.1.220, while 1.9 continues to establish the parallel between the two characters. Of course, you will want to read carefully the relationship staged in 4.5; critics have spoken here about the almost erotic intimacy shared by the two men at this point.

The second phase, of course, sees Aufidius splinter violently and suddenly away from the neat parallel established by the main body of the play. You will want to carefully trace how this break occurs and why. How does Aufidius become the political creature that Coriolanus never could?

Form and Genre

It seems as though Coriolanus's tragedy is sealed at his first entrance, blisteringly chastising the agitated Roman citizens: "What's the matter, you dissentious rogues, / That, rubbing the poor itch of your opinion, Make yourselves scabs?" (1.1.152–54). Throwing fuel on an already dangerous fire, it is clear that Coriolanus is someone whose way of being in the world does not have wide currency. We quickly learn and believe that Coriolanus is a remarkable warrior with a laurelled past. But as the roles shift, and Coriolanus is called to action in another arena, the political or court sphere, we sense at once that his opening lines define him and condemn him. An essay on the tragic vision of the play would allow you to draw heavily on a number of the sections above. If you choose to write an essay on the form of this play, on what it does and how it does it, you will have an abundance of material at hand. The initial task of focusing your essay will be vital, however. Coriolanus's personal tragedy is that outlined in the paragraph above: a man out of place, fatally out of tune with the world he inhabits. But this could be accomplished by Shakespeare in a variety of ways with differing "impacts" on the tone and mood of the play as a whole. The play could have limited, so to speak, the nature of the tragedy to Coriolanus's personal experience—a kind of Darwinian tragedy of someone who is not fit for his new world and does not survive, the extinction of a species. However, it seems that the scope of Shakespeare's tragic vision here is much wider than the loss of an individual, and, as has been often suggested by critics, *Coriolanus* looks and feels like a lament for the loss not so much of Coriolanus the man but of the world and past he represents.

Sample Topic:

1. **Tragedy:** How do you view the affairs of state as they are represented at the end of the play?

It is common for tragedies to end with a glimmer of light beaming over a stage full of corpses, the hope of something better to come. Often we can say that the state has been "purged," that a new and promising order is ready to take control. Young Fortinbras may play this role, for example, as he arrives onstage at the end of *Hamlet* (though Shakespeare may not want us to put much faith in a man who leads his men to battle and death largely for sport and recreation). More simplistically, in *Titus Andronicus,* the survival of Titus' son Lucius, and his final acts of condemning Aaron and ordering that Tamora be left unburied for the birds and beasts to consume, suggests strongly that order has been restored and the world righted—though at the cost of its tragic hero, of course. How do you view the state of play at the end of *Coriolanus,* however? We know that Rome will rise and one day fall, but what kind of seeds to we see planted in this play? What remains once Coriolanus is gone?

An important part of widening the tragic vision in this play, of course, is to consider not just Coriolanus's response to the world changing around him, but also the overwhelming and irresistible nature of that change itself. Paradoxically, though Coriolanus appears to be one of the most infuriating individuals in Shakespeare's canon, we have to ask just how much responsibility he can burden for this. The scheming of the Tribunes, the fickleness of the Roman citizens, the infidelity of the Machiavellian Aufidius, and even the misguided zeal of Volumnia all significantly contribute to making and undoing Coriolanus. In your essay, then, organize these elements as you like, but reach for some broad understanding of the play's tragic world rather than just the idea of an individual tragedy.

Compare and Contrast Essays

A number of compare and contrast topics emerge from character pairings. An analysis of Coriolanus alongside Aufidius literally allows you to compare and then contrast the two characters (see the entry on Aufidius in the preceding "Characters" section), while a paper treating the two female figures of Volumnia and Virgilia, Coriolanus's wife, would open up interesting possibilities for gender analysis and the representation of femininity, both in the idealized form of the near silent, dutiful Virgilia, and in the "hybridized" form of Volumnia's manly motherhood. The class divisions in the play also create natural compare and contrast possibilities as you examine the political maneuvering of the tribunes and the patricians, with the people and Coriolanus, in the end, equally powerless. Again, Aufidius will be a key figure here, someone who apparently embodies the same sense of virtue and honor seen in Coriolanus, but in the end possesses the skills of the new political order far more than the Tribunes. In a related essay, you could explore the relationship between the commoners and their "superiors" (see the entry on class tensions in the "Themes" section for more on this), focusing on large set pieces like 1.1 and the painfully awkward conferences between Coriolanus and the people, along with smaller, less memorable moments when ordinary folk such as soldiers and servants contest some issue with Menenius or Coriolanus.

Let us think here, however, about some options that place an aspect of *Coriolanus* alongside another Shakespearean tragedy. For more assistance with preparations for any of these essays, refer to the chapter in this volume for each of the respective plays. It is certainly interesting, for a start, to think about Coriolanus alongside other tragic protagonists in Shakespeare's work. We have been doing this intermittently throughout the chapter, but it may be helpful to group and clarify some of the possibilities together here. First, Coriolanus shares with Othello the warrior's nature and, like Othello, finds himself unable to translate his success on the battlefield into successful in another arena (for Coriolanus this is the public sphere of politics, while for Othello it is the domestic sphere of marriage). Another warrior figure is, of course, Macbeth, and we will explore the fascinating connection between Lady Macbeth and Volumnia in this section, but you could write on how the two men are alike in their vulnerability to a woman's will. Among the other Roman plays, a strong parallel can be forged between the titular tragic hero of *Titus Andronicus* and his more sober and sobering mirror image, Coriolanus. Both men vehemently adhere to the strictest moral code of Rome and suffer great consequences for their hyperdiligence.

It may be worthwhile to examine several more possibilities in more detail to glimpse how intertextual compare and contrast essays might be composed.

Sample Topics:

1. *Coriolanus* and *Hamlet:* How are the two tragic heroes in these plays connected? How are their situations similar but their responses so very different? And yet, how do they arrive at such similar fates?

As the somewhat convoluted nature of this question suggests, the web of differences and similarities between these two plays is mazelike. Wherever the connections lead you, the interaction between what is frequently understood as Shakespeare's greatest tragedy and the play we recognize as his final effort in the genre of tragedy is well worth discussing. The pairing of these two plays makes for a fascinating conversation and, if well controlled, a great subject for essay writers.

As has been frequently observed about both plays, they depict shifting political worlds transitioning from an apparently older order and way of doing things, one characterized by the valiance of Coriolanus and Old Hamlet, and a newer, Machiavellian world represented by such characters as the Tribunes, Claudius, and Young Fortinbras (and, possibly, it has been observed by some, Hamlet himself). Both Hamlet and Coriolanus are called to action in this new political order, and their responses differ dramatically. You could draw distinctions between Hamlet's inability to act emphatically and Coriolanus's inability to act subtly; it turns out these flaws are two sides of the same coin. And, of course, in the final act of his play, Coriolanus's narrative becomes a revenge tragedy as he sets about avenging his exile. Again, where Hamlet initially defers his search for justice, Coriolanus embraces it with characteristic ferocity. However, unexpectedly perhaps, while Hamlet is finally able to reach the degree of self-knowledge and self-assurance that permits him to take the final steps on his tragic path and slay Claudius, Coriolanus at the last moment equivocates and draws back from completing his revenge. Ironically, the fate of both men is the same, though almost certainly their state of mind in the final moments of action and the intellectual, moral, and emotional development they have experienced are far from equal. As you compare these two figures, the sharp personal and philosophical differences will emerge strikingly, but keep in mind the interaction of both similarity and difference as you map out an essay and reach for an insightful characterization of the important relationship between the pair.

2. **Comparing Lady Macbeth and Volumnia:** While Lady Macbeth is clearly intended to be one of the villains of her play, can we say the same about the overbearing Volumnia?

The balance between these two figures is quite a delicate one, so you could quite reasonably assert the dominance of similarities or differences as you see fit. Whichever way you lean on this, it may be a useful idea to outline, perhaps in some detail, the opposing evidence. So, for example, if your thesis is going to argue for fundamental and definitive differences between the two, you should probably spend some time after the introduction showing how the pair is nonetheless closely related. This has a twofold benefit: first, you demonstrate to your reader that you are aware of the nuances of your subjects. Second, you make your argument appear more ambitious and difficult if you have shown the reader how strong the case for the opposing side may be. Obviously, you don't want to overplay this hand; about one page of similarities to four pages of difference would be a good ratio in a five-page paper arguing for the observation of telling distinctions between the two women.

Let us look briefly at several points worth elaborating on in such an essay. Both women, for example, are gifted politicians, both hungry for a power that they can only obtain through a male surrogate. However, beyond these relatively simple similarities lie more ambiguous connections. The issue of gender is central to the complexity of both figures, for example. Think about how Lady Macbeth's call for the spirits to "unsex" her, to make her free of stereotypical feminine mildness, might be applied to Volumnia, directly or indirectly. Critical commentary on both figures has focused on the role of motherhood and images emerging from that role. Some of the most quoted and analyzed moments of each character's dialogue center on breastfeeding. Also, think about how each woman is viewed by her respective play. You may find that *Macbeth*'s view of Lady Macbeth, whose influence over her husband is viewed as aberrant and allied with the malign magic of the witches, is one of rigid, even misogynistic condemnation. But do you feel that *Coriolanus* also urges us to view Volumnia this way?

Bibliography for *"Coriolanus"*

Barton, Anne. "Livy, Machiavelli, and Shakespeare's *Coriolanus*." *Shakespeare and Politics.* Catherine Alexander and John Joughin, eds. Cambridge, England: Cambridge UP, 2004: 67–90.

Goldberg, Jonathan. "The Anus in *Coriolanus*." *Historicism, Psychoanalysis, and Early Modern Culture.* Carla Mazzio and Doug Trevor, eds. New York: Routledge, 2000: 260–71.

Kuzner, James. "Unbuilding the City: *Coriolanus* and the Birth of Republican Rome." *Shakespeare Quarterly,* 58, 2007: 174–99.

Ormsby, Robert. "*Coriolanus*, Antitheatricalism, and Audience Response." *Shakespeare Bulletin: A Journal of Performance Criticism and Scholarship,* 26, 2008: 43–62.

Pfister, Manfred. "Acting the Roman: Coriolanus." *Identity, Otherness and Empire in Shakespeare's Rome.* Maria Del Sapio Garbero, ed. Surrey, England: Ashgate, 2009: 35–47.

Sanders, Eve Rachele. "The Body of the Actor in *Coriolanus*." *Shakespeare Quarterly,* 57, 2006: 387–412.

Wheeler, David, ed. *"Coriolanus": Critical Essays.* New York: Garland, 1995.

HAMLET

READING TO WRITE

*H*AMLET IS one of the most celebrated pieces of literature in the Western tradition. The figure of Hamlet and the soliloquies he speaks are iconic, recognizable in some form to countless individuals, even those who would profess to have no familiarity with Shakespeare's works. As you make your way through the play, you come across one literary landmark after another, words and actions already so familiar to us but all the more stunning encountered directly in the text. This is the excitement and thrill of reading a text located at the heart of our culture. The vastness of the play, its intellectual and philosophical depth, and, above all, the enormous tradition of performance and criticism grown thick around the play contribute to the challenge of adding your own voice to the legions of scholars and laypeople who have already weighed in on this definitive work. Because the play contains so much—you will need to exercise a little discipline at the prewriting stage by reading carefully and identifying and tracking themes or issues that you might like to write about—it presents the essay writer with any number of viable inroads and directions to explore.

Any critical appraisal of *Hamlet* starts with its language and perhaps an analysis of one of those celebrated speeches by Hamlet. This passage comes from 2.2 as the luckless Rosencrantz and Guildenstern question Hamlet over the root of his melancholy:

> This most excellent canopy the air, look you, this brave o'erhanging, this
> majestical roof fretted with golden fire—why it appears no other thing
> to me than a foul and pestilent congregation of vapors. What a piece

of work is man! How noble in reason, how infinite in faculty, in form and moving how express and admirable, in action how like an angel, in apprehension how like a god—the beauty of the world, the paragon of animals! And yet to me what is this quintessence of dust?

While this passage appears to be about such universal, infinite subjects as the world and the people who live in it, the precise matter at hand is rather the mind of Hamlet, his perception of these large topics and abstractions. The play and the consciousness of its main character are indivisible, the latter taking the former to places that could not be reached without it. This might sound like a grandiose thing to write about a fictional character, but Hamlet is a remarkable and innovative presence, and most of the essays you could write on the play will succeed based on how much effort you give to understanding his character, the world of the play as it exists through him.

It is exactly Hamlet's imaginative power that we encounter in the passage. While most of us are content to be shaped by our world, Hamlet represents a kind of superbeing whose mind and imagination are powerful enough to shape the world in which he lives. Here, no less, Hamlet is revising and subverting the very principles on which the Elizabethan world was founded. The passage can be split into two halves, each forming one component of a remarkable argument. In the first, Hamlet envisions the wonder of the world, its awesome natural beauty and power, as "a foul and pestilent congregation of vapors." Aside from the transcendent capacity of Hamlet's mind, two key themes emerge from this chilling phrase. First, in the rankness of what Hamlet perceives we find a recurring image of disease and decay. From the first scenes of the play, we are asked time and again to think about the "rot" in Denmark, a pestilence that Hamlet suggests several times is by no means contained by the borders of his country. Many critics have attempted to diagnose the diseases of the play, and the writer might marshal this pattern of imagery in essays ranging from character studies of Claudius to thematic essays on gender or politics in *Hamlet*. With the word *vapors*, Hamlet goes further still. Here he invokes a sense of nothingness that becomes one of the most recognizable philosophical notes of the play. Not only is the world foul, but it is no more substantial, no more real than a mass of vapors evaporating into the air. This urges the writer to consider the play's obsession with undermining reality, whether that is through radical thought, as in this passage, or the act of putting on a play.

Following on, Hamlet turns his attention away from the stage of mankind's existence to the species itself. As he describes the virtues of man, we think perhaps of Hamlet himself. Not only does Hamlet's intelligence and consciousness seem to represent human faculty at its most acutely developed, but his description notably encompasses both "reason" and "action," two qualities infamously opposed to each other as Hamlet's psyche is confronted with the task of murdering Claudius. Yet it is the inevitability of the closing image, life reduced to "dust," that catches the eye and the mind sharply. Again, this moment becomes just one point in a sequence of images and thoughts connected through the play. This time the theme is death, and the writer might be drawn by this line into an essay touched by or directly engaged with the play's extended meditation on this most unhappy and universal of concerns. Certainly what will be clear to the writer by now—as if it was not before—is how dark and deep Shakespeare's text is and what opens it to a wide range of critical interpretations.

TOPICS AND STRATEGIES

Every essay requires a focus; you cannot write about everything in the play at once. In the section on how to write an essay, you will be presented with a number of ways of turning a focus into a thesis, observations into arguments. However, the starting point is nearly always finding an initial point of departure, making first observations. You can then seize on and develop the budding ideas you will have as you make your way through the play. By no means should you feel limited to these topics, however. Instead they can be viewed as triggering suggestions encouraging you to break out into your own critical directions.

Themes

While the character of Hamlet looms large over the play, there certainly are essays to be written that minimize his role or rather contextualize him. The topic suggestions in this section will certainly include Hamlet, but they will not necessarily be dominated by him in the way that the other subject sections, "Philosophy and Ideas" and "Compare and Contrast Essays," in particular, are. For example, the play forms a political parable charting the evolution of the state of Denmark from an old, chivalric order to a new system driven by the methods of realpolitik (politics based on practical rather than moral or ideological considerations; for important background on this term, see the section on Machiavelli in the *Julius Caesar* chapter). The writer treating this historicized theme could begin by looking at representatives of the old way of political life: Old Hamlet and Old Fortinbras. Read the early scenes of the play to establish a picture of how the previous generation had approached international relations. How would you describe the code of conduct in which the two kings duel for supremacy rather than commit to all-out war? Assess the characteristics of Old Hamlet in the ghost scenes. Pay close attention to the demands he makes of Hamlet, noticing the special request to leave Gertrude alone. Having established a picture of the old order, the essay would naturally proceed to the bigger task of mapping out the political system that appears to have replaced it. Look for small clues, of course, such as the court parasites and climbers (Rosencrantz, Guildenstern, and Osric) who suggest a world in which superficial pandering reaps rewards. The writer might employ some of the metaphors of disease and decay (like those highlighted in the introduction) to demonstrate how the play appears not to endorse the processes of political change forced onto Denmark. Useful as such motifs and details, however, the bulk of the study should focus on the way in which ambassadors of the new political way (Hamlet, Claudius, and Young Fortinbras) approach domestic and international politics. Try to define their styles and outline their ethics. Of course, there will be differences in the way they do things, but the key to this essay might be in identifying the core principles of the new order replacing the old.

Such an essay would make a nice historical approach, but other thematic avenues take the writer directly to the "universal" qualities so celebrated in the play.

Sample Topics:

1. **Death:** In what ways does death occupy and influence the living in *Hamlet?*

This question encourages the writer to arrive at a tentative idea of what deaths means in the play. Once you have crystallized your thoughts and are able to outline your position, you will be ready to produce a thesis statement on the play's darkest themes. Notice, first and foremost, that death is not a distant or removed event in the play. You might begin by identifying the ways in which the dead make their presence felt. For example, even before he sees the ghost of his father, Hamlet is engaged in an intense and overwhelming process of mourning (think, too, about Hamlet's dying request to Horatio at the close of the play, taking us full circle). Compare this to the advice of Claudius and Gertrude that death is natural, inevitable, and something not to preoccupy the living (1.2). Certainly Hamlet refuses to dismiss the subject of death from his mind, and as the play progresses his thoughts dwell increasingly on issues of mortality. Scrutinize the major soliloquies (3.1.58, for example), but look for contrasts in Hamlet's own thinking. For example, though Hamlet's meditations seem to conclude that death is unknowable to the living, an undiscovered country populated by shadowy prospects and dangers, this kind of philosophical dread is paralleled by frequent images of death as a tangible force of equality and realism cutting through the feeble constructions of human society. Death is sober and serious at the same time as it is a vulgar joke; it is nowhere (a place yet to be discovered) and it is everywhere (there are countless skulls beneath our feet). Key scenes for this latter, almost blackly comic vision of death are 4.3 and 5.1.

2. **Drama and theater:** In what ways is *Hamlet* a study of the practice of drama? What is the relationship between the stage and the "real world" of the play?

Such an essay might focus on at least three areas. First, writers might consider the way in which characters "act" their parts. For example, we might consider Claudius as a man performing the role of bereaved brother who inherits the throne. In other words, he is presenting to the world a version of reality that is false. Even Rosencrantz and Guildernstern, the court lackeys who seek Claudius's favor, are playing the part of interested friends of the troubled prince—a sordid performance that Hamlet sees right through. Of course, the true actor *par excellence* in the work is its star, Hamlet. Much has been written about Hamlet's "performances" through the play, especially the oft-debated issue of his pretended madness and his trouble assuming the popular "role" of revenge hero. This all resonates with the notion, key to the play, of a corrupt state; the business of acting, of performing, of staging is as important to the business of daily living as it is to theater. Are there any characters who do not act, however? If so, what do they contribute to the play's discussion of artifice and illusion?

The next strand of this complex topic to consider is the remarkably overt discussion of theatrics found throughout the play. From the recurring references to Polonius's theatrical past to the elaborate, frequently cited sequence of Hamlet's advice to the players (2.2), the writer should analyze both the details and the effects of the ever-present use of *metadrama* or *metatheater* (terms given to components of a play that somehow make drama the subject of the action rather than just the medium for it). In particular, 2.2 reveals Hamlet to be a connoisseur of the stage, with an elaborate set of opinions and preferences about how actors should best approach their lines and performances. One way of approaching this scene is to think about Hamlet's advice in relation to his own "acting" elsewhere in the play. More generally, why does Shakespeare foreground the illusion of drama, the fact that *Hamlet* is a play not a snatched vision of reality, so explicitly and deliberately here?

Finally, consider the use of the play within the play. Always consider the relationship between each layer of staging. For example, what might we make of the fact that in *The Murder of Gonzago*, the play with the play that Hamlet stages, it is the nephew of the king who sets about the murder? Think especially about how this detail helps us make new connections between Claudius and Hamlet.

Characters

Character criticism has traditionally formed the foundation of writing about *Hamlet*. Even the slightest of characters seem to offer substantial opportunities. For example, Young Fortinbras is mentioned early in the play and glimpsed briefly several times in the second half, but such a limited presence does not exclude him from taking center stage in an essay. He is one of the play's symbols of a new age in political life, but the writer could certainly draw out his qualities and contemplate his actions at length. Pay close attention to Fortinbras's intentions to war against Denmark, his motivations for doing so, and, finally, his alternate campaign against the Polish when his thoughts of invading Denmark are thwarted by his father. In the "Compare and Contrast Essays" section that follows, we will consider another function of Fortinbras's character, the ways he parallels Hamlet. Consider in some detail the brief appearance of Fortinbras in 4.4, asking about the ethics of his campaign against the Polish as it is related by one of his captains. Finally, assess the meaning of his centrality at the close of the play: How should we view the prospect of Denmark under Fortinbras? Similarly, the minor characters of Rosencrantz and Guildenstern (as well as Osric) could be made the focal point of a character study approach to the political sphere of Hamlet's Denmark. They show in miniature the vices of Claudius, Fortinbras, and (arguably) Hamlet.

Certainly critics have never tired of the melancholy Dane or run out of fresh things to say about his 400-year-old angst. While some scholarship has fought against the current of elaborate awe (T. S. Eliot famously wrote that Hamlet's character was flawed by an excess of emotion in relation to the situation he faces at the start of the play), the majority of writers have attempted to comprehend rather than refute Shakespeare's singular creation. Harold Bloom suggests that Hamlet is nothing less than "the most comprehensive of all literary characters." Strong praise indeed, but to many minds, the assertion is wholly justified.

One of the best ways to approach the character of Hamlet is to view him in relation to other characters in the play; they appear at times drawn not as independent characters but rather as reflections and inversions of Hamlet. Such approaches, however, are potentially more ideally suited for a compare and contrast discussion. For the writer who chooses to work first and foremost with Hamlet, there are endless routes available. You might begin by asking a question of yourself such as "Is Hamlet a misogynist?" or "In what way is Hamlet less than an ideal hero?" Such queries offer examples of precise and more narrowly defined approaches to Hamlet's character. There are broader questions, too, that allow writers a freer reign across the wide horizons of Hamlet's psyche.

Sample Topics:

1. **Hamlet:** Is Hamlet feigning madness or is he driven to it by circumstance? What does the play say about the division between "madness" and "sanity"? Can the difference even be determined in *Hamlet?* If it can, on what terms could such a distinction be made?

Such an essay will naturally draw on some of the material in the topic discussion of drama and theater in the preceding "Themes" section. After all, in so far as Hamlet is feigning his madness, he is acting or performing it. In this way, Hamlet's character becomes an entry point into a meditation on human character or identity in general; as Hamlet performs his role we—and it seems he—hopelessly struggle to distinguish where "natural" identity ends and invention begins. The key to this essay is to recognize that Hamlet himself may not be in possession of any answers. The writer should build on the idea that there may be a wide gap between Hamlet's "real" character and what Hamlet tells us about his character. So, it may be true that there is ample textual evidence to support the idea that, as Guildenstern puts it, Hamlet is suffering from nothing more than "crafty madness" (3.1.8). For example, you could marshal evidence to this effect from 1.5.171, 2.2.347, and 3.4.138, among other passages from the play. There is so much to suggest that Hamlet is feigning madness, centering your essay on that claim might not be the most exciting or revealing move. Instead, the writer might see if there is a friction or tension between such details and Hamlet's behavior. You might identify a moment at which the pretended madness is, unbeknownst to Hamlet himself, overtaken by something more "real." Another way to frame this approach is by asking if Hamlet is always in full control of his actions. For example, the scene in which Hamlet interrogates Gertrude prompts us to question exactly this. However, there is a problem—one that actually might itself make a good foundation for an essay—in that the Hamlet of 5.2 seems to have acquired—how?—a remarkable calmness and resolution. Critics have long sensed that at the close of the play Hamlet has "grown" or "developed" in some way, though identifying the precise nature of the change is difficult (and thus worth attempting all the more).

Another classic puzzle suggested by Hamlet's character arises from the divide between action and thought. For a long time, readers and writers have approached the dilemma of Hamlet's inaction, exploring psychological and emotional reasons for his delay in avenging his father. The formulaic response is that Hamlet is an intellectual made inactive or impotent by too much thinking. This statement may or may not be true—or just be part of the truth—but it is a well-worn in need of revision, expansion, and refinement. There is certainly room in this conundrum for many a good essay to tinker with—or, even better, completely overhaul—this argument. After all, as A. C. Bradley asserted in the early twentieth century, Hamlet actually leaps into action (such as with the pirate ship and at Ophelia's grave) a number of times throughout the play. Therefore, if you could offer a more specific reason for Hamlet's particular brand of inaction (that seems to be limited to the action of killing Claudius), and then support it, you would certainly be improving on the portrait of Hamlet as a somewhat wishy-washy, overly cerebral young man more inclined to acting than to action. For example, could we say that Hamlet struggles with killing Claudius because, consciously or not, he recognizes himself in his uncle?

2. **Gertrude and Ophelia:** Does the play *Hamlet* endorse the character Hamlet's disturbing view of women?

The most obvious example—and one much revisited over the years—is the issue of Gertrude's complicity with Claudius, extending out into a wider consideration of the play's matriarch as mother (and Hamlet as son). Ophelia, too, provides an interesting parallel to Hamlet's madness, one that is fatally, unambiguously authentic. If so much energy has been invested in exploring Hamlet's troubled psyche, then why not explore Ophelia's psychological decline too? Does Hamlet treat each of the women, from different generations and of different relations to the protagonist, differently or in a similar vein? Certainly, in effect, Hamlet makes no distinction between the two women, tarring all of womanhood with the same brush (3.1.135, for example). Look at this moment in the text, as well as others you find in which Hamlet rails against the inconstancy and impropriety of women. Is there a symbolic pattern to his comments? Does the play give us just cause to agree with Hamlet? Does our response differ from Gertrude to Ophelia? For any differences the writer might find, it is impossible to deny that both Ophelia and Gertrude are doomed to the same fate; the play punishes both equally. Do you agree with critics who suggest that the abuse and condemnation of the female characters, along with their tragic ends, encourages us to interpret the women as helpless victims of a male-dominated court? Or do you side with those who argue that Gertrude's muddied moral position in the play, along with, to a lesser extent, Ophelia's vulnerability and passivity, in fact requires us to accept Hamlet's famous condemnation of woman's frailty as the play's position too?

Philosophy and Ideas

Questions of reality and the real are central to the work, evident in the play's unrelenting attack on the unified concept of reality. By offering so many levels of reality, so many alternative variations of the real, the play undermines any single notion of what is real and what is not. Essays treating this theme might do well to focus on the play's foregrounding of theatricality, acting, and dissembling (see the preceding "Themes" section). It seems that everyone is playing or acting a role, and Hamlet himself has numerous roles or identities that finally make impossible any clear sense of who the "real" Hamlet might be (or even that such an singular identity could exist). Look at the myriad parallels and echoes that further add to the sense of fragmented identities scattered across the play—there are aspects and reflections of Hamlet detectable in Ophelia, Claudius, Fortinbras, Laertes, and even that theatrically inclined, lover of words Polonius. Look for other ways in which reality might be problematized, such as the shadowy alternative reality suggested by the presence of the ghost (a presence that itself is open to question when the ghost appears to Hamlet but is invisible to Gertrude). Philosophically minded students can explore this dissolution of the boundaries between reality and artifice, while also looking for other divisions interrogated or dissolved by the play, such as sanity and mental instability. To do so is very much to follow in Hamlet's footsteps.

Sample Topic:

1. **Existentialism:** Does the play finally suggest that we can construct our own realities through philosophy? Is this what Hamlet does? What is the relationship between Hamlet's interior world (his psyche) and the exterior world about him? Can we say that boundary is ultimately dissolved too?

In the passage cited in the introduction, we saw presented with Hamlet redefining his universe, distorting and diminishing the wonders of the natural world into a dead and decaying space. Denmark and the world can be transformed from vast expanses into confining prisons, all through the will and perception of the individual mind. Perhaps at the philosophical heart of such an essay, then, would be an assessment of how much power the play assigns to Hamlet's imagination. A good place to start this essay might be 2.2, in which the hapless Rosencrantz and Guildenstern are befuddled when they attempt to match wits with Hamlet. Try to puzzle through a statement like this one from Hamlet: "O God, I could be bounded in a nutshell and count myself a king of infinite space, were it not that I have bad dreams" (2.2.248–50). What does it seem to suggest about physical space, the world "outside" the individual, in relation to the inner existence of the self? Once more, the theme of acting and stagecraft might be useful as an example of the play's deep-rooted interest in humans creating and scripting their own reality. Still, it is important to remember that against this current of thought and meditation is set a countercurrent of action and events: Does the play finally suggest, then, given the wave of death, accident, and mischance that sweeps across its conclusion, that reality—whatever that might consist of—finally asserts itself even against the most contemplative of souls? Look, too, for other limits to the power of thought. Think, for example, about Hamlet's famous rejection of suicide precisely because his imagination cannot comprehend it. In a variety of ways, Hamlet's soliloquies will serve this topic well and give writers the opportunity to work closely and at length with complicated, dense passages.

Form and Genre

The story of *Hamlet* seems to have been a popular one with Elizabethan audiences as there was another, now lost version of the play (perhaps authored by Thomas Kyd) staged a few years before Shakespeare's. Though the exact evolution is not clear—the lost *Hamlet* is a kind of missing link that prevents us from knowing exactly how Shakespeare made the story his own—it is absolutely certain that Shakespeare worked exceedingly hard to make this play a terrifyingly dark tragedy. After all, the story, as part of Scandinavian folk tradition, has the hero, Amleth (Hamlet), avenge his father by killing Feng, the usurping, brother-murdering king who becomes Claudius. Amleth then assumes the throne. In other words, the original tale is hardly tragic as justice is fully served, the state purified, and order restored in the form of a triumphant revenge hero. Hamlet should be so lucky. As the dark, existential tones of the play suggest, *Hamlet* aspires to be more than the tragedy of an individual or small group of people. A version of the preceding topic suggestion on existentialism could certainly be written from the angle of *Hamlet* as "universal tragedy," the tragedy of existence as it is presented in the play. Another equally strong essay topic might be to consider the implications of the tragedy for the play's world. Always look for the ironies and uncertainties contained among the corpses of Shakespeare's tragic resolutions; ask what, if anything, has been achieved? What has been gained and what lost? As many critics have pointed out, one particularly striking irony is that by compelling Hamlet to seek revenge against Claudius, Old Hamlet actually ensures that Denmark falls into the hands of his old rival, the Norwegians, thus canceling out Old Hamlet's previous victories. Contemplate, too, the meanings of such apparently indiscriminant deaths in the final movement of the play. From the minor specks of Rosencrantz and Guildenstern, through the middling figure of Polonious, to the great majority of principal characters, it seems that Shakespeare's tragic vision is total and encompassing. An essay might attempt to assess exactly what the sum of that vision might be—recognizing that the play seems to resist single, clear answers on anything, of course. Is the great tragedy of *Hamlet* simply death, shuffling off a mortal coil? Or is the play perhaps more about the way we live than the way we die?

Sample Topic:

1. **Revenge:** Does the play endorse or denounce revenge?

> Revenge appears at part of the discussion of form and genre, rather than in the "Themes" section, because revenge tragedy was an extremely popular genre of the Elizabethan stage, and because Shakespeare subverts that genre so completely in *Hamlet*. It will not be necessary for writers to know much about the revenge tradition in order to tackle revenge as a topic, but a little background will be useful nonetheless.
>
> Obviously, the Elizabethans did not invent revenge tragedy; it was in many ways the staple of ancient Greek drama. Equally, it is an important motif in contemporary film and television. What Shakespeare and his fellow sixteenth-century playwrights did do, however, was to revitalize and even reinvent the tradition. After all, as citizens of the early modern world, Shakespeare's contemporaries were witness to a time of transition during which social and legal conventions shifted and changed. While in ancient societies revenge was not only acceptable but essential to the maintenance of individual honor and collective justice, by the sixteenth century revenge

was increasingly outlawed and replaced by the ideal of a state-supported justice system. If a man's father was killed, it was not the son's but the state's role to avenge the death. Of course, it is impossible for us to know if there was a general consensus among Elizabethans that this transition was a good thing or even if the change had occurred with any evenness by the time *Hamlet* had arrived on the scene. Certainly many of Shakespeare's contemporaries wrote against individual revenge, most notably Francis Bacon who dubbed it "wild justice." The intellectual, state, and religious institutions of Shakespeare's time all viewed revenge as not only imprudent but dangerous, a crime in and of itself. What of the ordinary people who largely made up Shakespeare's audience? What of *Hamlet?*

You might begin this essay with an examination of 1.5. Analyze the conversation between Hamlet and his father's ghost, studying the ghost's advice to Hamlet (his tone, his expectations, for example) and Hamlet's response. Pay close attention to Hamlet's speech beginning around line 92. What does he claim will be his approach to the task of revenge? Given Hamlet's character, is such an approach possible? Is there anyone in the play who adopts this approach to revenge? Certainly look at the way Young Fortinbras intends to avenge his father by waging war against Denmark and how Laertes becomes a vengeful fury in the name of Polonius. In contrast to these other characters, as well as his own frequent hot and bloody words about revenge (some critics have suggested that Hamlet, being such a fan of the stage and theatrics, is at times performing the stereotypical role of the dramatic revenge hero, bombastically launching into formulaic promises of vengeance), how does Hamlet actually approach the act of revenge? What is it that psychologically or emotionally separates Hamlet from Laertes? For example, you might argue that Hamlet consistently seems to require proof or knowledge of something and will not act without it; Laertes does not wait for certain knowledge before stirring up a riot in the name of revenge. The backbone of this essay, perhaps, will be an attempt to link Hamlet's character (as you have defined it) to his execution of the avenger's task. You might also consider whether the play judges Hamlet's "failings"; are we encouraged to regret his inability to avenge his father, or are we prompted to some other, more complex moral response?

Compare and Contrast Essays

The subject of revenge creates a number of compare and contrast possibilities among Shakespeare's works. Whatever it is that you conclude *Hamlet* suggests or argues about the nature of revenge, it would make for a potentially compelling essay to compare your findings with another play. Of the plays treated in this volume, points of comparison or contrast might be found most strongly in *Julius Caesar*. Alternatively, a comparison of Hamlet to other Shakespearean tragic heroes will certainly offer the writer a wealth of material. A close parallel might, for example, be found in Brutus from *Julius Caesar*. Like Hamlet, something in Brutus's nature (in this case, his commitment to "old-fashioned" ideals of honor that make him prey to a new breed of political machines like Octavius and Antony) makes him an ill fit for the task of political intrigue and machination. Interestingly, however, in *Hamlet,* the title character belongs precisely to that same new breed of political animal as Antony, while Old Hamlet resembles the anachronistic Brutus. For an alternative approach, think about a comparison of Othello and Hamlet. A strong essay could be possibly grounded in the notion that, while Othello demands proof of Desdemona's infidelity, just as Hamlet seeks proof of the ghost's honesty or Claudius's guilt, the pair must finally be contrasted because Hamlet ultimately rejects the idea of "truth" while Othello falls victim to the illusion of truth.

Of course, there are a great many compare and contrast essays to be found within *Hamlet* alone. Think, for example, about the comparison that could be made between the situations of Hamlet and Laertes, and the stark contrast to be seen in their responses to those similar situations. Again, even in the character of Hamlet, we can find enough progression and change to create a compare and contrast model of character essay: Assess the differences between Hamlet at the beginning and end of the play. What has he learned about the world and about himself? What in him has changed? These are all strong starting points, but there are two especially promising compare and contrast topics worth exploring.

Sample Topics:

1. **Comparing Hamlet and Claudius:** How much does Hamlet actually resemble his enemy?

This topic hinges on similarities rather than differences. The added potential value of pursuing this essay topic lies in showing how these two enemies and mortal rivals have much more in common than their antipathy for each other suggests. This could be approached in two ways—both will be useful, though the second should probably form the majority of the essay. First, you could suggest ways in which Claudius, despite his act of primal evil, can be seen in sympathetic ways. Some critics have pointed to his self-reflexive examination of his guilt, for example, or the way he appears to be in tune with the cycles of nature when he lectures Hamlet on the inevitability of death. On the other hand, and much more effective, is to show how Hamlet resembles Claudius. The bulk of the essay might effectively be taken up by bringing together and contemplating moments in which Hamlet's darkest character components are unmasked or revealed. For example, look at his murder of Polonious and its immediate aftermath, his harsh and heartless treatment of the blundering Rosencrantz and Guildenstern, his abusiveness to Ophelia and Gertrude, and—the episode that seems to disturb critics the most—the unthinkably cruel desire to consign Claudius not only to death but to eternal torment. Look, too, for other fascinating parallels such as Hamlet's strange casting of the nephew of the king as killer in the play within the play.

2. **Contrasting Hamlet and Fortinbras:** While Fortinbras seems to greatly impress Hamlet (and vice versa, as we learn at the end of the play), how are we supposed to interpret the play's comparison of these two young men?

An essay on this topic could potentially win praise for the way it foregrounds a seemingly minor figure. First, assess the relationship between the pair as it is constructed early in the play.

As we have seen, both are young men who desire revenge for wrongs against their fathers. From this point on, however, the dominating perspective appears to be mostly one of contrast. Consider Hamlet's attempts at revenge alongside those of Young Fortinbras. What do we learn of Fortinbras's ambitions to attack Denmark and then of the alternate campaign against the Polish? A close reading of 4.4 will stand at the heart of this essay. Consider Hamlet's response to Fortinbras's military campaign, but consider whether we the readers and audience are supposed to admire Fortinbras or not. Think carefully about the apparent pointlessness and recklessness of the forthcoming battle with Poland. If what separates Hamlet from Fortinbras is action, what does this scene, this comparison suggest the play has to say about action after all?

Bibliography for "Hamlet"

Bradley, A. C. *Shakespearean Tragedy: Lectures on "Hamlet," "Othello," "King Lear," "Macbeth."* 1904. 3rd ed. Basingstoke, England: Macmillan, 1992.

Bristol, Michael D. *Carnival and Theater: Plebeian Culture and the Structure of Authority in Renaissance England.* New York and London: Methuen, 1985.

Bloom, Harold, ed. *Hamlet.* New York: Chelsea House, 2004.

Garber, Marjorie. *Shakespeare's Ghost Writers.* New York: Methuen, 1987.

Mazzio, Carla. *The Inarticulate Renaissance: Language Trouble in an Age of Eloquence.* Philadelphia: U of Pennsylvania P, 2009.

Paster, Gail Kern. "'The Pith and Marrow of Our Attribute': Dialogue of Skin and Skull in *Hamlet* and Holbein's *The Ambassadors.*" *Textual Practice*, 23 (2), 2009: 247–65.

Sosnowska, Monika. "Gendering of the Eye: Representation of Visual Perception in *Hamlet.*" *Gender Studies*, 1 (8), 2008: 85–94.

JULIUS CAESAR

READING TO WRITE

WRITING AN essay on *Julius Caesar* gives the student a chance to participate in the play's open-ended debates. So much in the tragedy is uncertain; Shakespeare never clearly endorses one character over another, a single notion of what is best for Rome over any other. Therefore, the play becomes a conversation about the relationship between states and citizens, leaders and the populace, with no evident authorial guidelines for what the audience or readers should think or feel.

As you read the play, carefully consider the ideas voiced by each character. You will see an urgent political debate in progress. Read the dialogue closely not only for developing oppositions between characters but contradictions made by individuals.

The following passage, from 1.2, serves as a good window into the play. Using carefully crafted rhetorical gambits, Cassius persuades Brutus to join him against Caesar. After recalling a swimming race in which the apparently mighty Caesar needed to be rescued by him, Cassius continues:

> Why, man, he doth bestride the narrow world
> Like a Colossus, and we petty men
> Walk under his huge legs, and peep about
> To find ourselves dishonorable graves.
> Men at sometime were masters of their fates.
> The fault, dear Brutus, is not in our stars,
> But in ourselves, that we are underlings.
> Brutus and Caesar: what should be in that 'Caesar'?
> Why should that name be sounded more than yours?

> Write them together: yours is as fair a name.
> Sound them: it doth become the mouth as well.
> Weigh them: it is as heavy. Conjure with 'em:
> 'Brutus' will start a spirit as soon as 'Caesar'
> . . . .
> When could they say till now, that talked of Rome,
> That her wide walls encompassed but one man?
> Now is it Rome indeed, and room enough
> When there is in it but one only man.
> O, you and I have heard our fathers say
> There was a Brutus once that would have brooked
> Th' eternal devil to keep his state in Rome
> As easily as a king. (1.2.136–62)

The opening image of this speech is perhaps one of the most memorable of the play. Cassius paints the dramatic picture of a gigantic Caesar towering over Rome, a monstrous, unnatural threat that could squash the insectlike citizens who flit around his giant steps (but does this representation complement the image of a weak and feeble Caesar offered by Cassius in his speech moments earlier?). When Cassius adds that the rest "peep about / To find ourselves dishonorable graves," he suggests that an unrestrained Caesar does not merely pose a physical threat but a social and cultural one also: The small things under Caesar's feet do not just live powerless like insects, they die like them, unremembered and unmarked. It is this threat to honor that makes the risks of Caesar so great. Cassius quickly builds on this image, shifting slightly to the philosophical idea that men, and not the stars, make their fates. The first image stressed the powerlessness of the citizens against a tyrant Caesar, while the second offers a stirring counterargument to the threat. Cassius tells us no man is destined to be lowly; rather, an individual chooses to be so by not making it otherwise.

This line of thought might encourage the writer to reflect on the tension between the individual and the state found throughout the play. An essay on this topic could explore ideas of equality and freedom in the text. What is it about Caesar's power that seems to threaten the conspirators so much? However, the writer might also want to consider the possibility that when a character voices an apparent concern for the state, rhetoric may be masking nothing more than the desires of that individual to maintain political prominence.

As the passage continues, Cassius returns to his central thesis that all Romans are equal. Importantly, however, he frames this argument within a comparison of Brutus and Caesar. This is rhetorically astute, of course—Cassius knows his mark is Brutus and attempts to appeal directly to him—but it is more than that. For the first time we encounter, through Cassius's rhetorical devices, the relationship that, for many readers, structures the play: the opposition of Brutus and Caesar. Although Cassius is attempting to make the point that Caesar should not hold sway over Brutus, he is also setting up the important idea that these two men have much in common. After all, the final invocation of a grand Roman history is in reality nothing more than another personalized appeal to Brutus, a reminder of his own family history more than that of his city.

Clearly, we could also take from this passage another topic question: What is the symbolic relationship between Brutus and Caesar? This essay could certainly consider the motivations of Brutus, suggesting ways in which he is as interested in personal authority as Caesar is, but the essay might also look at the way Shakespeare makes both characters fatally flawed.

TOPICS AND STRATEGIES

Every essay requires a focus; you cannot write about everything in the play at once. In the section on how to write an essay, you will be presented with a number of ways of turning a focus into a thesis, observations into arguments. However, the starting point is nearly always finding an initial point of departure, making first observations. You can then seize on and develop the budding ideas you will have as you make your way through the play. By no means should you feel limited to these topics, however. Instead they can be viewed as triggering suggestions encouraging you to break out into your own critical directions.

Themes

Julius Caesar is a play primarily about politics. A chief concern of the work is with political systems, the way humans organize their societies into governed communities rather than the chaotic free for all of a natural state. How should this be done? What form of government is best? Should power be shared among many or concentrated in the hands of a few or even one? These were pressing questions in Shakespeare's time and will be discussed in greater depth in the "History and Context" section.

A close reading of *Julius Caesar* will offer the writer potential themes that might be developed in essay form. Using the passage cited at the beginning of the chapter, for example, think how you might write an essay on the theme of honor in *Julius Caesar.* Having selected the theme, it is necessary to ask how it functions in the world of the play. Cassius suggests that being stripped of political power is like a dishonorable death, but power may be just one component of honor in the play. Asking how the theme functions leads the writer to seek a definition of honor in the play, then to find parts of the text supporting that claim. What actions do you believe Shakespeare wants us to see as honorable? Of particular interest here might be moments in the text where there is a potential "gap" between an action or act and its motivation. For example, the killing of Caesar might be a dishonorable act brought to pass by nonetheless honorable intentions (or vice versa). A similar problem could be also found in the suicides of Cassius and Brutus, perhaps.

Sample Topics:

1. **Tyranny:** How dangerous is Caesar to Rome? Is he the monster that Cassius claims he is?

   An essay on this theme might naturally begin with a careful look at what Caesar says and does. Compare his actions to the complaints of the conspirators. Do you think the murder is justified? The other component of this essay might be a close look at the motivations of the conspirators. What do they want and why? Be careful, though, because you certainly should not take any of the characters in *Caesar* at their word. When characters talk about helping Rome, are they actually talking about helping themselves?

2. **The crowd:** How important is the crowd, or the "rabblement," as they are less favorably termed during the play, to the control of political power?

An essay on this theme might start at the beginning of the play. In the opening scene we see the tribunes, a group of men charged with looking after the interests of the working class, rudely abusing and harassing the people they are supposed to represent. What can we make of this? Isolate other scenes in which the crowd is depicted and see if you can build up a "profile" of them, of what function they serve. The key task might prove to be trying to determine whether Shakespeare is sympathetic to the crowd or not. This is no easy matter. For example, why does the poet Shakespeare have the crowd unjustly murder the poet Cinna? Look closely, too, at how the crowd functions during the funeral scene. Try to assess whether they are portrayed favorably or not in this key episode.

3. **Rhetoric:** How reliable is rhetoric, the art of persuasion, in *Julius Caesar?* Can we trust words, even if crafted elegantly and elaborately by brilliant speakers?

An essay on this topic will rely especially on close readings of key rhetorical moments. The question being asked is essentially: Is there any relationship between language and truth in this play? Find moments in the text where one character persuades a group or individual to do something they may not otherwise have done. Look carefully at these scenes to assess the consequences of rhetoric in the play. Shakespeare uses flourishes of linguistic brilliance, such as Antony's funeral oration, to study how language helps to build and organize human relations and political power. He wants us to think carefully about the art of language, to question it and look beneath the surface to understand its workings. What do you think he is encouraging us to see when we do so?

Characters

Julius Caesar has a relatively small cast of important characters, and the dramatic energy of the play comes from the tensions between the characters as much or more than the events of the plot. Critical approaches to the play have, in particular, centered on pairings of characters (Brutus and Antony, Brutus and Caesar, Cassius and Brutus, for example). While students might find themselves naturally drawn to working with two characters from *Julius Caesar* (see the section "Compare and Contrast Essays"), each of the principal figures certainly provides ample scope for a strong essay. Especially helpful to students writing about this play are character transformation and character duality. Antony, for example, is first seen as an athletic hero, quick of mind and rhetorically gifted, who seeks to avenge a murder. However, do we view him in this heroic light at the end of the play? Caesar, on the other hand, may not be in the play long enough to go through significant transformation, but his character is divided interestingly between the giant monster about whom Cassius cautions us, and a rather feeble old man who is hard of hearing.

Sample Topics:

1. **Brutus:** Though he claims to be motivated by a love of Rome and a desire to protect it from tyranny, to what extent is this motive mingled with or overshadowed by more selfish ambitions?

   This essay might start by asking how sympathetic we are supposed to be to Brutus. It goes without saying, of course, that a student writing this essay should focus on scenes in which Brutus is central to the action, but three episodes in particular might underpin the whole essay: the scene in which Cassius seeks to enlist Brutus; the murder of Caesar and the assassin's oration immediately following; and Brutus's suicide. To what extent does Cassius manipulate Brutus in their first conversation, or to what extent is Brutus a cautious but willing conscript? What does his funeral speech reveal about his character? What do you think we are supposed to feel at his death? This essay will certainly need to address the ambiguity of Brutus as a tragic hero. Do not let the complexity of the character become an obstacle; try to spot as many different (and no doubt contradictory) elements of his character as you can.

2. **Antony:** Can Antony be regarded as the play's hero? Is his revenge entirely driven by love for the dead Caesar?

This essay, like an essay on Brutus, must confront a nuanced character. We are drawn to his rhetorical power, but Shakespeare seems to caution that we should not embrace Antony unreservedly. Perhaps your thesis might reach for a multidimensional attempt to characterize Antony. Try to find scenes that reveal different sides of him, place them alongside one another in your analysis. You should be able to find quite radical extremes of behavior. For example, you might consider Antony's chilling conversation with Octavius at the beginning of act 4 alongside his apparently touching devotion to Caesar.

3. **Caesar:** What is it in Caesar that simultaneously provokes such intense love and fear?

This essay might begin by assessing who thinks what about Caesar at the beginning of the play. There is clearly a difference of opinion in Rome, and it could be said that the split runs along class lines. Consider why the masses might be infatuated with Caesar while the patricians seem possessed by a malignant mix of fear and contempt. Try making a list of the qualities and characteristics of Caesar before you begin writing, then see if you can use your list to formulate a thesis which characterizes him. Pay equal attention to his strengths and weaknesses. It might be profitable to ask how much Caesar is really in control of his actions, let alone the action of the play that bears his name. Consider, for example, his decision to go to the Senate. Finally, it will probably be necessary to think hard about the accuracy of the charges made by the conspirators, comparing them to what we actually know of Caesar's government of Rome. Again, the division between what the "masses" feel and what the elites perceive may be telling.

4. **Portia/Calpurnia:** Can these seemingly marginal figures help us better understand the characters of Brutus and Caesar? More important, how do they function as interesting and significant characters in their own right?

If the play gives little room to its two female characters, we as writers can go some way to correcting that imbalance. To counteract the lack of time these women spend on stage, beginning students might consider treating both Portia and Calpurnia in the same essay: the women of *Julius Caesar.* Certainly Portia seems to know that she inhabits a man's world, even going as far as challenging her own gender during her conversation with Brutus. Study the exchange closely, drawing significance from as many elements of it as you can. See if you can assess the type of marriage the pair have, focusing in particular on any mention of gender. Also, try to arrive at a symbolic or psychological meaning of Portia's wounded thigh. Moreover, why does she later take her own life in such a brutally unusual manner? Do not overlook the scene in which Portia waits to hear the outcome of the plot. If writing a comparative piece, how does Portia differ from Calpurnia? How much control does each woman have over her respective husband? Is there a difference between the way Caesar treats Calpurnia in public and the way he treats her in private? Gender may be a theme buried deeply in the play, but through study of these two characters, the political sphere of the play can be extended out to the relationship between the sexes.

History and Context

While Shakespeare sets his play in ancient Rome, he is a poet and not a historian. Unlike the historian, whose task is to reconstruct the past as accurately as possible, the artist is more likely to seek moral or aesthetic meaning. Therefore, in writing *Julius Caesar,* Shakespeare would have been responding to questions and issues surrounding him at the close of the sixteenth century. The implication here is that Shakespeare's play about ancient Rome has more to say about Elizabethan England than it does about antiquity. But how exactly does the play reflect the concerns of Elizabethan England? Literary critics have written a number of interesting essays about Caesar and Shakespeare's world. For example, Barbara Bono has suggested that in the debate over Caesar's murder can been found anxieties surrounding the impending death of Queen Elizabeth, while Wayne Rebhorn has written on the relationship between Caesar and the crisis in the Elizabethan aristocracy. Needless to say, these are highly specialized arguments, but beginning students could certainly find ways to approach Caesar historically. As it is principally a play about politics, one way to approach a historical essay might be to assess the relationship between Shakespeare's text and the political landscape of his day.

Sample Topic:

1. **Tudor and Stuart politics:** In what way does *Julius Caesar* reflect the political tensions and concerns of Renaissance England? How might Shakespeare be using a play about ancient Rome as a safe arena for topical debate?

   Written in 1599, *Julius Caesar* is composed literally on the eve of the most turbulent century of English political history. By the midway point of the seventeenth century, England would enter into civil war, the most critical moment of which was the execution of Charles I. Such things seemed cataclysmic at the time, and Robert Miola has suggested that *Julius Caesar* is an important part of the intellectual background of these events. Moreover, Shakespeare was living through an age of increasing state power, the machinery of power becoming more efficient and centralized. Elizabeth's government tried to exert control over many areas of an individual's life. For example, laws demanded church attendance on Sunday and dictated what clothes could be worn by each class of person (though historians disagree over how successfully such laws were enforced). For those interested in researching this topic,

Andrew Hadfield's *Shakespeare and Renaissance Politics* provides a lucid introduction.

An essay of this type would find an initial focus, such as the debate over concentrating power into the hands of a single figure such as an emperor or monarch. After having identified as many strands of this debate as possible in *Julius Caesar*, isolating key scenes and speeches for use in the essay, research about Tudor and Stuart political life might show how these debates were actually being conducted. The student might then compare the play to the historical record, asking how Shakespeare edits the debate for his text, what ideas he includes and excludes. Pay special attention to the different models of government offered in *Julius Caesar*, from monarchy to aristocracy to popular participation of sorts.

Philosophy and Ideas

Julius Caesar is an intellectual play, interested especially in the way power operates. As a writer, you can focus on at least two currents of this intellectual energy. The principal locus of this debate is the way humans construct political power, the different visions the play offers as to how Rome might be best governed. Yet power is not only something that the characters in Caesar exert and contest for. It is also something that is exercised upon them. As you read the play and prepare to write, think carefully about how power circulates through the work. Look closely at scenes where the balance of power changes, or, more troubling still perhaps, where human power appears to be an illusion, an impotent talisman that does little to protect Caesar, Brutus, and others from forces larger than themselves. The ultimate questions you address in this style of essay might actually be quite simple: What is true power in Julius Caesar? Where or with whom does it lie?

Sample Topics:

1. **Predetermination/free will:** What does the play have to say about the role of fate in the lives of its characters? How much control do individuals in *Caesar* have over the events that befall them?

An essay approaching this debate in *Caesar* might begin by assessing the philosophical alternatives found in the play. In part, students could focus on the power of fate and its dramatic agent, the supernatural. Consider the different ways supernatural events might be understood to direct the characters' fortunes: Calpurnia's dream, the soothsayer's vision, the remnants of an animal sacrificed the morning of Caesar's murder, and the strange portents the night before. However, do not forget that alongside this motif the play also treats the role of decision making seriously. Characters are frequently faced with pivotal, stark choices that have enormous implications. Look for the many instances where supernatural omens foreshadow these key moments of decision making. Further, consider the final implications of each major decision and assess in your essay how inevitable or avoidable each link of the play's tragic chain is. For example, could Caesar have avoided his assassination?

2. **Machiavelli:** Which character in *Julius Caesar* is the most Machiavellian?

An essay tackling this topic would begin with some reading from Machiavelli's principal work, *The Prince.* Writing almost a century before Shakespeare, Machiavelli argued that for leaders to be successful they should appear to be "good," but never shy away from almost any kind of "evil" in order to hold onto power. This sounds like devilish excess, and that is just how Shakespeare's England understood Machiavelli. But for all the bad press, his ideas are more subtle than they first appear. In fact, Machiavelli argues that the goal of a leader is simply the creation of a safe and stable state. In order to achieve this, he will have to lie, cheat, and even kill while all the time trying to appear honest, good, and pious.

Look for scenes in *Julius Caesar* where the patricians adopt the key Machiavellian strategy of saying one thing while intending or doing another. You could do this character by character, in fact. Pay attention especially to the role of soliloquies here, moments where the characters speak alone on stage to reveal their true thoughts and motives. Scenes of rhetorical performance would also be of great value to this essay, from Cassius's attempt to enlist Brutus in his plot through to Antony's funeral speech initiating the counterplot.

Form and Genre

Thinking about *Julius Caesar* explicitly as a work of literature, rather than as a living, breathing "world" inhabited by its characters, will take the writer in a new direction. When the student chooses this approach to the play, she is looking not so much at what *Julius Caesar* says but at how it says it. The difference may sound slight, but it dramatically changes how you read and write about the text. Shakespeare, as the author of *Julius Caesar,* comes to the foreground, and the essay writer's task is no longer to assess the choices of Brutus or Caesar, but of the playwright as he goes about his job. In this play he is writing a tragedy, doing so against a backdrop of expectations about what such a play will contain and do. Consider what it is that Shakespeare might want his audience to take or derive from Julius Caesar and offer evidence of how he is manipulating his drama and its spectators through his art. As you do so, consider how Caesar works in comparison to other Shakespearean tragedies you have read, or what you understand by the basic idea of tragedy in general.

To do this, you must consider key structural moments that determine not only what happens in the drama, but the tone produced as a result. Alongside this, you could ask why Shakespeare makes certain structural decisions in *Julius Caesar.* For example, you might ask why, in a work titled *Julius Caesar,* Caesar himself appears relatively little and his death, which could have been the tragic end of the play, is actually only its middle.

Sample Topic:

1. **Tragedy:** How cathartic is *Julius Caesar?* Is there an adequate sense of resolution at the close of the play?

Writers addressing this topic should pay especially close attention to the final act of the play. Catharsis is the idea that a play ends with a sense of release, the final events cleansing the reader emotionally and the world of the play literally. Reflect on what the characters of Cassius and especially Brutus have come to mean by the close of the play, reflecting then on what is "accomplished" by their deaths. You could ask a similar question about Caesar's death, too. Has Rome been purified by any of the tragic deaths? Is it any better off at the end than it was at the beginning? Consider also that Shakespeare will assume that some of his audience know that the "real life" Octavius lived to be made Emperor Augustus (and, as staged by Shakespeare in *Antony and Cleopatra*, become Antony's enemy). Judging the cathartic value of the play, therefore, is difficult and requires the writer to assess carefully the outcome of the play in relation to the tensions and problems raised by the work as a whole.

Compare and Contrast Essays

Julius Caesar is a play that seems to particularly welcome compare and contrast essays focusing on character. The characters overlap and oppose one another in interesting and often unexpected ways, uniting members of rival factions and even murderers with the man they kill. The play works hard to create symmetries between characters that deserve our attention as writers. For example, both Brutus and Cassius conspire to kill Caesar, tussle for the right to define the behavior of the anti-Caesar camp after the murder, and commit suicide at the close of the play. An essay focusing on this relationship would do well to capture its intensity (witness, for example, the emotional fervency as the pair iron out their differences before battle), though perhaps the essay's principal energy might come from identifying the differences that exist amid all this similarity and apparent brotherhood.

Julius Caesar is also a play that invites many connections with other works in Shakespeare's canon. Not least, of course, students could make use of the "sequel" to the play, *Antony and Cleopatra*, comparing how characters (Antony and Octavius) develop from one play to the next, or how Shakespeare continues to work with similar themes. However, perhaps the closest play in terms of political tone and theme might be Shakespeare's *Richard II*. Both plays ask what right powerful aristocrats have to overthrow their rulers under extreme circumstances, but do both plays take this debate in the same direction? Assess how much Caesar is similar to the equally ill-fated Richard, or what, if anything, distinguishes Brutus from Bolingbroke.

Sample Topics:

1. **Comparing Brutus and Caesar:** Are these two characters linked by shared weaknesses?

   You might structure this essay by first treating Caesar's weaknesses, then those of Brutus, before offering a third section that reflects on the relationship you have suggested. A little more challenging, perhaps, would be an approach that moves from fault to fault (the desire for power, susceptibility to flattery, failure to take counsel from their wives, for example), considering both characters simultaneously. Do not feel obliged to argue that Brutus and Caesar are identical even as you argue they are similar. Within the process of demonstrating shared weaknesses, you can reveal even greater sensitivity for the characters by showing the reader important distinctions between the two men.

2. **Contrasting the tragedies of *Julius Caesar* and *Macbeth*:** How are these two Shakespearean tragedies about killing kings different? Although the action of both plays centers on the plot to murder a ruler and the unhappy consequences of the deed, do the plays finally assert or say different things about this same theme?

   This essay would examine the structural similarities the plays share and consider both the differences and the meaning or import of those differences. For example, Duncan in *Macbeth* is an idealized, good king, while Caesar is arguably a tyrant in the making. The effect of this is to make Macbeth's deed seem more obviously despicable than Brutus's, but it also opens up

two very different thematic concerns. Because of this key difference, *Macbeth* becomes a play about the tension between
the natural and unnatural (focused on this most unnatural
murder of the fatherlike King Duncan). On the other hand, in
Caesar, by making Caesar a more ambiguous figure and the
motives for his murder more murky, Shakespeare takes the
action of regicide as the focal point for a complex discussion
of political alternatives.

3. **Comparing the domestic scenes of the play:** Shakespeare
   gives us two parallel scenes in *Julius Caesar*, one showing
   Brutus and Portia in private conversation, the other Caesar
   and Calpurnia. In what ways do these scenes mirror each
   other?

Such an essay would begin with careful scrutiny of these
two scenes alone (utilizing the kind of close reading skills we
have stressed throughout), though ultimately it would want
to make connections between the words and actions of these
two limited portions of the text and the themes of the play as a
whole. Think about what the scenes reveal about the male figures and the female characters individually, as well as assessing the dynamics of their relationships. Look for differences
in the way Caesar interacts with Calpurnia when the two are
alone and how he treats her during more public moments.
Think carefully about the qualities displayed by Caesar and
Brutus during these scenes, comparing them to their characters as a whole. Do we see the two men fundamentally as they
are elsewhere in the play, or are there differences to be noted
in this more intimate setting?

Bibliography for "*Julius Caesar*"

Bloom, Harold. *Julius Caesar*. New York: Penguin, 2005.

———, ed. *William Shakespeare's* "Julius Caesar": Modern Critical Interpretations. New York: Chelsea House, 1988.

Bono, Barbara. "The Birth of Tragedy: Tragic Action in *Julius Caesar*," *English
Literary Renaissance*. 24 (1994): 449–70.

Del Sapio Garbero, Maria, ed. *Identity, Otherness and Empire in Shakespeare's Rome.* Surrey, England: Ashgate, 2009.

Kahn, Coppelia. *Roman Shakespeare: Warriors, Wounds, and Women.* New York: Routledge, 1997.

Marshall, Cynthia. "Portia's Wound; Calpurnia's Dream: Reading Character in *Julius Caesar.*" *English Literary Renaissance.* 24 (1994): 471–88.

Miola, Robert. *Shakespeare's Rome.* Cambridge: Cambridge University Press, 1983.

Sims, Matthew. "The Political Odyssey: Shakespeare's Exploration of Ethics in *Julius Caesar.*" Harold Bloom and Blake Hobby, eds. *The Hero's Journey.* New York: Chelsea House, 2009: 95–105.

KING LEAR

READING TO WRITE

KING LEAR is a long play. The play is so immense in scope it may be useful to keep a log as you read, writing a short summary of each scene. If you jot down important episodes, ideas, and speeches in one place, navigating the play in your prewriting and writing stages will become easier (and a detailed essay plan or outline will also be even more essential here than ever). Try to keep the log relatively brief, otherwise it will itself become a daunting text. The play is also an intellectually demanding work of literature, pressing us to see and perceive despite the tragedy's reoccurring bouts of blindness, even to find something in the play's obsession with "nothing."

A first step is required to enter the play's motherless world of rival-rous, murderous siblings and conflicted, deluded fathers. A close reading of a passage from the play will help to introduce and provide some definition to the various themes and issues coursing through the text. An ideal passage to scrutinize perhaps is Edmund's soliloquy at the beginning of 1.2:

> Thou, nature, art my goddess; to thy law
> My services are bound. Wherefore should I
> Stand in the plague of custom, and permit
> The curiosity of nations to deprive me,
> For that I am some twelve or fourteen moon-shines
> Lag of a brother? Why bastard? Wherefore base?
> When my dimensions are as well compact,
> My mind as generous, and my shape as true,

> As honest madam's issue? Why brand they us
> With base? with baseness? bastardy? base, base?
> Who, in the lusty stealth of nature, take
> More composition and fierce quality
> Than doth, within a dull, stale, tired bed,
> Go to the creating a whole tribe of fops,
> Got 'tween asleep and wake? Well, then,
> Legitimate Edgar, I must have your land:
> Our father's love is to the bastard Edmund
> As to the legitimate: fine word,—legitimate!
> Well, my legitimate, if this letter speed,
> And my invention thrive, Edmund the base
> Shall top the legitimate. I grow; I prosper:
> Now, gods, stand up for bastards! (1.2.1–22)

Edmund's speech begins with a rejection of law in favor of nature. He understands the latter to mean a chaotic, disordered free for all in which human "custom" is trumped by a kind of Darwinian survival of the fittest or smartest. However, this interpretation forms just one strand of the play's thinking on the theme of nature, and an essay writer could take Edmund's anarchic vision as the starting point for a much broader essay. If human laws and customs represent the unnatural for Edmund, while brutal self-reliance is for him the sole character of the natural world, does the play agree? If not, what does nature mean in *King Lear?* Look for the way in which human customs and natural laws actually seem to overlap in the play. For example, the devotion of children to their parents, tender and respectful treatment of the aged, and the integrity of a nation are all human precepts so entrenched in our lives that they appear as part of nature. Look for ways in which these and other "natural laws" are abused and broken. Assess signs that nature is "angry" at these breaches of faith, for example, Gloucester's superstitious foreboding (1.2.101) and the great storm at the center of the play (see the "Themes" section). Finally, the fates of the characters might be used to discuss the role of nature in the play's tragedy. In his final line of the passage above, Edmund exclaims, "Now, gods, stand up for bastards!" But do they do so in the play? How exactly do the gods or nature "behave" toward the characters? Does nature triumph? At what cost? Perhaps the most chilling conclusion to reach is that Edmund's assessment of nature and the play's assessment of nature are in many ways alike. Some writers will finally argue that the play also believes nature is chaotic, random, and brutal, that nature itself is a human construct that masks the disordered universe of *King Lear*.

The passage might also lead the writer to an essay based on character analysis. Edmund is certainly a remarkable creation that deserves intensive study. For writers attempting such an essay, 1.2 is an important scene. Not only does it contain the passage cited at the beginning of the chapter but several others that provide insight into Edmund's motivations and malign independence (1.2.109–25; 1.2.102–08). Think carefully about the social limitations placed on Edmund as an illegitimate child, but more important reflect on his philosophical challenges to those limitations. Ask what makes Edmund an attractive or at least seductive character not only to Goneril and Regan but to the audience as well. Finally, no paper on Edmund would be complete without consideration of his perplexing behavior at the play's close (5.3). Assess not only his commitment to the speedy execution of Lear and Cordelia, but the curious conversion of his final lines (242–46). Formulate an explanation for his desire to "do some good," and consider what he means when he says to do so would be "Despite of mine own nature." Does Edmund, the memorable villain of the piece, finally have his own tragedy to suffer as well?

TOPICS AND STRATEGIES

Every essay requires a focus; you cannot write about everything in the play at once. In the section on how to write an essay, you will be presented with a number of ways of turning a focus into a thesis, observations into arguments. However, the starting point is nearly always finding an initial point of departure, making first observations. You can then seize on and develop the budding ideas you will have as you make your way through the play. By no means should you feel limited to these topics, however. Instead they can be viewed as triggering suggestions encouraging you to break out into your own critical directions.

Themes

King Lear takes for its themes some of the most important issues central to human existence; we might even argue that it is transcendent, stretching beyond the limits of this world and the common mind. Certainly the play's greatness (and it is routinely talked of as Shakespeare's finest, most powerful work) is located in the text's ideas and themes, rather than in its story. Its plot has prompted much criticism over the centuries, and it is difficult to see how the story alone could make an enduring work of literature. Yet somehow the glaringly silly mistakes of an old man, potentially implausible and contemptible, are the starting point for one of the most celebrated works of art in Western civilization; the themes of the play quickly soar far beyond the narrative starting point, and writers must be willing to follow. This is no small commitment. Many of the themes considered in this chapter immediately betray their philosophical, transcendent substance: vision, nature, nothingness. There are, however, some more worldly themes offered by the play. For example, writers with an interest in gender could certainly engage the play successfully from a feminist stance. You might take as your starting point the oft-noted absence of a wife for Lear, contemplating why Shakespeare might omit the figure of a wife and mother and what effect it has on the domestic dynamics of the play. The figures of Goneril and Regan clearly offer much material for the writer of this essay, along with Lear's misogynistic declarations throughout the middle section of the play. And, of course, for contrast, there is Cordelia. But what is gained by this contrast? What does the play seem to say about female authority (think about the treatment of fathers and husbands)? If Cordelia is to be seen as the play's idealized vision of woman, assess exactly what that vision entails.

This material or political approach to the play, examining the text's conscious and unconscious revelations about Shakespeare's treatment of gender, is hugely important and a vital part of reappraising *King Lear.* However, many students are rightly drawn to the challenges of *King Lear*'s universal aspirations, its timeless study of human folly and suffering.

Sample Topics:

1. **Vision:** What are the limits of human vision in *King Lear?* Is it possible to truly "see"? What would true sight reveal?

   Such an essay might start with the idea that there are two types of blindness and two types of sight in the play: literal sight and blindness (what we see or cannot see with our eyes) and the superior "vision" of true perception, the mind's eye. Catalog and interpret examples of both literal and symbolic blindness in *King Lear*. For example, assess how Lear's blindly misguided actions of 1.1 (the disowning of Cordelia, the banishment of Kent, and the division of his kingdom) mirror the literal (and symbolic) blindness of Gloucester. Catalog other parts of the text where sight is mentioned, using such examples both as evidence of the play's preoccupation with sight and as part of your own formulation of what sight means in *King Lear*. Particularly important scenes include 3.7 (where Gloucester's eyes are plucked out to Cornwall's grisly cry of "out, vile jelly!") and the powerful 4.6 in which Edgar leads his blind father to an imaginary cliff (analyze the way so much that is not real is "seen" in this episode). Importantly, treat the idea that it is possible to have literal vision while seeing nothing at all (Lear in 1.1; Gloucester's pitiful acknowledgment in 4.1 that he "stumbled when I saw"). Equally, contemplate the way in which the play suggests that sight and true vision can be achieved even when literally blind (Gloucester) or maddened (Lear). What is it that Lear and Gloucester finally come to see? While you can certainly begin answering this question by noting the fathers finally see which of their children can be trusted and which cannot, the more powerful insights will address what the two aging men "see" or realize about themselves and their behavior.

2. **The storm:** What symbolic power does the storm of act 3 possess?

Storms are important symbols in Shakespearean drama (for those who might be interested in a comparative approach to the theme of storm, other examples can be found in *Twelfth Night*, *Othello*, *The Winter's Tale*, and *The Tempest*), but nowhere does Shakespeare imbue a storm with more meaning and complexity than in *King Lear*. Shakespeare tends to associate the power of the storm with a moment of change or transition. Yet in *King Lear* the storm is not merely a catalyst but rather the centerpiece of the drama, a presence as strong and memorable as any of the characters. Perhaps the most accessible way to approach this essay would be to examine the storm's effects primarily on Lear, but a broader approach could be taken as well. An essay of the former type might begin by assessing Lear's character before the storm and end with an evaluation of Lear after the storm. The bulk of the essay, however, should probably be devoted to a close reading of the storm scenes (3.2, 3.4, and 3.6) and the steady transformation of Lear taking place during his encounter with the storm. The best essays will chart a progression rather than a sudden enlightenment, seeing in each of the three scenes a different stage in Lear's transformation. One model, for example, might focus on Lear's anger in 3.2 as the violence of the storm mirrors his rage, then move into 3.4 looking for evidence of newly acquired insights on Lear's part, and the final, overwhelming collapse of 3.6 into a tempest of madness and pain.

Characters

King Lear contains some of Shakespeare's most complex and memorable characters. The thematic ambitions of the play demand characters that develop and change, bend and twist in the ferocious storm of the play's tragedy. Even the most minor characters in the play are capable of offering enormous interest and provoking extended meditation. For example, as Cornwall gouges out the eyes of Gloucester, one of Cornwall's servants tries to intervene and stop his master (3.7.73–85). The servant has only nine lines, fails to stop Cornwall, and is killed by Regan, but only after fatally wounding his lord. There is something enigmatic about this fellow who is so unimportant in the grand scheme, tries to do a good deed, harbors dreams of justice and heroism, but dies almost as quickly as he arrived on the scene. There is something human and tragic about this nine-lined creature. While it might be a bit much to attempt an entire essay on this ill-fated but well-intentioned figure, he could become a meaningful part of wider essays. For example, a paper on servant characters in the play would allow a nice blend of character study and thematic analysis. Two other characters who would certainly belong in such an essay are the chivalric Kent and the toadying Oswald.

Using these three characters, such an essay might explore the servant's place in the social or "natural" order (perhaps likening it to the parent-child relationship also explored in the play; thus, the servant becomes another example of a person born into a "natural" place who must come to terms with the limits of that existence and determine how to live best within those confines. This is precisely what Edmund cannot do, for example, and what Kent appears utterly devoted to), assess how a servant should serve his master according to the thematic structure of the play, and look for telling similarities and differences between the apparently divergent Kent and Oswald. Once you have defined how the play defines good service, it will be possible to explore the paradoxes and complexity of this concept. For example, the minor character who tries to stop Cornwall from ripping out an old man's eyes does so by reminding his master of the lifetime of faithful service he has given to Cornwall and by framing this intervention as part of that service. Yet to Cornwall and Regan he is an impudent "peasant," a bad servant who deserves no more thanks than to be stabbed in the back.

Sample Topics:

1. **King Lear:** What has Lear's tragedy taught him?

> A character study of Lear is a large task, but by no means unmanageable. In some ways, the more there is to say on a subject the easier it is to write an essay on it. You certainly will not run out of things to say in a five- or ten-page paper on this topic. However, there are several important strategy points to be made before we start. First, while the basic technique of a character study is to trace the progression and development of a character, this is rarely a straight line. Perhaps this is no more true than with the figure of Lear; the play takes him to enormous depths of anguish and suffering, anger and blindness, before his "sight" is restored. Lear's progress is imperfect and filled with "lapses"; be prepared to trace a winding path as you follow Lear's passage from the start of the play to the close. Nor is it clear what Lear achieves, what his newly found vision perceives. This is for you to decide, an assessment that would make for an excellent thesis statement with which to

start the paper. The body of the essay would then track and interpret the steps in Lear's journey.

It is arguably much easier to know where Lear starts than to understand where he ends. Such an essay should surely begin with a detailed examination of 1.1, identifying the nature of what Kent calls Lear's "hideous rashness" (1.1.151). Try to understand the king's apparently inexplicable behavior, characterizing the possible psychological motivations behind it. You might follow these same faults as they appear in the build up to the storm scenes. See, for example, Lear's insistence on keeping a large retinue of men and Goneril and Regan's calculated efforts to strip him of his train. Then a careful consideration of the storm scenes is required, recognizing again that the storm does not cause an instant epiphany for Lear but a gradual weathering of self (see the preceding "Themes" section). The essay might follow analysis of the storm scenes with an explication of Lear immediately after the storm as his madness slowly transitions into vision, or, as Edgar puts it, Lear develops "reason in madness" (4.6.169). Close read 4.6 and 4.7, looking in the former for growing wisdom and in the latter for Lear's redemption through Cordelia. It is possible to argue that Lear's "education" is complete by the end of 4.7, and that the remainder of the play intensifies his suffering and destroys him. You may or may not agree with this position, but a careful consideration of his death scene in 5.3 will probably be a good idea regardless. So, as you can see, there is a lot of material to work with, so give yourself ample time to write and a put together a detailed plan before starting the essay. This will help avoid spending too long, for example, on the prestorm Lear and running out of time, energy and pages before the final gusts of the storm have blown. The writer could give significantly more weight to the storm scenes and the scenes immediately after. It is these scenes of Lear's complicated transformation that the reader will want your help in understanding.

2. **The Fool:** Why does the Fool disappear in the second half of the play?

Such an essay understands the Fool more as a function than a character and seeks to understand why he is no longer needed after the storm scenes. The writer might begin by evaluating the Fool's contribution to the play in the earlier scenes. Clearly, he is an example of a traditional type called the "wise fool," a figure whose position as a clown grants him the freedom to speak truths that would be punishable from the lips of other characters (see Kent's banishment, for example). What truths does the Fool reveal to Lear? Examine the corrective reproaches offered by the Fool in 1.4 and other following scenes. In order to account for the Fool's disappearance, it might be useful to say that perhaps Lear no longer needs the clown's blunt chastisements. But why, do you think? What is it that Lear now understands that he did not before? You might also see the Fool as a childlike figure, and assess the treatment he receives in the storm scenes from Lear. This angle adds to the idea of the Fool "teaching" Lear traits and insights he must gain in order to find redemption later in the play. In this light, you might want to tackle and explain the puzzling blur between the identities of Cordelia and the Fool in 5.3. As Lear clutches the body of his daughter he exclaims: "My poor fool is hanged." While "fool" is a term of endearment not out of place here, given the audience's awareness of the character called the Fool, and his sudden absence, the line resonates with a strange double meaning. A difficult but praiseworthy final step for this essay, then, might be in assigning the Fool a place in the resolution of this tragedy, explaining why he reappears in this perplexingly ghostly manner.

3. **Edgar:** Edgar is often described as being a collection of characters rather than a single, unified "person." Is this correct? If so, what importance does each of his "characters" have in the play?

Such an essay might begin by establishing Edgar's function in the play before 2.3. Principle to this might be the contrast of Edgar with Edmund. Close read the brief episode of 2.3 which culminates with Edgar's "I nothing am." An enigmatic statement like this is a gift to the essay writer because it opens up numerous interpretive possibilities. The statement could be connected to the theme of "nothing," a motif so prominent in the play from Lear and Cordelia's early quibble over the word (1.1.86–90). Alternatively, the writer could interpret the statement in terms of Edgar's mutability, his ceaseless changing and transforming from this point on. Certainly Edgar's most memorable disguise is Poor Tom, the deranged and homeless beggar who haunts the open country. Assess the functions of Tom, perhaps connecting him with the Fool. What "truth" emerges from Tom's apparently fearful babble? What purpose does Tom serve in the slow transformation of Lear and Gloucester? Consider the symbolic importance of other disguises adopted by Edgar, the kindly peasant who finds Gloucester at the bottom of the imaginary cliff and the nameless knight who triumphs over Edmund.

Related to the issue of disguise is the idea of ambiguity in Edgar's character (if we see enough continuity through the sequence of disguises to call Edgar a cohesive character, of course). Critics have pointed to at least two causes for concern here, and the writer of an essay on Edgar would do well to treat both. First, some have suggested that Edgar unnecessarily prolongs the anguish of his father by not revealing himself earlier. An important counterargument to deal with here, of course, is that Edgar has a reason to delay the revelation of his identity, that Gloucester requires more anguish in order to find his redemption. Second, scholars have also taken Edgar to task for his belief that a kind of justice runs through the play, vindicating and explaining the play's great heap of suffering with his final claim that the "gods are just" (5.3.171). Consider whether this is a heartless and rather ugly statement given his father's plight, or whether it is perhaps the view of the play as articulated through Edgar.

Form and Genre

For some readers and theatergoers, confronting *King Lear* provokes a heightened emotional response that derives from the overwhelming force of the play's tragic movement. In the eighteenth century, audiences preferred to watch an adaptation of *King Lear* that ended happily, the original tragic resolution being deemed simply unwatchable. To avoid or turn away from Lear's tragedy, however, is not an option available for the student writing an essay on the play; instead, she must harness for her essay the brutal energy of the text's vision. For many critics, *King Lear* is Shakespeare's most compelling and perfect engagement with the tragic form. A. C. Bradley, for example, an early twentieth-century scholar who wrote extensively on Shakespeare's tragedies, argued that *King Lear* is "the most terrible picture that Shakespeare painted of the world. In no other of his tragedies does humanity appear more pitiably infirm or more hopelessly bad." A writer might attempt a paper that looks for good and for hope in *King Lear,* but the task of identifying and characterizing the nature of the tragedy is philosophically simpler and allows the student to draw material from the entire play. What is at the heart of the picture Shakespeare paints of the world in *King Lear?* You might agree with Bradley that it is the infirmity and immorality of mankind, but this is simply a place to start rather than a place to finish. In what ways does the play highlight our frailties and weaknesses? Does the play offer an explanation for the wickedness that corrupts us?

Sample Topic:

1. **Tragedy:** What is the significance of the recurring "nothing" motif? What might the idea of "nothing" contribute to the play's tragic vision?

A good beginning for such an essay might be to identify and close read several passages that seem to powerfully articulate the spirit of tragedy animating *King Lear.* Among the various passages that do exactly this are Gloucester's terrifying observation that the gods are like naughty children and humans like the flies these children "kill for their sport" (4.1.37–38), or Lear's no less chilling "stage of fools" speech (4.6.176–81). Having characterized the nature of the tragedy the essay could continue by connecting these dark visions with the motif of "nothing" so prominent in the play. Look for utterances of the word "nothing" (see the discussion of Edgar in the preceding "Character" section for one example), but do not simply catalogue these instances. Instead, try to spot philosophical patterns developing with each example. Connect the idea of "nothing" with the tragic movement of the play. One way to do this might be to focus on connecting "nothing" with the idea of disorder, of chaos. Here "nothing" becomes a watchword for the kind of unruly and chaotic world that allows old men to be abandoned and betrayed by their children and Poor Tom to be abandoned by the comforts and good fortune that others enjoy. A writer might play with the word *further* to find other ways in which it articulates what the play has to say about the world. But is "nothing" the dominant force in the play, or can it be challenged? For example, the writer might feel obliged to treat a number of issues: the goodness and devotion of characters such as Cordelia and Kent; Edgar's claim that the "gods are just," suggesting, of course, a very large "something," rather than "nothing," giving order to the play's action; the redemptions that Gloucester and Lear *do* experience, regardless of their exceptional price; the deaths of all the principle villains; and even Edmund's ambiguous turnaround. When writing about comedy or tragedy, the final scene of the play must always be considered as this is where the shape of the drama is completed. A writer might consider the neatness of Albany's closing declaration (5.3.294–303), Kent's haunting promise that sounds unhappily like a suicide note (5.3.320–21), and, of course, Lear's final lines over Cordelia's body (5.3.304–06). If there is a "something" in the world of the play, what is it? If there is only void and nothingness in *King Lear,* what other names does the text assign to "nothing," how do we come to know a force that is inherently an absence or a lack?

Bibliography for *"King Lear"*

Bloom, Harold, ed. *Modern Critical Interpretations: King Lear.* New York: Chelsea House, 1987.

Bradley, A. C. *Shakespearean Tragedy: Lectures on Hamlet, Othello, King Lear, Macbeth.* Basingstoke, England: Macmillan, 1904.

Danson, Lawrence, ed. *On King Lear.* Princeton: Princeton University Press, 1981.

Foakes, R. A. *Hamlet versus Lear.* Cambridge: Cambridge University Press, 1993.

Goldberg, Jonathan. "Perspectives: Dover Cliff and the Conditions of Representation." *Shakespeare and Deconstruction.* Douglas Atkins and David Bergeron, eds. New York: Peter Lang, 1988.

Khan, Coppelia. "The Absent Mother in King Lear." *Rewriting the Renaissance: The Discourses of Sexual Difference in Early Modern Europe.* Chicago: University of Chicago Press, 1986.

Taylor, Gary and Michael Warren, eds. *The Division of the Kingdoms: Shakespeare's Two Versions of King Lear.* Oxford: Clarendon Press, 1986.

MACBETH

READING TO WRITE

*M*ACBETH PROVIDES the writer with any number of directions and choices for essay topics. There are several psychologically complex and vivid characters, a variety of thematic concerns as well as prominent marks of Shakespeare's engagement with Jacobean politics. Despite this abundance, the play is often noted for its economy. It is an efficient piece of theater that does not waste a scene. As a result, you can find significance and meaning throughout *Macbeth*, with nearly all points of the text connected to every other point in narrative, symbolic and thematic terms. Close reading is especially important here because so many speeches are dense and contain strong material for the writer, but also because spotting patterns within the rapid and consequential action will help prevent your essay from becoming a "hurlyburly" of disjointed observations or from missing out on important parallels.

Lady Macbeth's soliloquy, spoken during 1.5 as she anticipates the arrival of Duncan, is a good passage from the play exemplifying how character, theme, and tone are compacted so tightly in *Macbeth*.

> . . . Come, you spirits
> That tend on mortal thoughts, unsex me here,
> And fill me, from the crown to the toe, top-full
> Of direst cruelty! Make thick my blood,
> Stop up th' access and passage to remorse,
> That no compunctious visitings of nature
> Shake my fell purpose, nor keep peace between
> Th' effect and it! Come to my woman's breasts

And take my milk for gall, you murdering ministers,
Wherever in your sightless substances
You wait on nature's mischief! Come, thick night,
And pall thee in the dunnest smoke of hell,
That my keen knife see not the wound it makes,
Nor heaven peep through the blanket of the dark,
To cry "Hold, hold!" (1.5.41–54)

The first three words of this passage make an important thematic statement, as well as forging a key connection between characters. In invoking these spirits, Lady Macbeth solidifies the already clear presence of the supernatural in the play, showing how the reach of the mysterious and occult is far from limited to the isolated heaths; she also symbolically but unmistakably connects herself with the witches. The role of the supernatural will be discussed in greater depth in the "Themes" section, but consider how to develop the second observation, that Lady Macbeth is linked to the witches through her incantation, into an essay (an alternative approach to the topic can be found in the "Compare and Contrast" section). Having made this connection, we might begin with a section of the essay establishing the characteristics of the witches and—more important—what they cause to transpire in the play. This might be usefully followed with a similar section treating Lady Macbeth, followed by a third, longer portion discussing the overlap between Macbeth's wife and the witches. Look for similarities of function within the play. Both appear to drive Macbeth forward initially, molding his thoughts and deeds, though both eventually become superfluous to his multiplying acts of violence. However, there will be few moments that help make the connection as directly as Lady Macbeth's conjuring in the cited passage, so you will need to establish the link through careful use of the play's thematic content.

For example, two such connections grow out of the second line of our quotation. In Lady Macbeth's demand that the spirits "unsex" her, we see a parallel to the witches' androgyny, but, vitally, we also see how Lady Macbeth desires to be unnatural and monstrous, a status that connects her with the cruelty of the witches and allies her with the darkest forces operating in the play: broadly, of the "unnatural" in opposition to what the play appears to deem natural. To oppose nature, whether that is the laws of the organic world or the divinely ordained (and thus natural) order of society, is to be evil in the world of *Macbeth*.

This power is nowhere seen more clearly than in the repeated allusions to infanticide (child killing) hinted at here in Lady Macbeth's desired transformation of her breast milk into venomous gall. This is a great example of how Shakespeare peppers the play with patterns for the reader to discern and contemplate. Read carefully through the text for inferences to child killing or the Macbeth's childlessness, and you will find numerous appearances of this disturbing theme. However, this is just one element of a much bigger thematic movement that asks the writer to identify as many strands of the unnatural in the play as she can find. Such a list will be of enormous help in writing about many aspects of the play as it will encourage you to read the play as a web of interconnected motifs and ideas. However, when you write avoid merely making a list that shows Shakespeare is concerned with the tensions between the natural and the unnatural; instead, try to characterize that tension. For example, you might want to draw a connection between the murder of children in the play (actual and symbolic) with the disruption Macbeth temporarily causes in the "natural order" of royal descent.

See, too, how yet another theme emerges from the passage following these ghoulish demands of Lady Macbeth and striking a clearly different note. The references to her acts being hidden, from heaven and even the knife she murders with, anticipate the enormous role to be played in *Macbeth* by the power of guilt. Try to establish links between such seeds of emotion and fear planted in the first part of the play and their fruit grimly growing later in the text. Also note that the tone of this whole passage suggests that even with these nascent anxieties, Lady Macbeth is still very much in control. You could use this confidence and surety as the starting point for an essay considering the relationship between Lady Macbeth and Macbeth, exploring in particular the balance of power between the two and how that power is maintained. Obviously, moments in which this married couple is alone together will be the key. Ask yourself, moreover, at which point this relationship shifts and the balance of power alters with it.

TOPICS AND STRATEGIES

Every essay requires a focus; you cannot write about everything in the play at once. In the section on how to write an essay, you will be presented with a number of ways of turning a focus into a thesis, observations into arguments. However, the starting point is nearly always finding an initial point of departure, making first observations. You can then seize on and develop the budding ideas you will have as you make your way through the play. By no means should you feel limited to these topics, however. Instead they can be viewed as triggering suggestions encouraging you to break out into your own critical directions.

Themes

Thematic approaches to *Macbeth* are as plentiful as they are rich. One soliloquy opens many doors to the writer seeking her topic. This creates an even higher than usual need for self-control and the firm establishment of boundaries in your essay plan. For example, let us say you take as your theme the natural versus the unnatural. This theme overlaps with many others in the play, such as gender roles or witchcraft. Both gender roles and witchcraft could by themselves be the subjects of excellent essays, of course, and so the problem might be in allotting these "subthemes" enough space to explore the main theme of the natural versus the unnatural thoroughly without your paper unintentionally becoming an essay about gender roles or witches (and the witches, in particular, have a tendency to take over an essay). A key tip here is to acknowledge in your work any elements of *Macbeth* that you will only briefly touch on or will pass by entirely. So, let us say you are assigned or decide to write a short paper on gender in the play. You may feel that, given a limited page count and a desire for depth of analysis more than breadth, your essay should focus on the shifting gender roles of the Macbeth and Lady Macbeth. An acknowledgment that the witches are an important part of the play's discourse on gender, but beyond the scope of the current essay, shows the reader that you are aware of the connection and have not missed something important. Instructors often assess and grade an essay with one eye on what the student has *not* written about, so it is always important to know the parameters of your essay and to make sure your reader is aware of them also. This is particularly helpful when writing about a dense but concise work like *Macbeth*.

Sample Topics:

1. **Gender:** Gender concerns of many kinds seem ever present in *Macbeth*, but how exactly do these issues become integral to the tragedy?

An essay such as this might start by establishing how gender functions at the beginning of the play, then tracing a series of subtle shifts that by the end of *Macbeth* have produced an entirely different gender dynamic. One subtle point to consider early on might be Macbeth's "manliness" before the play begins. All you have to go on here is the captain's report to Duncan in 1.2. What kind of man does the captain describe? Compare this to Lady Macbeth's anxieties about Macbeth, sometimes expressed in private or as taunts expressed directly to her husband. How is gender an important component of Lady Macbeth's attempts to impel Macbeth to murder Duncan? Most important, perhaps, try to assess how each of the couple compares to the commonplace ideal of "man" or "woman." Look for moments where each character comments on the gender role of the other, such as Macbeth's remark that his wife could only bear male children because she has nothing of woman in her. Finally, from this first part of the play, you might try to describe to your reader how Lady Macbeth constructs her gender identity, and what that identity is.

Consider carefully, then, how the gender roles change by the end of the play. How has Macbeth's gendering changed? What has happened to Lady Macbeth to change her role in the play? Describe the gender roles that each of the pair has by the fifth act, but be sure to also account for these changes.

2. **The natural versus the unnatural:** What are some examples of unnatural behavior in the play? What does the text propose as a natural state of affairs? How might we describe the status of this conflict between natural ideals and unnatural powers at various moments in *Macbeth?*

Many critics have observed that Shakespeare begins his play with a world in chaos; the movement of the play's action from this starting point is the gradual and costly process of nature's return to preeminence. Although students are certainly not obliged to agree, accepting this basic shape gives good structure to an essay while still allowing enormous intellectual and interpretive freedom for the writer. How is the world of the opening acts under the shadow of unnatural forces? How has natural order been restored at the close? You might think about the debate on many different levels: moral, social, political, and, of course, the play's supernatural elements; they are all interweaved tightly by Shakespeare here. In the play's vision there is no distinction between a wife who controls her husband, an aristocrat who murders his king, or the baleful and bearded witches who conjure mischief. All of these things are opposed to the natural order as many in Shakespeare's audience would have understood it, and you might want to draw parallels between the various elements as you write. Look for other manifestations of the unnatural as the plot unravels.

Importantly, ask yourself what "solutions" the play offers for each unnatural problem—these solutions are not always kind or easily arrived at. Think about the political order after Macbeth's death, for example, to explore one way in which "natural order" has been restored.

Characters

The psychological terrain of this play is dominated by only two characters. Lady Macbeth and Macbeth offer complex reflections on their future actions at the beginning of the play and profoundly harrowing emotional and intellectual responses to those actions once taken. Even more advantageous to the writer, these complex characters also grow and change markedly during the play. This combination of psychological complexity and discernable transformation means that essays on the two main characters might benefit from the formulaic but reliable character-study approach of identifying what a character is like at the beginning, then what she or he is like at the end, drawing to the reader's attention in detail the various factors that brought that change about

There are, of course, other characters in the play worthy of consideration. Macduff earns his own topic in this section, and the witches will be discussed in more detail in the "History and Context" section. Malcom, too, is a character that, given his important role at the end of the play, might merit an essay. However, selecting a relatively minor character for a detailed study presents challenges as well as the rewards of an original topic and a clear, tight focus. Malcolm's scenes are few, but pay special attention to his curious and perhaps unsettling exchange with Macduff in 4.3. What do you make of the way Malcom "tests" Macduff, as well as his response to Macduff's sorrow at the loss of his family? Overall, try to assess how we are to judge Malcom's role as the "natural" curative to Macbeth's unnatural blight of Scotland. Look for troubling moments or words that might conceivably complicate our sense of hope accompanying Malcolm's ascendancy.

Sample Topics:

1. **Macbeth:** How does Macbeth's character change during the play? How does he respond to his crimes?

An essay on this topic might explore Macbeth's reluctance to assassinate Duncan at the beginning of the play, as well as identifying what tactics Lady Macbeth employs to coax him to perform the murder. It may appear an obvious difference, but Shakespeare seems to want us to think about the relationship between Macbeth's bloody and uncompromising performance on the battlefield and his reticence to kill his king. Exploring these differences may allow you to get a better sense of Macbeth as well as his society. Look closely at his immediate response to the murder, and guide the reader through the shifting psychological decline that sets in. Consider the role of guilt but also the much more complicated feelings of hopelessness and fear that follow. Lastly, how does this dangerous mix of emotions and thoughts further deform Macbeth into a serial killer? Consider throughout the fatal tension in Macbeth's psyche between internal and external voices; to what extent are his greed and then arrogance the product of his own innate character or the counsel and prophecies of others?

2. **Lady Macbeth:** If Lady Macbeth initially appears to be the stronger or more ambitious half of the couple, how do we account for her decline into a state of debilitating emotional weakness by the end of the play?

In many ways this essay might share the same basic shape as an essay on Macbeth: an exploration of the character in the build up to the key dramatic moment of Duncan's murder, and then a careful consideration of the spiraling psychological degeneration that follows. Assess what motivates Lady Macbeth in the early acts, and what measures she takes to prepare herself for the event. Look carefully at her decisive and domineering behavior in the immediate wake of the murder, comparing this to her descent into a deep-rooted and destructive guilt in the following acts. It is noticeable that the immensely strong figure we come to know at the start of the play is reduced to such a weak presence who simply vanishes offstage in a reported suicide. How do you account for this? What changes have occurred in Macbeth's character that essentially sideline Lady Macbeth? Think, too, about the role her death may have in the play's restoration of natural order.

3. **Macduff:** How are we to understand the play's nominal hero? How does he fit into the complex thematic puzzle of the play?

Such an essay might pay close attention to two key areas; first, think about the problem that arises for Macduff's character when his family is murdered. He has essentially left them undefended and alone, vulnerable to an attack that he could have anticipated and perhaps prevented. Certainly, before she is killed, Lady Macduff expresses harsh words about her "traitor" husband. Compare this attack on Macduff's domestic honor to Ross's defense of Macduff's political honor and his flight to England. How do you think Shakespeare wants us to interpret this action? Second, reflect on the important connection between Macduff and Macbeth; the play appears to offer Macduff as the "anti-Macbeth," but how does he come to play this role not just in narrative terms but symbolically too? Think, for example, about how Macduff might fit interestingly into the play's debates about the relationship between men and women as well as the natural and the unnatural. The death of his family, and the infamous circumstances of his own birth might be good places to begin making these thematic interpretations.

History and Context

The only version of *Macbeth* that has come down to us appears to have been written for a court performance for King James I. Moreover, Shakespeare certainly did his homework in preparing a play that would appeal to (and flatter) the new king; the text is filled with references and themes that would have drawn the royal audience into the entertainment before them. As a result, the student writing on *Macbeth* can follow Shakespeare's lead, doing her own homework to uncover these plentiful and telling historical traces. Historically focused essays on *Macbeth* can take a number of directions, though students might do well to keep in mind Shakespeare's primary target as they research and write.

James I was a controversial figure in a number of ways. When he came to the throne, many in England were relieved to see the uncertainties of the late Elizabethan era safely buried with Good Queen Bess. Where Elizabeth I was unmarried and childless, James, already king of Scotland, brought with him a wife and children. The honeymoon between king and country, however, if it existed at all, did not last long. The problems and concerns of James's reign palpably shape English drama of the early seveteenth century and are unmistakably discernable in *Macbeth*. Tensions between the Scottish king, along with his Scottish favorites who traveled south with him, and the existing English court are perhaps wished away in the alliance of England and Scotland forged at the end of *Macbeth*. Moreover, James saw himself as quite the scholar, writing tracts on subjects as varied as royal power and witchcraft; it is no coincidence that these kingly interests become important thematic concerns of the play. A good text to begin with when researching the connections between James' court and Shakespeare's work is Alvin Kernan's *Shakespeare, The King's Playwright: Theater in the Stuart Court, 1603–1613*.

Sample Topics:

1. **Witchcraft:** How does Shakespeare employ the witches in *Macbeth*? How do they become pivotal elements of the tragedy rather than merely atmospheric and peripheral figures?

Such an essay might begin by describing Shakespeare's use of witchcraft mythology, proceeding then to argue how this representation of the witches complements other thematic concerns in the play. There are two key sources for the student of witchcraft in Shakespeare's world: the enormously influential medieval text *Malleus Maleficarum* (or "The Hammer of Witches," to give the translated title), and the early seventeenth-century writings of Reginald Scot. Both of these, along with a useful modern introduction to the history of witchcraft, can be conveniently found in *Witchcraft in Europe: 1100–1700*, edited by Alan Kors and Edward Peters. Scot's writings embody the skeptical and enlightened view of witchcraft dawning in Shakespeare's lifetime, but it is the stereotypical witch of the *Malleus* that Shakespeare explicitly and somewhat sensationally uses. Using your research and understanding of the play as drama, consider the various reasons why Shakespeare—an otherwise enlightened man who elsewhere treats his marginalized figures with at least some trace of sympathy—might employ stereotypes so blatantly in crafting his witches. You might identify a symbolic meaning for the sisters, discussing how they are more than a cheap, theatrical thrill. For example, you will not have to get too far into the text of the *Malleus* to recognize that it harbors a deep mistrust of women, theorizing in detail why women are weak and vulnerable to the temptations of the devil. Think about how this merging of demonology and anxiety over female power is also important in *Macbeth*. More generally, describe how these medieval witches contribute to Shakespeare's broader vision of evil in *Macbeth*.

2. **The divine right of sovereigns:** What does *Macbeth* say about the politics of monarchy, a subject close to James I's heart in both theoretical and practical terms?

The thesis for this essay might be relatively straightforward, but the difficulty will lay in compiling and structuring your evidence. A popular reading of the play asserts that *Macbeth* endorses James's writings on the divine authority of monarchs, identifying Macbeth's murder of Duncan and challenge to the natural political order with other manifestations of frightening disorder in the play. As critics often point out, Shakespeare alters the historic record, erasing from his play the successful ten-year reign of Macbeth before his real life tragedy unfolded. Why did Shakespeare make this change? What point does it help him to make about royal power and challenges to it?

Think, too, about the allusions to Banquo's bloodline leading down the centuries to James I. While this has obvious sycophantic charm for the play's intended audience, consider how it fits into the more serious discussion of kingship and destiny.

Form and Structure

While Shakespeare takes his source material for *Macbeth* from Raphael Holinshed's *Chronicles* of British history, the same place he finds the material for his English history plays, few if any talk about the text as a history play. There is no mistaking this play as anything but a tragedy of the darkest kind. Macbeth's terrifying description of life as "a tale / Told by an idiot, full of sound and fury / Signifying nothing," is perhaps the most concise and powerful articulation of the tragic world in Shakespeare's works, or anywhere else in literature for that matter. This line is so raw and brutally powerful that we are encouraged to think about the structural, generic makeup of the play that engenders such sentiments. As you read *Macbeth*, look for other phrases and speeches describing the spiritual or moral value of the world in which its characters live. The chief spokesperson for this tragic vision is, of course, Macbeth, so pay close attention to his ever-decreasing estimation of the world after Duncan's death. Identify what forces are at work against the characters of the play, attempting to see both external and internal factors at play in the tragedies of each individual.

Sample Topic:

1. **Tragedy:** Can we arrive at a description of Shakespeare's tragic vision in *Macbeth?* How does the play consider the function of fate in Macbeth's life, and how does this debate form a core part of the tragedy?

This is a potentially challenging essay to write because it involves organizing a lot of dense and difficult lines of discussion into a single, clearly stated thesis. Such an essay might begin by asking what forces drive Macbeth (if you make Macbeth the centerpiece of your essay) to his tragedy. One of the key functions of the witches, for example, is to raise the question of how much control Macbeth holds over his fate. Read the opening scenes of the play closely, trying to assess the extent to which Macbeth's actions are governed by his own volition. Look carefully at the relationship between the predictions the witches give to Macbeth and his preexisting desires and ambition. At this point you might also include some discussion of Lady Macbeth's seductive promptings, of her influence over him. This analysis might lead you to ask if the outcome of Macbeth's life as the play gives it to us could have been different. Consider whether the overlap of supernatural and psychological elements create an insurmountable enemy set against him. You might also return to the idea of the natural versus the unnatural so prominent in the play, asking whether or not the mere existence of a natural order relieves the overwhelming sense of darkness in the play and challenges Macbeth's fatalistic assertion that life "signifies nothing." In other words, are there sources of hope and inspiration in the play, a sense that there actually is "something" behind the play's looming "nothing?" Think about the repetition of the word *done,* and the notion that Macbeth can never find peace of mind once his plot is set in motion; nothing is ever "done" in this play, so consider what factors conspire to prevent Macbeth from resolving the events of his own life. Macbeth's uncontrollable and insidious plotting, the absence of a truly "done" or finished deed, should act as a caution to the writer looking for fixed meanings in this play. However, by reaching for an understanding of why Macbeth commits murder, how he and his wife cope with the moral and emotional implications of their crimes, and how the world of the play craftily ensures his tragic fate, you will be well placed to suggest what

Shakespeare is using tragedy in *Macbeth* to say about human behavior and human evil.

Compare and Contrast Essays

Puzzling through the many dualisms and parallels in Macbeth is a major part of the play's critical heritage. There are so many "mirrorings" within the play's narrative and symbolic structure, so many characters and actions with distorted equivalents elsewhere in *Macbeth*. These pairings can be unexpected or have unexpected consequences. David Scott Kasten, for example, has written provocatively on how Macduff's killing of Macbeth mirrors Macbeth's murder of Duncan. This final murder, Kasten argues, might have been as troubling as Duncan's assassination for proponents of absolute royal power (including James, who argued that even a tyrant king should not be killed).

Another pairing for an essay might be Lady Macbeth and Lady Macduff. Although we see the latter only briefly, we learn a good deal about her views on the value of domestic versus political life. She seems to be the counterweight to the "fiendish" Lady Macbeth, a portrait of an idealized model of femininity that contrasts with the aberrant wife of Macbeth. Such an essay would gather evidence for this contrast but explore also the more complex problem of why the play kills both the natural and unnatural examples of womanhood in the play. The play also clearly invites us to see a relationship between Macbeth and Banquo. Assess what Banquo and Macbeth have in common before the former is killed, focusing perhaps on each man's reaction to the witches' prophesy. Then the essay might interestingly explore how the relationship changes after Banquo's death, with Banquo lingering on as a psychological or ghostly presence in Macbeth's conscience and banquet hall.

As we have seen, *Macbeth* is a play structured by change and progression toward a tragic resolution. While this is true of many plays, of course, transformation really is the key trait of this play's dramatic form. Therefore, many thematic and character essays on *Macbeth* can also be presented as compare and contrast essays if desired or needed: Macbeth at the start and end of the play; Lady Macbeth at the start and end of the play; the status of the natural order at the beginning of the play and at the end, and so forth.

Sample Topics:

1. **Comparing Lady Macbeth with the witches:** What is the relationship between these female figures? How do they share similar roles in the play?

A strong thesis on this topic might argue that Lady Macbeth can reasonably be termed the fourth witch of the play. While her territory may be distinct from the heath-bound witches, she is nonetheless tied to the trio. Note, however, that because this is such a commonplace of *Macbeth* criticism, reading against this idea may make for a distinct essay. Such a paper might be forced to take as its starting point the observation of broad similarity, but then proceed to argue for distinctions between Lady Macbeth and the witches. This could take the subtle form of finding differences of motivation and approach; how is the way Lady Macbeth "works on" Macbeth, the strategies she uses to beguile him into murder, different from those of the witches? A telling observation to integrate into the essay might be the identification of two types of seductive magic in the play, one supernatural and one earthly but unnatural.

2. **Contrasting the play to Roman Polanski's 1971 film adaptation:** What strategies does Polanski use in his adaptation of Shakespeare's text?

Polanski's solid version of *Macbeth* is probably the most commonly viewed film of the play in schools and colleges. As with any essay treating an adaptation of Shakespeare's text, look for visible and interesting directorial choices, intriguing casting decisions, as well as prominent omissions from and additions to the text of drama. The important move is to characterize the sum of these changes in a thesis before exploring them in detail throughout the body of the essay. Your thesis might follow a simple formula: Roman Polanski's adaptation produces a *Macbeth* that argues . . . In other words, try to imagine that the director has a thesis about the play just as you do as a reader.

With Polanski's film, think about his casting of young and attractive actors in the roles of Macbeth and Lady Macbeth. What aspect of their relationship is made more prominent by emphasizing the beauty of Lady Macbeth in particular? You might also consider the look of the film, gloomy and violent. Think, too, about the representation of the witches, as well as the possible gender implications of a coven of witches in one scene rather than a mere three weird sisters. Finally, reflect on the ominous (and historically accurate) ending of the film.

Bibliography for "*Macbeth*"

Adelman, Janet. *Suffocating Mothers: Fantasies of Maternal Origin in Shakespeare's Plays*. New York: Routledge, 1992.

Calderwood, James L. *If It Were Done: Macbeth and Tragic Action*. Amherst: University of Massachusetts Press, 1986.

Kasten, David Scott. *Shakespeare After Theory*. New York: Routledge, 1999.

Khan, Coppelia. *Man's Estate: Masculine Identity in Shakespeare*. Berkeley: U of California Press, 1981.

McAdam, Ian. *Magic and Masculinity in Early Modern English Drama*. Pittsburgh, PA: Duquesne UP, 2009.

Norbrook, David. "*Macbeth* and the Politics of Historiography." *Politics of Discourse: The Literature and History of Seventeenth-Century England*. Ed. Kevin Sharpe and Stephen Zwicker. Berkeley: University of California Press, 1987: 78–116.

OTHELLO

READING TO WRITE

A LTHOUGH THERE are many possible approaches to writing on
Othello, one of the most interesting if not obvious to explore is
the role of race. As you read the play, then, be sure to carefully follow
the complex meanings and function of this theme. Do not fall into the
trap of seeing this as simply a black man victimized by the racism of
a white society. While that dynamic is certainly present in the work,
what the play has to say about Othello's relationship with the white
Venetian community, as well as his own sense of racial identity, is far
more intricate.

Let us look at a passage from the play to illustrate this point more
clearly. The following lines come from a key, early moment in 1.3. Othello
is hoping to convince the court he has won the hand of Desdemona honestly, explaining how she came to love him.

> Her father loved me, oft invited me,
> Still questioned me the story of my life
> From year to year, the battles, sieges, fortunes
> That I have passed . . .
> Wherein I spoke of most dangerous chances,
> Of moving accidents by flood and field
> Of hair-breadth scapes i'th' imminent deadly breach,
> Of being taken by the insolent foe
> And sold to slavery, of my redemption thence . . .
> And of the Cannibals that each other eat,
> . . . the Anthropophagi, and men whose heads

> Do grow beneath their shoulders . . .
> She [Desdemona] loved me for the dangers I had passed,
> And I loved her that she did pity them.
> This is the only witchcraft I have used. (3.1.127–68)

This short passage reveals to the writer an enormous amount that could form the foundation for an essay. Notice the quotation begins with a significant clue to Othello's status in white Venice. Brabanzio, Desdemona's father, now outraged by the marriage of Othello to his daughter, was once comfortable inviting Othello into his house. At this point, the writer might reflect on the degree to which Othello has been accepted by and welcomed into Venetian society, asking what the limits of this acceptance are and the specific terms under which it is given.

Othello continues by telling us how he entertained those gathered at Brabanzio's house with stories of his past. These stories open up to the writer one of the most important concepts in the play: the conscious and unconscious ways Othello's actions are determined by his race. Notice the exotic sights and curiosities populating his tale, the fantastic and monstrous symbols of a dark world far away from the "civilization" of Europe. Is Othello merely recollecting things he has seen and done, or is he wittingly using his "otherness" to appeal to his audience (and perhaps Desdemona)?

So far, we may believe that race is playing a powerful though not entirely negative role in Othello's Venetian life. While he relies on military skill to counteract the discrimination he would otherwise face, Othello is able to use these differences to his advantage for public and, as Desdemona comes to "pity" him, perhaps private gain. (Certainly do not ignore Othello's use of the word *pity* in describing Desdemona's responses to his tales. The writer may take this as a cue to think carefully—as Othello himself will do to a fatal extent—about the roots of the play's central marriage.) Notice how the final lines of the passage encourage us to once again think about Othello's difference in terms of what we would today call racism. Consider the implications of Brabanzio accusing Othello of employing "witchcraft" to woo Desdemona—he is at a loss for other ways to explain what is to him and his society such an inexplicable decision on his daughter's part. The dark and mystical elements of the story Othello told to his advantage are reflected in the preexisting cultural imagination of white Venice. They are brought to the surface when Othello wants to be more to Venice than a fascinating curiosity or sideshow, when he wants to become a member of the European "family." As you write, focus on other ways in which racially motivated feelings emerge from hidden places in unexpected ways.

As this small cross section of the play's racial discourse suggests, the writer should resist the assumption that because Shakespeare's play is four centuries old it is from a simpler time. The best way to approach the social issues contained in *Othello* is to recognize that while different, the racial relationships in Shakespeare's lifetime were as fraught and complex as they unfortunately can be today.

TOPICS AND STRATEGIES

Every essay requires a focus; you cannot write about everything in the play at once. In the section on how to write an essay, you will be presented with a number of ways of turning a focus into a thesis, observations into arguments. However, the starting point is nearly always finding an initial point of departure, making first observations. You can then seize on and develop the budding ideas you will have as you make your way through the play. By no means should you feel limited to these topics, however. Instead they can be viewed as triggering suggestions encouraging you to break out into your own critical directions.

Themes

While many students will be drawn to the theme of race in *Othello,* there are many alternative avenues available to the writer. For example, we can see in *Othello* a stark and frightening contemplation of the nature of evil, of unlimited hatred. An essay on this subject would not necessarily require the writer to discuss race at all. A paper treating gender in the play, focusing perhaps on Desdemona's restricted control of her fate and selfhood, might or might not include analysis of race. Yet as race is a particularly popular choice among student writers working with this play, a discussion of it cannot be neglected. Clearly, the key to writing about the role of race in the play is to have a sharp focus on a specific aspect of that theme. While race may be presented here as one theme, the writer should craft a thesis statement that is defined and targeted enough to make sure her essay avoids becoming merely a broad discussion of the issue in the play.

Let us once more look at the passage cited at the beginning of the chapter. The opening and closing lines encourage the writer to think about how Othello is viewed by the white denizens of Venice. This perspective on race in the play might make for a good, sharp essay. What exactly does Othello mean to the state he serves? The student should certainly consider the hypocritical opinions expressed by Brabanzio but also the seemingly different point of view held by the Duke. Why does the Duke defend Othello against Brabanzio's charges? Look closely, too, at Lodovico's response in 4.1 to Othello's violence. Of course, as with any essay, the writer must think about what limits he should place on his study. For example, should Iago be included in such an essay? What about Desdemona?

No matter what you choose to include or leave out, this essay would clearly have a more or less limited scope, for example, analyzing how Othello is viewed by other people and in that way building an understanding of the society in which Othello lives. A similar effect could also be achieved by the writer without placing such rigorous textual limitations on herself, however. To do so, think about questions offering the chance to discuss race in the play more broadly while still ensuring a tight focus. For example, the student might ask some variation of the following question: To what extent is the play racist? To write this essay, you would look for evidence of Shakespeare's sympathies for Othello, and/ or, conversely, the playwright's reliance on and perpetuation of racial stereotyping.

Sample Topics:

1. **Race:** How central is race to the play's action? To what extent is the action driven by race?

   Such an essay might begin by identifying explicit statements of racism in the play. Don't simply list them, however. See if you can characterize the patterns and central principles of racial discord as they appear in *Othello*. For example, we have already seen the way Brabanzio naturally slips into identifying Othello as a magical, witchlike figure born of some oth-

erworldly place. Look, too, at the opening exchange between
Iago, Roderigo, and Brabanzio. Try to spot commonalities
of image and metaphor that shape the racist slurs abound-
ing in the first scene. How does society perceive the marriage
between Othello and Desdemona? Read for patterns of language and symbolism invoking the unnatural or the bestial.

Perhaps, however, the most intriguing element of this
theme can be found by the writer in Othello's own conflicted
sense of racial identity. Try to gain psychological insight into
Othello's perception of himself by locating passages in which
he expresses anxieties about his marriage that are anchored
in his racial identity. Identify the ways in which Iago brings
these deep-seated anxieties to the surface in Othello. Then
find evidence of a growing division in Othello's sense of selfhood. How might Shakespeare be intending us to see Othello's
transformation in the second half of the play through a racial
lens? Be sure to include a discussion of Othello's final speech,
unraveling the complex layers of racial metaphor and meaning
that surround his suicide. The key to such an essay might lie in
identifying the nature of Othello's divided self. How does this
"split personality" stem directly from the racial conditions of
the life he tried to lead in Venice and the social anxieties that
appear to have weighed heavily on him all along?

2. **Love:** Although we hear much from the Venetians condemning Othello and Desdemona's marriage, how does Shakespeare
   actually represent the love between them?

Again, a good place to begin this essay might be the opening scene in which Iago's vulgar jibes caricature the physical
relationship between Othello and Desdemona. Compare this
view from the outside to moments where the lovers characterize their marriage. What is the dynamic of the marriage
as the play opens? What kind of husband is Othello? What,
for him, appears to be the "correct" way to love Desdemona?
What draws Desdemona to Othello in the first place? As you
write, you might then work backward from Othello's final

observation that everything has gone wrong because he "loved not wisely but too well" (5.2.353). Was excessive love really the root of Othello's fall? The most important thing might be to recognize that love here does not exist in isolation from the social and psychological ghosts that haunt Othello from the start. Try to identify the various pressures exerted on the love between Desdemona and Othello, perhaps finding scenes that challenge Othello's final, too-neat judgment of what went wrong.

Characters

Character essays rooted in this play are likely to overlap significantly with consideration of the play's themes. A character essay on Othello might obviously draw on many of the same questions and textual moments as the theme of "race" above. Similarly, a study of Desdemona would be difficult to execute without also considering some of what we have already discussed. Meanwhile, a character study of Iago presents clear problems of its own. Principally, the main appeal of Iago for many students is precisely what makes him difficult to write about; he is an enigmatic presence about which there is arguably little concrete to say beyond a few textual clues to his purposes. Certainly none of this means that students should avoid character analysis essays on *Othello*. On the contrary, such an approach opens up different aspects of Othello's character for study or might provide a good way to narrow the focus of an essay on race or some other theme. For example, an essay asking whether Shakespeare's presentation of Othello is sympathetic, given the absolute centrality of race to an understanding of Othello's character, is finally a specific reformulation of a thesis seeking to evaluate how Shakespeare handles race. The key to a character essay on this play, then, is recognizing that each character is a product of his or her society, mired in the same swamp of conventions and prejudices as the rest.

Sample Topics:

1. **Othello:** How can we explain Othello's transformation from military hero, darling of the Venetian elite, to a murderer who appears to kill his wife based on nothing more substantial than a handkerchief?

An essay on this topic will integrate many of the same concepts and textual moments as an essay on the theme of race. A good structure for this essay might obviously be to start by briefly showing the reader Othello as he is at the beginning (perhaps confident and somewhat secure), then proceed to a more substantial analysis of the character at the end of the play, focusing on the idea of Othello as a divided, torn man. The remainder of the essay would cover the play's center and detail the complex mix of social and psychological elements that led to his transformation (act 3 will be especially vital here). Do not forget, though, as we have seen, the seeds of this transformation might not be found in Iago's machinations but in the workings of European society and Othello's attempts to be an accepted part of it.

2. **Desdemona:** Is Desdemona merely a passive victim of the tragedy that overcomes her? Or does she help bring disaster on herself, as some critics have suggested, through her desires?

As you read, look for ways in which Desdemona is marginalized. There seem to be similarities between Othello's status as a black man in Venetian society and Desdemona's as a woman: Both are clearly outside the white, patriarchal center of the community. Pay close attention especially to the early scenes in which she is argued over as if a belonging, an object whose ownership is contested between father and husband. Even more controversially, are we supposed to see Desdemona as being "punished" for her desires, succumbing to erotic fantasies centered on the other? Look for ways in which she is increasingly associated with images of darkness instead of the language of purity and whiteness that surrounds her at the start. For example, try to wrestle meaning from the link between Desdemona and the servant Barbary (almost certainly intended to have been black), emphasized by the "Willow" song moments before Othello kills Desdemona. Has Desdemona finally undergone a transformation that mirrors Othello's progression to a divided racial identity?

3. **Iago:** What are Iago's motivations as a villain? Are they substantial enough to give meaning to his character and the actions he takes?

Many students are drawn to this essay, but exercise care; this is a difficult one to write well. The romantic poet and critic Samuel Coleridge complained that Iago's motives were inexplicable and insufficient to make the action of the play believable. Look carefully through the early scenes of the drama in which Iago offers a number of explanations for what he is about to do. Do you find these convincing? If not, you should embrace Iago's lack of concreteness; think about Iago as a symbolic character, a representation of evil rather than a well-rounded, multidimensional figure. This approach connects him to the medieval stage tradition of the vice, a character simply representing a negative quality such as greed or lust, for example. If we view Iago as symbolic, what exactly is Shakespeare saying about evil?

You should certainly not hesitate to disagree in your essay with this take on Iago if you are not in accord; this will take you in a different, but no less profitable direction. If we accept Iago's early justifications as substantial enough to propel him forward, we might want to claim that his jealousy mirrors that of Othello and thus shapes the play into a warning against excessive envy. This approach argues for Iago's complexity and humanness, perhaps the most frightening of all possible interpretations of this character. If we see Iago as more than a symbol, how might we begin to explain a figure of such unmitigated evil?

History and Context

Much of the intellectual energy surrounding *Othello* in recent decades has been generated by a school of criticism known as postcolonial studies. Along with several other Shakespeare plays, *Othello* has received attention from these critics who hope to obtain a better understanding of Europe's encounter with the ever-growing outside world in the early modern era. From this perspective, *Othello* becomes a historical document of considerable importance because it takes as its thematic focus precisely this encounter.

This type of approach gives the student a wonderful opportunity to write about and participate in recent critical trends. As with any historically minded essay, you will need to follow the basic strategy of researching the historical moment and comparing it to the episodes and characters of the play.

Sample Topic:

1. **The African or Moor in Europe:** What was the relationship between Europeans and the Africans or Moors existing at or within their borders? In what ways does Shakespeare engage real issues and anxieties of his time in *Othello?*

There were relatively few people of African origin living in Shakespeare's England. However, their presence was enough of an issue for Elizabeth I to give a proclamation that they should be removed from the land. To the east of Europe, the Turks represented a grave military threat to "Christendom." Finally, of course, the empires of Europe in the New World were being built by African slaves whose lives were cheaply expended to realize colossal profits for the ruling elite from crops such as sugar in the Indies. In short, we can see a mix of fear and subjection that in many ways is replicated in Othello's story. G. K. Hunter's classic study *Dramatic Identities and Cultural Tradition* is a slightly dated but nonetheless good place to begin research in this area. More contemporary, but perhaps less accessible, is the impressive body of work being written by postcolonial critic Ania Loomba.

As you write this essay, compare the historical record to two components of the play. On the one hand, look at what characters say and do throughout the play. You will find many of the same anxieties and prejudices in the words of the characters as you do in the historical record. Then try to view the play as a statement about the European encounter with the African or Moor distinct from the sentiments of its characters. Ruth Cowhig argues that, in writing *Othello*, Shakespeare breaks new ground of sympathy and tolerance for a black character. She points out that irrespective of Othello's flaws, Shakespeare consciously avoids the otherwise inevitable stereotype of the villainous black man that audiences would have expected. Shakespeare seems to deliberately soften his version of Othello compared with the more sinister Othello character found in his source material. Assess Shakespeare's voice against the historical record, the typical sentiments and opinions of his day. Find how he is of his time in this way, as well as other ways in which he is "ahead" of it.

Philosophy and Ideas

Othello seems to be a play about passions more than it is a play about ideas; the heart and not the head seems to be the primary motive force in the text. Othello's great weakness, as he understands it, is precisely that he does not think enough. (How, by the way, might this be considered one more of the stereotypical traits of Shakespeare's tragic hero?) Iago, however, thinks quickly and spontaneously, but, as we have seen, it might arguably be difficult to identify any overarching or grand philosophy animating his thoughts. Many have argued that Iago's significant intelligence is ungoverned by any cohesive intellect. Nonetheless, there is still scope for writing an essay about the philosophical content of the play. Iago's rejection of a guiding philosophy creates a philosophical problem for the writer considering the nature of evil in this play. Othello's self-division could also be viewed as a philosophical problem of consciousness that is as much internal as it is social. These essays might encourage the writer to take on philosophical questions hand in hand with analysis of the play's social conditions. However, *Othello* also asks philosophical questions that attempt to evade social context and approach the universal.

Sample Topic:

1. **The relationship between appearances and reality:** What does the play have to say about the relationship between perceptions and actualities, what we see and feel compared to what actually is? To what degree can the characters of *Othello* (and by implication, the rest of us too) trust their senses?

An essay exploring this topic must be willing to look at many different aspects of the play. This philosophical theme manifests itself frequently and in many different contexts. As you read and prepare to write, identify moments where appearance and reality are at odds. Look for ironic details such as the frequent labeling of Iago as "honest," or for moments when speech and language appear to be persuasive and clear but are merely lies. Perhaps more important and more troubling is the way in which Othello's demand for "ocular proof" results in Iago staging the convincing but utterly false scene of Cassio's "confession." It might be inevitable that we cannot always trust other people when they talk, but what is Shakespeare attempting to say by showing how Othello's most reliable sense, his sight, is as vulnerable to deception as his ears? Follow closely, too, the passage of the handkerchief, perhaps the clearest and most famous symbol of how truth is so difficult to discern in *Othello*. Look for and comment on ways in which the meaning of this piece of fabric shifts several times throughout the play. Finally, and perhaps most difficult of all, you might want to consider how this theme is connected to the play's consideration of race. The strongest case for a racially sympathetic *Othello* might rest in the play's obsession with inaccurate and mistaken perceptions, cautioning against the failure to look beneath the surface and see what truly matters.

Form and Genre

For a long time, *Othello* was maligned by many critics. They perceived a number of dramatic failures that supposedly compromised the play's success. Questions of Shakespeare's workmanship in *Othello* have largely been supplanted (or explained) by the kinds of critical interests we have already discussed, but they nonetheless offer good material for students interested in the mechanics of the play. As you write, however, be sure to look for connections between form and content. In other words, are Shakespeare's "mistakes" really mistakes at all? Do they in fact help to illuminate the themes treated in the play?

Sample Topics:

1. **The "failures" of characterization in *Othello:*** To what extent
   are Shakespeare's characters in *Othello* plausible? Are their
   motives and actions naturalistic or psychologically real enough
   to earn our "belief"?

An essay of this type might address two of the most common
charges against Shakespeare's development of character in
Othello. First, that Iago's murderous scheme is not explained
or adequately justified by any compensating motive (see the
preceding "Character" section and the topic discussion on
Iago for suggestions on how to approach this matter). Second,
Othello is too gullible to earn our respect, too thinly realized
when compared with Shakespeare's great tragic heroes. Perhaps you agree with one or both of these statements, in which
case your essay will be an attempt to support these familiar
claims. In the case of Othello, you will focus on what appears
to some to be a frustrating lack of healthy suspicion or awareness of those around him. It might be more interesting, however, to challenge one or both of these objections. Again, to
take Othello as an example, it might be that his apparently
inexplicable naivety is actually nothing less than justifiable
self-doubt born from an acute awareness of his vulnerable
position in Venetian society.

2. **The "quality" of Othello's tragedy:** What is the tragic catharsis of *Othello?* Does its tragic movement compare well to Shakespeare's other great tragedies?

Tragedies were expected to contain a certain number of characteristics, including a clear cathartic value likened to a purging of fearful emotions. Plays subscribing to the genre were
expected to be grand, with great men falling in the face of
obstacles of universal magnitude. Such an awesome spectacle cleansed the audience member by instructing him or her
at the expense of the tragic character. In short, the criticism
often leveled at *Othello* over the last 400 years has been that

it is not serious or grand enough, that Othello's decisions and his circumstances are too poorly contrived and explained to function as a tragedy should. Your essay, naturally, would proceed from this charge, defending it or attacking it as you wish. The latter approach might begin by identifying a substantial cathartic effect at work in the play, showing how *Othello* is more than a mere domestic drama driven by foolish decisions and a lady's handkerchief. Where is the significant dramatic power located in the text? In what way have critics misinterpreted or undervalued the tragic elements of the play? You might develop a number of ideas from throughout this chapter to help you make your case, but also consider the interesting possibility that this tradition of devaluing the play is a product of the same kind of social prejudices visible in the action of the play itself. After all, until as recently as the mid-twenieth century a good deal of criticism on this play had a distinctly racist tenor (see, for example, M. R. Ridley's notorious discussion of the play in his introduction to the *Arden Shakespeare* edition of *Othello* in the 1950s).

Compare and Contrast Essays

Othello lends itself more easily to certain kinds of compare and contrast essays than others. It may be a little difficult to find "internal" compare and contrast options, or elements of character, action, or structure within the play that invite comparison or contrast. Nonetheless, set about looking for pairings in *Othello* and you will find them. For example, a student could write an essay comparing the only two women in the play, Desdemona and Emilia. In this essay, you would want to pay close attention to the conversations they have with each other, especially the remarkable exchange about adultery shortly before their deaths. Shakespeare seems to be presenting two different models of womanhood, but be careful not to jump quickly to judgment against Emilia. After all, her speech might be read as the only moment of female empowerment in the play. Try to characterize the two models of feminine conduct that these women represent, but try to see ways in which Shakespeare might intend them to be complementary as well as oppositional.

Some of the most energetic student essays, however, look outside the play for reference points. One play that encourages comparison of this kind is *The Tempest,* another of Shakespeare's works dramatizing the encounter between white Europeans and a foreign other. Although the settings may differ, look for ways in which the Europeans' treatment of Ariel, Caliban, and the island itself reflects the Venetians' treatment of Othello.

Sample Topics:

1. **Comparing Shylock in *The Merchant of Venice* to Othello:** To what extent do these marginalized figures resemble each other? Does Shakespeare make similar or different points about "otherness" through these characters?

An essay on this topic could focus on moments in which sympathy is created for each of these outsiders. Look, of course, at Shylock's well-known speech in 3.1.45–61 but also at other moments that bring Shylock and the audience together. These might include Jessica's desertion of Shylock (and her sale of his treasured engagement ring for a monkey), as well as the complex emotional makeup of the trial scene. Both Shylock and Othello are able to eloquently express themselves and articulate their place in society, so look for moments in both plays when this occurs. Are their fates in any way similar, brought about by related social dynamics?

2. **Contrast Shakespeare's *Othello* to Tim Blake Nelson's 2001 film adaptation, *O:*** What changes occur in the process of updating *Othello* by 400 years?

Contrasting a Shakespeare play to a film adaptation can make for a strong and compelling essay, but in this case the possibilities are especially varied because the 2001 film takes more liberties with the text than a traditional adaptation might. That version entirely abandons Shakespeare's language in the process of modernizing the story, though it manages to remain thematically true to the spirit of the text. Watch the film closely for shifts, omissions, or additions to the narrative of the play. Consider the way in which race functions differently in the movie. The relationship between Odin (Mekhi Phifer) and Desi (Julia Stiles) is now less outwardly controversial than Othello and Desdemona's, but look for moments when race inevitably influences this modern tragedy. For example, can we still say that Desi is drawn to Odin at least in part because of his difference? Watch for moments where the lovers discuss race with an openness and candor unavailable to Shakespeare's stage. Think, too, about shifts in the motivations of Hugo (the Iago character in the movie, played by Josh Hartnett), which help to make his behavior more comprehensible, in particular his use of steroids and the addition of a troubled relationship with his father, Duke, who appears to love Odin more than his own son.

Bibliography for "*Othello*"

Cowhig, Ruth. "Blacks in English Renaissance Literature and the Role of Shakespeare's Othello." *The Black Presence in English Literature.* Ed. David Dabydeen. Manchester: Manchester University Press, 1985.

Hall, Kim. *Things of Darkness: Economies of Race and Gender in Early Modern England.* Ithaca: Cornell University Press, 1995.

Hendricks, Margo and Patricia Parker, eds. *Women, 'Race,' and Writing in the Early Modern Period.* London and New York: Routledge, 1994.

Loomba, Ania and Martin Orkin, eds. *Post-Colonial Shakespeares.* London and New York: Routledge, 1998.

Thompson, Ayanna. "The Blackfaced Bard: Returning to Shakespeare or Leaving Him?" *Shakespeare Bulletin: A Journal of Performance Criticism and Scholarship,* 27 (3), 2009: 437–56.

Vitkus, Daniel. "Turning Turk in *Othello:* The Conversion and Damnation of the Moor." *Shakespeare Quarterly,* 48 (2): 145–76.

ROMEO AND JULIET

READING TO WRITE

PERHAPS ONLY *Hamlet* can match *Romeo and Juliet* for familiarity; the star-crossed lovers and their passage from balcony to tomb are instantly recognizable to many millions around the world. For many, too, that familiarity is based on more than just the cultural background Shakespeare presents. The play is a staple of high school English classes from Chattanooga to Calcutta. Why? Part of its continued and universal appeal is due to its accessible and compelling storyline. More than most Shakespeare plays, *Romeo and Juliet* appears to be plot driven rather than animated or colored primarily by thematic and intellectual concerns. This is not to suggest that the play does not have intellectual depth or merit but rather that the narrative is strong and the story demands the reader's attention. In light of this, *Romeo and Juliet* can actually be difficult to write about precisely because it seems so simple. A student who knows that good essays require much more than plot summary can sometimes be left wondering what exactly to write about in the wake of this well-known tragedy. The answers naturally lie or are initially suggested by the text.

In reading the play, explore it slowly; do not get swept up by the riptide plot. For example, in 1.4, we as readers are headed to the Capulet ball in 1.5. We want to see Romeo and Juliet meet for the first time, but if we read for plot alone, we might miss the following odd and unsettling speech by Mercutio on Queen Mab. Responding to Romeo's lovestruck talk of dreams, the skeptical Mercutio brings to his friend's attention the legend of Mab:

She is the fairies' midwife, and she comes
In shape no bigger than an agate stone
On the forefinger of an alderman,
Drawn with a team of little atomi
Athwart men's noses as they sleep
. . . .
And in this state she gallops night by night
Through lovers brains, and then they dream of love;
O'er courtier's knees, that dream on curtsies
straight;
O'er ladies lips, who straight on kisses dream,
Which oft the angry Mab with blisters plagues
Because their breaths with sweetmeats tainted are.
Sometime she gallops o'er a lawyer's nose,
And then dreams he of smelling out a suit;
. . . .
Sometimes she driveth o'er a soldier's neck,
And then dreams he of cutting foreign throats,
Of breaches, ambuscados, Spanish blades,
Of healths five fathom deep; and then anon
Drums in his ear, at which he starts and wakes,
And being thus frightened, swears a prayer or two,
And sleeps again. This is that very Mab
That plaits the manes of horses in the night,
And bakes the elf-locks in foul sluttish hairs,
Which once untangled much misfortune bodes.
This is the hag, when maids lie on their backs,
That presses them and learns them first to bear,
Making them women of good carriage.
This is she—   (1.4.55–94)

This passage is highly representative of the play it is taken from. As
Mercutio begins to speak, it looks as though the content and tone of the
passage will be simple, even whimsical. However, by the end of the passage, it is clear that something much more complex, much more unsettling has been expressed. Like *Romeo and Juliet*, then, this passage at
first promises simplicity and an entertaining story but finally delivers
something troubling and difficult to comprehend.

Immediately after introducing the figure of Mab, Mercutio continues to create a light and benign mood. Mab at first appears a positive force, the carrier of romantic dreams to lovers; but the mood is quickly tainted when we hear of Mab blistering the lips of ladies, apparently because their breath is sweet and fair. Fairies, of course, in popular folklore were often ambiguous entities, far from the benevolent, wand-waving sprites they are often portrayed as. Nonetheless, this image still marks a striking and unexpected turn in the passage, undermining the benign characteristics of the preceding lines.

This process of undermining romance continues, however, as Mercutio's narrative of Mab grows ever darker. If the image of blistered lips instead of kisses is disturbing, Mab's generation of a soldier's bloody and murderous dreams initially establishes the play's tragic association of love and death; the soldier's blood lust here has the same root and origin as a lover's dream of desire. By now the thematic relevance of this passage to the whole of *Romeo and Juliet* should be clear: The play presents more than one version of love, and the writer must be aware of this multiplicity. As you approach the romantic elements of this play, do not be seduced by custom into believing that *Romeo and Juliet* offers a unified, unqualified vision of love as bright and good.

Of additional interest in Mercutio's speech are issues of gender. Critics have been long interested in uncovering and scrutinizing the play's gender dynamics, considering elements such as patriarchy and the oppression of women or the homoerotic or homosocial connections between male characters, including Mercutio's relationship with Romeo. This speech, functioning as part of Mercutio's ongoing attempt to challenge Romeo's heterosexual passions, may play a part in such a debate. The antifeminine tones of the passage's last lines, moreover, and in particular the anxiety surrounding female sexuality, have also been noted by critics. While the writer would do well to pursue some of these gender concerns, the main point here is that the relationships in *Romeo and Juliet* are open to interrogation and interpretation, and that it is chiefly in these relationships that the "simplicity" of the plot is checked and infinitely complicated.

TOPICS AND STRATEGIES

Every essay requires a focus; you cannot write about everything in the play at once. In the section on how to write an essay, you will be presented with a number of ways of turning a focus into a thesis, observations into arguments. However, the starting point is nearly always finding an initial point of departure, making first observations. You can then seize on and develop the budding ideas you will have as you make your way through the play. By no means should you feel limited to these topics, however. Instead they can be viewed as triggering suggestions encouraging you to break out into your own critical directions.

Themes

As with all texts, some of *Romeo and Juliet's* themes are visible at the surface, while others must be uncovered and interpreted. To give an example of the former, one plot element that has received attention over the years is the theme of vendetta. As with all surface-level themes—motifs that essentially function as plot devices—there is the danger of plot summary. After all, in some ways to explain vendetta in the play might be to simply restate part of the plot. It is obviously not enough to have a thesis arguing that vendetta is an important part of the play; this much is clear to anyone who has read *Romeo and Juliet*. To turn theme into thesis, look for function: what does vendetta *do* in the play, what role does its presence serve? One answer—and therefore one potential thesis—is that vendetta acts as a destabilizing force and is strongly condemned by the play. To support this claim you might look at the figure of Prince Escalus, for example, who struggles to exert control over his state in the face of unrelenting gang warfare. Of course, more pressingly, the fatal consequences of vendetta tear friend from friend and lover from lover. Arguably, in a play that is not driven by tragic flaws (such as Macbeth's susceptibility to dreams of power, or Othello's naïve jealousy), vendetta, the business of habitual hating, is the primary catalyst of tragedy. Writers could also take such an essay down the historical path, situating the clan feuds of Shakespeare's Verona within the real-life practices of Renaissance vendetta and revenge. Edward Muir's *Mad Blood Stirring: Vendetta in Renaissance Italy* is a good (but dense) text on this subject and even takes its title from a line in *Romeo and Juliet.*

Of the second type of theme, the kind buried deep within the muscle of the play, we might select time as an important example in the play. As you read a text, look for patterns, words, or actions repeated several or more times. Such a reading would reveal that there is much talk of time throughout the play. For example, during a fascinating glimpse of Capulet servants preparing the hall for the party, there is a vivid sense of their scramble to ready the feast in time. More noticeably, time functions as an important part of the exaggerated language of love employed by Romeo and Juliet; it is the kind of time that can turn the duration between tonight and tomorrow into 20 years in the absence of the beloved. We also get a clear sense of a generational rift, a division between the older characters and their children, a clear symbol of time's passage. Of course, time also becomes the bitter vessel of tragedy, as old Friar Lawrence's legs carry him too slowly to tell Romeo that Juliet is not dead at all, not victim to time's ultimate resolution to human life. Though the identification of the pattern is by no means easy, the challenge is to crystallize all this textual evidence into a sharp, cogent thesis such as: In a play where everyone except Romeo and Juliet seems to recognize that time is rushing on, the motif of time becomes an important metaphor for the way in which their model of love is unrealistic and at odds with the logic of the "real" world. Not only is this thesis inspired by the theme of time, it is also, of course, rooted in the play's greatest theme: love.

Sample Topics:

1. **Love:** How are we to understand or characterize the love between Romeo and Juliet?

   Such an essay could go in at least several directions and arrive at a variety of conclusions (though, of course, it might be a strong move to argue for *one* interpretation of the pair's love over other plausible interpretations). Certainly this is an issue that has excited generations of critics. I suppose the question could be crudely put as follows: are Romeo and Juliet really as in love as they think they are? If you feel they are, then your essay will perhaps move toward highlighting the maturity and spirited rebelliousness of the lovers, their heroic standing. If you doubt it, you are most likely steering your essay toward an analysis of the play's own skepticism about the relationship. Consider some important pieces of evidence. First, what of Rosaline? What purpose does she serve, and how does her presence in the play shape our sense of Romeo? Think whether you agree with critics who argue that Rosaline functions primarily to make Romeo seem fickle and immature. Whether you agree or not, you may want to include in your analysis the Chorus from the beginning of act 2, often sighted as "proof" that the play wants to highlight Romeo's flighty and inconstant heart. At this point it may also be worthwhile asking if the play morally condemns excessive passions and desires; in other words, does the play agree with Friar Lawrence when he counsels Romeo to "love moderately" in 2.6? Look for evidence for or against this idea. Be aware, though, that modern scholars have suggested that the sympathetic perception of Romeo and Juliet might well be a popular twentieth-century invention. In the Renaissance, this argument continues, the pair would have been viewed quite clearly as foolish and reckless. Perhaps, then, the play mocks the impassioned idea that two young lovers can fall so swiftly and completely in love and punishes them accordingly.

2. **Confusion:** What does the play's obsession with confusion and indeterminacy contribute to the philosophical world-view of the play?

The core of this essay is in the concept, often and quite deliberately employed in the play, of exploring the relationship between words and the objects they represent. Some possibly helpful theoretical terms here are *signifiers* or *signs* (the words that represent concepts or objects) and *signified* (the concepts or objects represented). Perhaps the most famous moment in which the relationship between signifier and signified is explored can be found in 2.1. In this scene, Juliet famously asks "what's in a name?" and continues to point out that a rose by any other name would still smell as sweet. The philosophical crux here is that the connection between language and the objects or concepts it represents is weak: a rose could be identified by any word, that particular signified would do nothing to alter the flower's odor. The debate that triggers this deconstructive musing is, of course, Romeo's last name. What exactly does "Montague" signify? As far as the Capulets are concerned, it signifies hate, war, and generations of blood feud. Romeo imagines that his name could be a scribbled word, one that could be torn up, and to an extent this is precisely what the lovers do by challenging the meaning of "Montague" and "Capulet." All of this is teasingly playful, but the writer needs to do more here than philosophize; these complexities still need to be organized by the conventional demands of the essay.

First, look for other instances of "confusion" between signs and signified. For example, think about conversations similar to those we have just considered around the word *banishment* in 3.2 and 3.3. What do you make of the strange confusion between Romeo and Tybalt in the Nurse's account of Tybalt's death? Look for other instances of word slippage and word play. Next—and this is the hard part—you must formulate a thesis that organizes such observations. Why, exactly, does Shakespeare invest an apparently simple tale with such philosophical problems? There are a number of ways you could go here. Is it to show how Romeo and Juliet are right to fall in love as they do and that social conventions such as vendetta and feuding are no more "natural" than language? Could it be to show, rather, how despite all the free play of language, for all the artifice of "Montague" and "Capulet," the concepts of "Montague" and "Capulet" are real enough to cause the deaths of Romeo, Juliet, and others? Or, perhaps, could all of this philosophical quibbling be intended to show how love itself, a relationship between word and concept that the lovers never think to question, is no less vulnerable than "rose" and "Montague" to the collapse or blurring of meaning?

Characters

Though inevitably the titular pairing receives the most attention, the play actually has a deep cast of characters worthy of further study. For example, as the strange and unsettling passage cited in the chapter introduction suggests, Mercutio is a complicated figure. Like many of the minor characters in the play, he appears to function as a plot device, a catalyst for some kind of action on the part of Romeo or Juliet. However, Shakespeare invests in him much more. An essay on Mercutio might focus on an unexpected division within his character. On the one hand, as we have seen, Mercutio is perhaps the play's dominant voice against love, and through his rhetoric, love becomes not merely a childish game but a grim and ugly corner of human existence. Yet modern critics talk about the homoerotic or homosocial nature of his devotion to Romeo, suggesting at least the possibility that his opposition to love might simply be a manifestation of his desire not to share Romeo's affections with a woman. With this in mind, a key part of the writer's task will be in assessing how male friendships work and the expectations placed on men in the play. For example, the writer might want to consider the way in which Mercutio, along with Tybalt, is conditioned to continue the feud and, above all, prize the maintenance of honor. Obviously 3.1 will be a key scene for understanding not only Mercutio but the psychological and social codes that contribute to masculinity in Verona. Notice the changing pattern of Romeo's behavior in response to Mercutio's unwavering and self-destructive commitments to the ideals of honor and vendetta.

If Mercutio represents one of the most ferociously male figures in the text, the Nurse offer a vivid portrait of female hypersexuality; both characters are drawn to operate at extremes of the gender spectrum. While an essay on Mercutio would ultimately be an assessment of masculinity in *Romeo and Juliet,* an essay on the Nurse might study the relationship between her role as wetnurse or surrogate mother and her intense interest in sexuality. In other words, she offers a picture of femininity that appears to contrast sharply with the idealized figure of Juliet and, with her ribald talk, the Nurse offers yet another interpretation of the romantic relationship. While Romeo and Juliet talk of eternity, the Nurse equates romance and love exclusively with the sexual act; she is always pragmatic and candid in her advice to Juliet. A good crux, indeed, for an essay on the Nurse might be to assess how her vision of coupling differs from Juliet's and, more importantly, what the implications of these very different tones might be. You might also want to gather examples of the Nurse's interest in Juliet's sexual life, as well as what you can about the Nurse's function in the Capulet household (she is essentially a mother to Juliet, for example, and we hear open talk from her, in 1.3, about her years of breastfeeding Juliet as a baby). How does this symbolically situate the Nurse in relation to Juliet, or even Lady Capulet? What do you make of the so-called betrayal by the Nurse when she encourages Juliet to partner with Paris in 3.5? Perhaps the question that hovers over a study of the Nurse might be one of disruption. For example, does she finally undermine the idealized talk and hopes of the young lovers with her resolute and untiring insistence on the tangible and fleshy nature of human bonding?

Sample Topics:

1. **Juliet:** Does the play encourage us to see Juliet as a strong woman?

It is a myth that women married at a young age in the Renaissance (probably a myth perpetuated by *Romeo and Juliet,* in fact). While some high-level aristocratic marriages could be arranged at a young age for the future—especially international marriages that acted as cornerstones of foreign alliances—the majority of women married in their twenties. As critics have pointed out, then, Juliet would certainly have been widely perceived by Shakespeare's audience as too young to marry (see, for example, her own father's declaration of exactly this in 1.2.8–11). This fact makes Juliet an intentionally controversial creation and thus rich subject matter for writers. There are at least two avenues to pursue here. The first is that, despite her youth, Juliet matures quickly and can be viewed as a strong woman, intelligent and self-reflexive. If the writer favors this idea, she might suggest a turning point at which "girl" becomes "woman," as well as catalog examples of strength of character. An alternative path to take is viewing Juliet as not a strong presence and arguing that the play encourages us to see her as naïve or worse (see the preceding discussion on love for further points relevant to this approach). A potentially appealing third way is to identify how a modern audience commonly rejects the play's intended interpretation of Juliet in favor of a postfeminist interpretation that stresses her strength. In short, using the text, show how and why Juliet has been and continues to be reinvented by modern audiences seeking positive female role models in the literature of our past.

2. **Romeo:** In what ways does the text undermine Romeo's character?

As with an essay demonstrating the text's ambiguity (or even something more negative) toward Juliet, this topic requires students to assess how and why we might find Romeo less than heroic. To put it bluntly, however, it is easier to find the flaws in Romeo's character than in Juliet, and to see how the text creates a figure of ambiguous sympathy. A writer might offer a thesis that posits Romeo as an immature and emasculated character, one who falls well short of his society's codes of masculinity, a figure designed to win little enthusiasm from an Elizabethan audience. We have already seen how Romeo begins the play, arguably, cast as a vacillating and faithless wooer of women, someone whose loud protestations of love for Rosaline are silenced all too quickly. But the opening scenes do even more to give us pause in regard to Romeo. For example, what do you make of his excessive melancholy or highly stylized and rhetorical language of love? If you have read more widely in Shakespeare, you may recall the foppish and lovesick Duke Orsino of *Twelfth Night* or the benign but ridiculous Orlando from *As You Like It.* The first appears to relish and embellish the pain of unrequited love, leading readers to feel that he is more in love with himself and with the conventions of love than with any woman. Likewise, Orlando's elaborate, poetic, and unrealistic statements of love for Rosalind are mocked by the play as well as by his beloved, and it is the task of the grounded and pragmatic Rosalind to bring the lyrical Orlando down to earth before they can marry. Romeo can be placed alongside these figures, and he is thus in quite dubious company. These three men speak the language of a ritualized and courtly form of love known as Petrarchism. This highly artificial and dressed-up mode of speaking about love originated in the sonnets of the Italian poet Petrarch and is characterized by a quite stable set of conventions. Among these are the impossible beauty of the beloved (the woman to whom the poetic expressions of love are aimed), the cruelty of the beloved in toying with or ignoring the speaker's affections, and the paradoxical pleasure found in the pain of unrequited love. With this fashionable tradition in mind, how do you assess Romeo's approach to both Rosaline and Juliet?

Alongside the problems raised by such superficial performance, the text clearly encourages us to see Romeo as a highly feminized character. What do you make of the numerous instances where Romeo is perceived as effeminate by those around him (and by himself in 3.1.109) and reprimanded as such by such disparate characters as Friar Lawrence, Mercutio, and the Nurse? Look carefully at 3.3, for example, where Romeo can be found throwing a teary tantrum on the floor and is thus paralleled with Juliet. Why is Romeo emasculated in this way? How does this character detail add to the thematic fabric of the play? Can we identify these traits as Romeo's tragic flaw?

3. **Friar Lawrence:** Are we to view the Friar as a sage friend and counselor to the lovers or a meddling old man whose misjudgment initiates the tragic death of Romeo and Juliet?

This topic belongs to a type of essay both difficult to execute and much appreciated by those who spend time marking student papers. We might call it the "from edge to center" approach, as it involves taking a relatively minor character, episode, or theme as the centerpiece or primary preoccupation your essay. The advantage of this type of approach is that few other students are likely to write the same essay (and never underestimate the importance of this if your reader is plowing doggedly through a large pile of papers, many of which noticeably echo one another), and it typically evinces a strong and comprehensive knowledge of the text on the writer's part. However, such essays are often difficult to write because of limited textual material. An essay focusing on Friar Lawrence, though, might well benefit from all the advantages without the risks; while he is indeed a relatively peripheral character, there is a great deal to say about Friar Lawrence and a strong, intractable central dilemma surrounding him. Are we invited to see Friar Lawrence as a figure of wisdom attempting to check the excesses of young love, or as a man whose decision-making powers are little better (or far worse, precisely because he does not have the excuse of youth) than the impetuous Romeo and Juliet?

Whichever way you lean, you will have to deal with the opposing viewpoint in your essay. So, for example, the Friar's first speech is a good example of his wisdom, and Shakespeare carefully crafts the Friar's view of the good and evil in all things to encourage respect and sympathy (2.3.1–30). In a similar vein, look for moments when the Friar seems to guide Romeo with grave responsibility (especially 2.6). Alternatively, assess his two principal decisions: marrying two plainly immature adolescents and the ill-fated poison scheme. Even though his intentions were good in both cases, critics have argued these blunders were likely to invoke exasperation or even contempt in early audiences (often citing, too, a possible anti-Catholic bias in the Friar's ineptitude). If you view the Friar negatively, however, you must not only judge him but assess his purpose within the play. Is he simply one more example of hotheadedness in a play that cautions against rashness, or are we to see him as more central even than this? For example, might his purpose be as a kind of moral lightning rod that conducts our frustration away from the two lovers to an older generation that fails its young charges?

Form and Genre

From the perspective of genre, *Romeo and Juliet* is a complex work (yet another way in which the play's reputation for simplicity is belied and subverted). It is, of course, a tragedy, but there are some important caveats that complicate any tidy definition of the term. First, the play does not treat the great and grand figures demanded of tragedy by Aristotelian decorum. Instead of a Macbeth or a Hamlet, a King Lear or a Julius

Caesar, the tragedy centers on the love life of two tempestuous teenagers. Today we might argue that tragedy is certainly no less powerful, and perhaps even more so if it represents the lives of ordinary people rather than the great and the good (certainly this seems to be the opinion of many filmmakers who rework Shakespeare's great tragedies into stories of ordinary folk. Yet in Shakespeare's time this was somewhat controversial. Sir Philip Sidney, one of the great poets of the age, lamented that plays that mingled kings and clowns together onstage were guilty of sullying the classical conventions of ancient drama. Yet many of the tragedies being written went even further in this vein, overlooking the kings altogether. A genre known as domestic tragedy became popular during Shakespeare's lifetime, and critics sometimes refer to *Romeo and Juliet* as an example of this type. However, the matter is not even as simple as labeling *Romeo and Juliet* as a certain type of tragedy. The play was written in the mid-1590s, a period in which Shakespeare appears to have been deep in thought about the limits and possibilities of genre. At roughly the same time he wrote *Romeo and Juliet,* Shakespeare composed two comedies that flirt with tragedy and mix ample darkness into the bright and festive tones of mirth. The first is *A Midsummer Night's Dream,* which in many ways seems to be almost a companion play to *Romeo and Juliet* (we will think about how to write an essay on this pairing of plays in the "Compare and Contrast" section). The second play is *The Merchant of Venice,* a comedy so stained with tragedy that its formulaic comic movements seem consciously artificial and hollow. At first glance, *Romeo and Juliet* might not appear to belong with these two experimental works, but on closer inspection the play has some puzzling generic qualities.

Sample Topic:

1. **Comedy:** What elements of comedy can be found in *Romeo and Juliet?*

Students pursuing this topic should certainly stand out from the crowd. It is another example of a paper topic with a built-in surprise factor. Just as an essay on Friar Lawrence (see the preceding "Character" section) impresses because it makes central a relatively marginal figure, this essay draws its surprise value, its uniqueness from reading against the grain, or moving in the opposite interpretive direction to that which a casual reader might migrate. Even a seasoned reader of student writing—someone who no doubt is well aware of the generic complexities of the play—will typically be impressed by a writer's desire to challenge the "obvious."

Such an essay might start by looking at the subject matter of the play. The theme of young lovers was not the traditional subject matter of classical tragedy, but it is the staple and mainstay of comedy. Everything about *Romeo and Juliet* up to a certain point in the play telegraphs comedy. The story of two young lovers kept apart by a harsh law or difficult parents is the essence of new comedy, the type of romantic comedy that dominated the 1590s. Look for other comic elements in the early scenes, especially characters. Look for comic tones, too, such as examples of lust-tinged talk. Then look for a turning point in the text, a moment where the forces of tragedy engulf the text. Critics cite 3.1 as just such a moment. What happens in this scene that has the power to turn the play around, so to speak? Think, too, of the frequent blurring of marriage and weddings (the principal "glue" of new comedy's resolutions) with funerals (definitive symbols of the destructive capacity of tragedy). Finally, think about ways in which the ending, despite the pitiful deaths of Romeo and Juliet, offers a faint vision of the comic feast, the coming together of characters and the community, which rounds off a typical Renaissance comedy.

Compare and Contrast Essays

We have already seen a number of parallels that might usefully be turned into compare and contrast essays. In particular, much of the material in the preceding "Character" section could be skillfully manipulated into a compare and contrast approach. For example, a writer might assess whether the play encourages us to see one of the lovers in a more admirable light than the other (Juliet is the more likely candidate here), or whether we are intended precisely to see them as alike (with all of the emasculating gender implications that contains for Romeo). Moreover, we could look at each or both of the characters and compare them at the start of the play to their characters as we see them at the close of the work. In what way(s) have they changed, if at all? Much of the material presented in the discussion of Romeo in the "Character" section invites a comparison with other men in the play, particularly Tybalt and/or Mercutio. The Nurse and the Friar seem made for comparison also. In addition, as the preceding "Genre and Form" section suggested, *Romeo and Juliet* is so distinct from Shakespeare's other great tragedies that a writer could turn to a contrast with any of those great plays, from *Hamlet* to *Othello.* A particular focal point for such essays could be the overriding tragic vision of the respective texts. What do we learn about or see of the world in each tragedy. For example, *Macbeth* arguably offers the bleakest tragic vision of all, summed up in Macbeth's terrifying summary of life as a tale told by an idiot that signifies nothing. You might think, too, about the role of the supernatural in *Macbeth,* the way in which the universe arguably conspires against Macbeth to ensure his fall. What is the tragic vision of *Romeo and Juliet?* Why does tragedy befall the young lovers? This is just one of many correlations you can draw among the works making up Shakespeare's canon.

Sample Topic:

1. **Comparing *Romeo and Juliet* to *A Midsummer Night's Dream:*** What is the relationship between these two plays? How do they explore the same material? Do their "conclusions" differ at all?

   To compare and/or contrast these two popular plays, the writer might begin by assessing the thematic continuity between the two plays. What do the two plays say about love? Think about the role of Rosaline in *Romeo and Juliet* alongside the shifting affections of the four Athenian lovers and the mercurial powers of Puck's love potion in *A Midsummer Night's Dream.* Study the darker elements of the forest world in the latter play that appear mirrored by the lighter elements of *Romeo and Juliet*'s tragic tale. Above all, closely read and study carefully the play performed by Bottom and his troupe at Theseus and Hippolyta's wedding. The play, for all intents and purposes, is *Romeo and Juliet* by another name. What does this say about love? What about comedy and tragedy? Are each of the plays different versions of the same story, one comic and one tragic? Do you agree? Or do these works complexly and disarmingly court comic and tragic sensibilities simultaneously?

Bibliography for *"Romeo and Juliet"*

Brook, Nicholas. *Shakespeare's Early Tragedies.* London: Methuen, 1968.

Callaghan, Dympna. *The Weyward Sisters: Shakespeare and Feminist Politics.* Oxford: Blackwell, 1994.

Forse, James H. *"Romeo and Juliet:* A postmodern Play?" *Popular Culture Review,* Summer; 20 (2), 2009: 59–67.

Khan, Coppelia. "Coming of Age in Verona." *Modern Language Studies,* 8.1 (spring 1978).

Knowles, Ronald. "Carnival and Death in *Romeo and Juliet:* A Bakhtinian Reading." *Shakespeare Survey,* 49 (1996).

Porter, Joseph. *Shakespeare's Mercutio: His History and Drama.* London: University of North Carolina Press, 1988.

TIMON OF ATHENS

READING TO WRITE

*T*IMON *OF Athens* is one of the strangest plays in Shakespeare's canon. Along with the oddities of *Love's Labour's Lost,* a comedy that in the last 200 lines suddenly lurches into unexpected and unparalleled tones of sadness and frustration, and arguably even more problematic than the so-called problem plays *All's Well That Ends Well* and *Measure for Measure, Timon of Athens* is a wild card subject for the essayist. Part of the play's legendary peculiarity no doubt stems from the ambiguous history of its composition. For a long time, scholars have disagreed over whether the play is co-authored by Shakespeare along with someone else—Thomas Middleton is the name typically offered as Shakespeare's writing partner here—or authored by Shakespeare but left in an unfinished state. To some, both of these suggestions have merit. There are many passages that to many do not read like Shakespeare's writing, and the work in its entirety feels as though important finishing touches had not been applied. Further, historians of the play reciting the origins and publication history of *Timon of Athens* often recall that it appears to have been added to the First Folio, the volume of Shakespeare's collected works assembled by several friends shortly after the dramatist's death, last minute and under circumstances that suggest this particular tragedy was not originally intended for inclusion. Perhaps, then, these good friends who wished to preserve Shakespeare's memory and art were at least a little reluctant to have *Timon of Athens* as part of that project. So the picture is a complicated one. If you are an avid reader of Shakespeare, you may want to join the debate on authorship, yet more practically, the question of whether the text is "finished" might be accessible to students writing an essay focusing on form and genre, reflecting on the quality of the play's tragic vision and whether it seems completely developed and effectively articulated by the play and its author(s).

Most of all, however, this information about the play's background will inform general essay writing on *Timon* by alerting the student to the somewhat bumpy terrain she is about to enter. The play never seems quite sure what it wants to be, and its central division can be cast in terms of complexity and simplicity. On the one hand, certain aspects of the play are strikingly simplistic (Timon loves all men and then he hates all men; *all* of Timon's aristocratic friends fail him). On the other hand, the play is ferociously ambitious in its morality and obsessive in its devotion to explicit philosophical debate. Also, as more recent commentators have written, the play is potentially subversive in its condemnation of the decadence and luxury-infused Jacobean economic life (Kahn 1987, for example). This is all intended to encourage the student not to reject *Timon of Athens* on the grounds of its idiosyncrasies or any perceived simplicity; rather, when these interpretive problems are turned into "puzzles" by the essay writer, the possibilities open up. The play's simplistic structure can serve as a form of support for the writer while he ventures productively deeper into the material.

To start with an exploration of the text, consider one of Timon's soliloquies. This passage comes at 4.1.1–41, as Timon departs for the wilderness.

> Let me look back upon thee. O thou wall,
> That girdlest in those wolves, dive in the earth,
> And fence not Athens! Matrons, turn incontinent!
> Obedience fail in children! slaves and fools,
> Pluck the grave wrinkled senate from the bench,
> And minister in their steads! to general filths
> Convert o' the instant, green virginity,
> Do 't in your parents' eyes! Bankrupts, hold fast;
> Rather than render back, out with your knives,
> And cut your trusters' throats! bound servants, steal!
> Large-handed robbers your grave masters are,
> And pill by law. Maid, to thy master's bed;
> Thy mistress is o' the brothel! Son of sixteen,

> pluck the lined crutch from thy old limping sire,
> With it beat out his brains! Piety, and fear,
> Religion to the gods, peace, justice, truth,
> Domestic awe, night-rest, and neighbourhood,
> Instruction, manners, mysteries, and trades,
> Degrees, observances, customs, and laws,
> Decline to your confounding contraries,
> And let confusion live! Plagues, incident to men,
> Your potent and infectious fevers heap
> On Athens, ripe for stroke! Thou cold sciatica,
> Cripple our senators, that their limbs may halt
> As lamely as their manners. Lust and liberty
> Creep in the minds and marrows of our youth,
> That 'gainst the stream of virtue they may strive,
> And drown themselves in riot! Itches, blains,
> Sow all the Athenian bosoms; and their crop
> Be general leprosy! Breath infect breath,
> at their society, as their friendship, may
> merely poison! Nothing I'll bear from thee,
> But nakedness, thou detestable town!
> Take thou that too, with multiplying bans!
> Timon will to the woods; where he shall find
> The unkindest beast more kinder than mankind.
> The gods confound—hear me, you good gods all—
> The Athenians both within and out that wall!
> And grant, as Timon grows, his hate may grow
> To the whole race of mankind, high and low! Amen.

The passage could be used in a number of essays: first, of course, character essays on Timon but also essays on themes such as friendship, money and materialism, and the Cynical philosophy underpinning the play's intellectual preoccupations.

From a narrative point of view, the passage marks the key spatial transition of the play as Timon leaves Athens for the wilderness that will become his last home and final resting place. In classic Shakespearean style, a character leaves the court or city in order to find some peace in the environs of nature. This is most commonly seen in the comedies and the employment of the "green world" space, a place where problems can be resolved free of the corruptions and problems of "civilization." The play's idea seems to be that Athens is mired in a general corruption, but, also typical of Shakespeare, the green world does not prove to be so very different. Just as the forest of Ardenne in *As You Like It* or Prospero's island in *The Tempest* turn out to be spaces filled with intrigue and power struggles, so Timon's ascetic life in the woods quickly fills with the same cursed wealth and empty flattery he is fleeing.

Yet Timon cannot know this as he bitterly departs Athens. The passage is a starkly angry one, of course, demanding an obvious and sharp contrast with the warm benevolence expressed by Timon at the beginning of the play. There is a notable riff on the theme of betrayal in the passage, moving from a desire to see individual Athenians betray their compatriots (for wives to commit adultery, slaves revolt against masters, bankrupts turn on creditors, for example), to a broader more abstract desire to see the social institutions of Athens dissolve (religion, manners, and customs). That his thinking should fixate on the issue of betrayal is, of course, entirely appropriate, and that he should wish to see the fabric of the society dissolve, with all its institutions and mores that failed to protect him, is equally fitting. From here, though, the anger spreads outward. Timon's more precise and thematically targeted visions lapse into a general, biblical-style curse on Athens, complete with itches and blights. The railing now has an unstoppable energy, and the passage ends with Timon's wish that his "hate may grow / To the whole race of mankind, high and low." This misanthropy has philosophical consequences in the play, linking Timon to the Cynical philosopher Apemantus, who will be discussed in greater depth later in the chapter, and showing that Timon, at least, believes his tragedy is an epic one rather than a local one of customs and manners.

In light of these issues and concerns, we can see how this passage fits nicely into work on Timon's character, the philosophical fabric of the play, and the formal quality of the play's tragedy. The lines also serve as a useful reference when discussing the play's parable of materialism and luxury when Timon tears off his clothes and rejects all Athenian possessions.

TOPICS AND STRATEGIES

Every essay requires a focus; you cannot write about everything in the play at once. In the section on how to write an essay, you will be presented with a number of ways of turning a focus into a thesis, observations into arguments. However, the starting point is nearly always finding an initial point of departure, making first observations. You can then seize on and develop the budding ideas you will have as you make your way through the play. By no means should you feel limited to these topics, however. Instead they can be viewed as triggering suggestions encouraging you to break out into your own critical directions.

Themes

This is another of Shakespeare's plays in which theme trumps character. Like *The Two Gentlemen of Verona* and *The Comedy of Errors* among the comedies, and *Titus Andronicus* from the tragedies, *Timon of Athens* is more concerned with discussing issues explicitly rather than finding diversion in such things as complex characters and psychological realism. However, these other plays all originate in the early years of Shakespeare's career, while *Timon* is among the latest works written by the author. Critics have been quick to note both the thinness of characterization and the particularly aggressive pursuit of thematic clarity, and to remark further that it is alone in these characteristics among Shakespeare's mature drama. I would contest this a little. The play has often been linked with *Coriolanus* because, among other similarities, it depicts a tragic hero (if we can call Timon this) out of tune with the world around him and unable to function in an environment where others do not share his simplistic, even naïve ideology. Yet Coriolanus can also be viewed as something of a one-dimensional character, too, a figure not invested with the same self-awareness as other Shakespearean tragic heroes. Furthermore, Leontes of *The Winter's Tale* could added to this list of characters that become bodies on the stage through which the dramatist explores ideas rather than individual minds. So we can begin to see an interest, potent but certainly not dominant, late in Shakespeare's career in composing powerful thematic structures at the expense of careful characterization. Perhaps the intricacies of the great tragic heroes had exhausted the dramatist's ability to meticulously create such figures, or perhaps situations rather than individuals came to compel him more. Perhaps, as has been suggested, in the case of *Timon of Athens*, it was the influence of a colleague on the work that pushed so strongly in this direction. Critics have argued that the play reflects Thomas Middleton's intense interest in the drama of money and capitalism. However it came to be, the play is almost a dramatic essay on money, greed, and economic systems. Other themes and currents are present, but by and large they flow out of the work's central preoccupation with how money circulates and how societies are structured by economic principles.

Sample Topics:

1. **Money:** What economic system does the play advocate?

This essay could be done in at least two primary ways. The first, we might call a historically centered approach to the theme of money in *Timon of Athens*. This would involve using research to provide a context for the play's apparent anxieties over materialism and greed. Exploring how Shakespeare's world was witnessing massive changes to the way wealth was distributed (the emergence of a middle class and a new mercantile elite, for example) and how it was spent (massive increases in opportunities for consumer spending and the systems of credit that support such spending) will allow you to make claims about the intellectual energy of the play, giving this strange work a sense of urgency in its time. Organizing such an essay can be a little difficult, and the question is always about how to balance close reading of the literary text and usage of the historical research. The simplest model, of course, is to keep the two separate, perhaps starting with a detailed exploration of the history and then proceeding into the text to show how Shakespeare adapts the world around him to the stage. A slightly more difficult model has the close reading and the historical material intermingling. This is probably the stronger model, but it requires quite meticulous organization at the prewriting stage. If in doubt, discuss such organizational dilemmas with your instructor before writing.

As for where to look for research, you will find chapters on finance and money in almost all historical overviews of the period. A more specialized text is Lisa Jardine's important work *Worldly Goods: A New History of the Renaissance* (W. W. Norton, 1998). Another strong text in the area is *The Social Life of Money in the English Past* (Cambridge University Press, 2006), by Deborah Valenze (though this text picks up the story of money in early modern England a few decades after *Timon of Athens* was written). Perhaps more germane still is *Theatre, Finance and Society in Early Modern England* by Theodore B. Leinwand (Cambridge University Press, 2006, part of the Cambridge Studies in Renaissance Literature and Culture series).

Of course, it is possible to write this essay without substantial emphasis on the historical moment. A more formalist approach to the issue of money would evaluate how the issue is handled in the play without too much concern for historical context. Either essay is fine, of course; you should choose your approach based on your own interests and the requirements of the paper you have been asked to write.

Returning to the text itself, then, let us outline a few key moments that demand the writer's attention. Obviously, 1.1 is loaded with material for use here. Evaluate the nature of Timon's "generosity," what it is he does and what, if anything, he expects or hope for in return. How do those around him view his behavior? You may certainly want to contrast the opulence of scene one with the intrusion of stark fiscal reality in 1.2 and 2.2 as we learn the illusory nature of Timon's wealth. How would you describe Timon's philosophy of money? How is it at odds with the economic system that actually exists in the play? What is the moral of Timon's discovery (and rejection) of gold in the forest? As you study, try to determine whether you think the play sides with Timon or not. Critics have with great results weighed the question of whether the play scorns Timon's fiscal irresponsibility more, less, or the same amount as it does the brutal economic system that surrounds him.

2. Friendship: In what ways may the play be less cynical on the issue of loyalty and friendship than Timon himself becomes?

The theme of friendship in the play grows directly out of the theme of money and asks "what effect does money have on our personal relationships with other people"? In many ways, of course, the play paints a gloomy picture in response to this inquiry. It has been pointed out quite movingly by some, for example, that Timon's optimistic understanding of what friendship means, the rights and responsibilities are attached that accompany it, is at the heart of his tragedy. Look at such moments as 1.2.17 and 1.2.94 to establish what Timon believes friendship entitles both himself and his friends to. This optimism continues as far as another moment worth considering in your paper, 2.2.168–74. Although by this point, of course, we have heard Flavius anticipating the failures of friendship (2.2.159–67). Certainly you will want to give much space in your essay to an account of how the play brilliantly realizes this failure in the parade of fair-weather friends seen in act 3.5 You may or may not want to also include Alcibiades's defense of his nameless friend in 3.6, and the consequences, both for himself and his friend, of the senators' refusal to hear his plea. Of course, 5.1 presents another opportunity to see the falsity of the Poet and the Painter, but this time Timon's worldview has been radically altered.

Some critics, however, encourage us to pay close attention to the behavior of the common citizenry in the play, the way in which they provide touching models of sympathy and devotion to Timon. Flavius is of particular interest here, but the motif is widespread in the play.

Characters

Theme dominates character in the play. The implication of this is an unusually large overlap between essays on character and essays on theme. For example, an essay on Apemantus is largely an essay on his brand of cynicism because he is little more than a mouthpiece for it (look for a discussion of this character in the "Philosophy and Ideas" section). Equally, an essay on Flavius is likely to become an essay on fidelity and faithfulness, something that Timon's steward seems to embody in the play. The character of Alcibiades is a little more difficult to define, but that complexity comes less in the form of psychological realism than it does in the simple difficulty of trying to identify what he represents within the symbolic framework of the play. You may want to explore him as something of a distorted mirror image of Timon, for example, someone out of tune with the city's morals and soon betrayed by Athenian callousness. Certainly by the end of the play, Alcibiades wants to make the connection between him and Timon as explicit as possible, and he claims his revenge, at least in part, in Timon's name too.

Furthermore, as has been noted frequently throughout the critical history of the play, even the central antagonist is hardly an especially complex figure. Nonetheless, he is a compelling presence and though the writer may not have to grapple with the metaphysical subtleties of a Hamlet-like soliloquy, there are nonetheless pressing questions surrounding Timon that need to be addressed.

Sample Topics:

1. **Timon:** How much should we pity Timon?

> We may be frustrated by Othello's gullibility, but we still pity him that his life is cursed with Iago and fear that we ourselves could also be undone by such evils in the world. Hamlet, of course, is a remarkable creature, and we are truly saddened that his young life ends as it does. We are unsettled, too, by the realizations he shares with us on his brief passage to tragedy. By contrast, Timon seems somewhat little, and his problems and flaws, frankly, a little trivial by comparison. In Hamlet we see ourselves reflected at a great distance, able to make out something of us as we look on him and his pain. With Timon, the mirror is embarrassingly close, and we see our everyday faults and mistakes in all their foolish ugliness. We can necessarily directly identify with Timon. Perhaps this is why many find him so annoying a presence—we see an unattractive part of ourselves or someone close to us in him and we project

resentment as a result. Alternatively, some may be frustrated and appalled by the kind of spending and materialism they see on all sides every day, and they may condemn Timon as just another weak culprit of such superficiality. Though 400 years divide us and the author(s) of *Timon of Athens*, then, the problems of the play and its central protagonist feel unquestionably contemporary. You should consider your feelings toward Timon before writing, then, thinking particularly on issues of sympathy, perhaps trying to distinguish any differences that may exist between how you view him and how the play views him. Once you have a sense of the character in these terms, you should return to the text in search of material for your paper. The play's first act, of course, gives us much, both in terms of what other characters say about Timon and what Timon himself says and does. Pay close attention to his gestures of largess and the commentary he provides on them. This first section will probably be quite lengthy, but you will eventually come to the moment when the illusion of wealth collapses. What do you make of Timon's reluctance to take responsibility for his actions (2.2.123–27)? His turn in the third act takes place quickly and dramatically. Assess his transformation from benevolence to misanthropy carefully, though. A telling moment to help with this pursuit occurs at 3.7. Act 4, of course, explores the embittered Timon's ongoing lamentations, but critics have asked a key question: is his response disproportionate? Many have taken this question as an effective starting point for their consideration of the play's second half. Do the apparently rather trivial events that lead to his ruin warrant the theatrical, stylized nature of his conduct in the second half of the play? Is he right to turn personal failings into universal hatred, blaming others for his own mistakes? Are the terms of these questions false, though? Is there a way to argue that what leads to Timon's ruin is by no means a trivial set of circumstances? Is Timon solely to blame at all? To help you move in this direction you can think about issues of grand social change or the alienation of the individual from the world in which he lives. We see this in Coriolanus, where the man bred to be nothing but a warrior and use nothing but a sword cannot function in the world of politics where a cloak must be used with the dagger. Also to consider, one final piece of text likely to enrich your paper is Timon's epitaph, read aloud at 5.4.72–79.

2. **Flavius:** How does Flavius function to soften the tragedy of the play?

Draw on material discussed in the "money and materialism" and "friendship" entries as part of the preceding "Themes" section. In addition, perform a close reading of his interactions with Timon at the end of 4.3. You may connect Flavius with the other servant depicted in such scenes as 3.4 and 4.2.

Philosophy and Ideas

The play flaunts its philosophical content, explicitly drawing on the ancient school of Cynic philosophy and making allusions to one of its chief practitioners, Diogenes. At the heart of both Cynic philosophy and *Timon of Athens* is a meditation on the individual's relationship to society. In the play, this is compounded by concerns over emergent capitalism, a force rapidly changing the early modern world.

The conversation about Cynical philosophy that follows is naturally limited by the space and scope of this chapter. For readers who would like to explore the ideas involved further, a few recent studies are worthwhile: *The Cynics: The Cynic Movement in Antiquity and Its Legacy*, edited by R. Bracht Branham and Marie-Odile Goulet-Caza (University of California Press, 2000); *Cynics*, by William Desmond (University of California Press, 2008); and *Diogenes the Cynic: The War Against the World*, by Luis E. Navia (Humanity Books, 2005). If you are looking to write an essay that treats Cynical philosophy in the play, consult one of these works or a comparable volume. Attempting such an essay armed with little more than a few loose scraps of information found online is unlikely to yield good results, putting the essay at risk of becoming a study of Apemantus or Timon with a few lines of philosophical trivia thrown in at the start.

Sample Topic:
1) **The Cynic philosophers:** How do the teachings and tenets of the Cynic philosophers appear in the play? What are we to make of the school's chief practitioner in the play, Apemantus?

The Cynics, broadly speaking, rejected social norms in favor of a spontaneous and ascetic life. Diogenes, the most celebrated adherent of Cynicism and whose association with dog imagery carries over into the play's representation of Apemantus, embraced a life of penury in order to live more naturally and "honestly." As the image of the dog suggests, Diogenes's aim was to achieve a life outside the limitations of human society and folly, to live with the integrity of an animal rather than the superficiality of a human. To my mind, the play presents an exaggerated and darkened version of Cynicism, but the author(s) might have suggested that society had moved a lot further in the wrong direction since Diogenes had rejected the comforts of Athens. As you begin to read a little into the actual ideas of Cynicism, do you agree that the playwright(s) distort the philosophy for dramatic effect and emphasis?

A discussion of Cynicism in the play might be framed around Timon's character in the second half of the play or the figure of Apemantus. Closely follow Apemantus' dialogue in the first act, characterizing his motivations and his ideas. His version of "grace" at 1.2.61 is often quoted and is succinctly illustrative of the man and what he stands for. You will likely also want to spend some time unpacking the conversation between Apemantus and Timon in 4.3. Finally, how do you fit Apemantus and the use of Cynical philosophy into the broader moral and intellectual movement of the play? Does the play agree wholly or only partly with the Cynical doctrines?

Form and Genre

The nature of Timon's individual flaws and tragedy, the failures of those around him and his bitter rejection of mankind, all allow us to characterize the formal and generic aspects of the play. Two useful questions may be asked as we talk about the tragic vision of *Timon of Athens*, and responses to both will draw on much of the material discussed previously in the chapter. So the task of this section, then, is to synthesize and slightly reformulate some of the material we have already highlighted in order to better address these formal questions. In addition, we can introduce some reflection on the end of the play and the shape of Athenian society after the curtain goes down.

Sample Topic:

1. **Tragedy:** To what extent is Timon's tragedy limited to his own experience? In other words, is the tragedy in this play only the size of one man? If not, how is it grander or more far reaching? Moreover, as many critics have asked, is Timon's response, his performance of the tragic hero in such dramatic fashion, warranted or disproportionate?

   Use the structure of the play to organize and guide your thinking here. When Timon embraces a kind of nihilistic contempt for humanity and perceives nothing but hollowness and infidelity in his fellow men, are we convinced by him or do we keep a respectful distance from the character? Look back to the first half of the play and ask yourself whether Timon's bitter views in the second half are justified. Certainly he is treated disrespectfully by his friends and their lack of charity is unkind, but hardly surprising or "evil" in a flamboyant, theatrical sense of the term. And, most important, do you feel that Timon's naivety is the true root of his misfortunes, rather than the behavior of others? Equally, critics have suggested that the loyal conduct of Flavius and other members of the serving class is a challenge to the unrelenting gloominess of Timon's final, troubled worldview. Do you agree?

   You may also want to reflect on the resolution of the play. Some critics feel that Alcibiades's purging of Athens, promised in the final lines of the play, should be viewed skeptically. Do you feel that Alcibiades has gained enough moral currency during the play to be viewed as a legitimate cure to Athens' ills, or do you sense that the play wants us to feel that the behavior witnessed in the play is hardly isolated to a few mean-spirited Athenians, and that human nature, the true "enemy" of Timon, is hardly likely to be mended by a few token punishments to be meted out after the play's close?

Compare and Contrast Essays

So starkly can Timon's behavior before his turn in act 3 be contrasted with his thinking after it, a character study of Timon is likely to look and feel like a compare and contrast essay. Equally, there is a natural division to be seen between the behavior of the servants and their masters in the play, and that, too, can be structured in the compare and contrast format. Apemantus and Timon have an interesting relationship in the second half of the play, and this also could be turned into an essay. Though they appear to have much in common at this point, a natural tension seems to continue between them. Why do you think this is? For those looking for an unexpected pairing, a tricky but promising essay could be made by comparing Timon to Alcibiades, Timon's fellow outcast, or, even more interestingly still, perhaps, to Alcibiades's nameless friend sentenced to death in 3.5.

Among other plays in Shakespeare's canon, *Timon of Athens* may be written about in conjunction with *King Lear,* most likely through some variation on the themes of generosity and giving. For another possible comparative character study, Timon, like Othello, could claim that he had loved not wisely but too well.

Sample Topics:

1. **Comparing *Timon of Athens* to *Coriolanus:*** To what extent are the two tragic protagonists alike? Can we discern any important differences?

   These two plays appear to have been written around the same time, and the two tragic protagonists may be said to mirror each other in some important features. When working with *Coriolanus,* establish how the tragic hero is "out of tune," how he is alien to his own culture. You may want to work the connection between Coriolanus's stubborn adherence to old-fashioned ideals of martial valor, and Timon's blinkered belief that his generosity will somehow be returned. Interesting parallels could be drawn, for example, between two structurally similar scenes: the parade of the citizens in conversation with Coriolanus as he attempts to win their support, and the parade of fair-weather friends through act 3 as Timon's servants attempt to secure financial support on their master's behalf. The scene, along with other broad parallels such as the characters' departure from their respective cities and their demise in the "wilderness" outside the city walls, seems to demand careful comparative work.

2. **Comparing *Timon of Athens* with *The Merchant of Venice*:** Paired together, do these two plays provide a coherent, anticapitalist commentary?

Critics often make the connection between these two plays and find a compelling relationship based on an apparent distrust of the new economic conditions to be seen in early modern Europe. You may find that what could be termed an anticapitalist motif is, in fact, nothing of the sort. Or you might feel that while the two plays meditate on the same theme, they arrive at different conclusions and assert different arguments. Obviously you will draw on the "money and materialism" entry in the preceding "Themes" section for some of your material on *Timon of Athens*, but for *The Merchant of Venice* pay close attention not only to the obvious anxieties about credit and lending witnessed in the main Shylock plot but also the crass materialism of the Christians in the play, most explicitly witnessed in Bassanio's gold-digging mission to wed Portia. Perhaps pairing the figures of Timon and Antonio will provide the hinge needed for the essay.

Bibliography for "*Timon of Athens*"

Barasch, Frances K. "Performing Apemantus in Shakespeare's *Timon of Athens*." *Acts of Criticism: Performance Matters in Shakespeare and His Contemporaries: Essays in Honor of James P. Lusardi.* Paul Nelsen and June Schlueter, eds. Madison, NJ: Fairleigh Dickinson UP, 2006: 111–25.

Dawson, Anthony. "Is Timon a Character?" *Shakespeare and Character: Theory, History, Performance, and Theatrical Persons.* Paul Yachnin and Jessica Slights, eds. Basingstoke, England: Palgrave Macmillan, 2009: 197–213.

Hadfield, Andrew. "*Timon of Athens* and Jacobean Politics." *Shakespeare Survey: An Annual Survey of Shakespeare Studies and Production,* 2003, 56: 215–26.

Jowett, John. "Middleton and Debt in *Timon of Athens.*" *Money and the Age of Shakespeare: Essays in New Economic Criticism.* Linda Woodbridge, ed. New York: Palgrave Macmillan, 2003: 219–37.

Kahn, Coppelia. "'Magic of Bounty': *Timon of Athens,* Jacobean Patronage, and Maternal Power." *Shakespeare Quarterly,* 38, 1987: 34–57.

Nutall, A. D. *Timon of Athens.* Harvester New Critical Introductions to Shakespeare. Hemel Hempstead, UK: Harvester Wheatsheaf, 1989.

TITUS ANDRONICUS

READING TO WRITE

*T*ITUS ANDRONICUS is an outrageous play, sometimes darkly funny, sometimes genuinely disturbing. Like a number of Shakespeare's early plays, it has often been dismissed as immature and inferior to his more sophisticated, later work. However, setting thoughts on quality aside, the play contains a number of powerful issues that resonate with modern audiences and provide strong, politically minded topics for the essay writer. The play is among Shakespeare's most dense with regard to gender studies and second only to *Othello* in providing material for papers that focus on race.

Amid the gloriously lurid antics of *Titus Andronicus*, then, is a thematically rich text that demands the writer strive for intellectual responses to a play that first and foremost demands emotional ones (disgust, shock, and guilty laughter, for example). For example, let us look at a passage from one of the memorably brutal episodes in *Titus Andronicus*. Here Titus readies himself to butcher Tamora's sons, Chiron and Demetrius, and turn them into a pie to feed their mother. Lavinia, the mute victim of the brothers' hideous crime of rape and mutilation earlier in the play, is standing by with a bowl to catch the blood that will be flowing.

> Come, come, Lavinia; look, thy foes are bound.
> Sir, stop their mouths, let them not speak to me;
> But let them hear what fearful words I utter.
> O villains, Chiron and Demetrius!
> Here stands the spring whom you have stain'd with mud,

This goodly summer with your winter mix'd.
You kill'd her husband, and for that vile fault
Two of her brothers were condemn'd to death,
My hand cut off and made a merry jest;
Both her sweet hands, her tongue, and that more dear
Than hands or tongue, her spotless chastity,
Inhuman traitors, you constrain'd and forced.
What would you say, if I should let you speak?
Villains, for shame you could not beg for grace.
Hark, wretches! how I mean to martyr you.
This one hand yet is left to cut your throats,
Whilst that Lavinia 'tween her stumps doth hold
The basin that receives your guilty blood.
You know your mother means to feast with me,
And calls herself Revenge, and thinks me mad:
Hark, villains! I will grind your bones to dust
And with your blood and it I'll make a paste,
And of the paste a coffin I will rear
And make two pasties of your shameful heads,
And bid that strumpet, your unhallow'd dam,
Like to the earth swallow her own increase.
This is the feast that I have bid her to,
And this the banquet she shall surfeit on;
For worse than Philomel you used my daughter,
And worse than Progne I will be revenged:
And now prepare your throats. Lavinia, come,
[He cuts their throats]
Receive the blood: and when that they are dead,
Let me go grind their bones to powder small
And with this hateful liquor temper it;
And in that paste let their vile heads be baked.
Come, come, be every one officious
To make this banquet; which I wish may prove
More stern and bloody than the Centaurs' feast.
So, now bring them in, for I'll play the cook,
And see them ready 'gainst their mother comes. (5.2.166–205)

First, thinking in terms of form or genre, the passage illuminates the production of grim humor that can be seen throughout *Titus Andronicus*. The scene depicted here is at once terrifying and absurd, something so hideous that we take the excesses as a grim cue for laughter. The style is familiar to fans of contemporary filmmaker Quentin Tarantino, whose *Pulp Fiction, Kill Bill,* and other films also use extreme excesses of violence as part of a dark comic palette. This episode, along with lines like "This one hand yet is left to cut your throats, / Whilst that Lavinia 'tween her stumps doth hold / The basin that receives your guilty blood" could play a part in an essay on comedy, genre, and violence. Equally, as critics of the play routinely note, this passage shows how Shakespeare's excess of violence is a calculated and conscious strategy. When Titus tells the brothers that "worse than Philomel you used my daughter, / And worse than Progne I will be revenged," we understand that one of Shakespeare's source stories for *Titus Andronicus,* the rape of Philomel and her subsequent revenge, is not simply being evoked but interrogated and perhaps even parodied for comic effect. The violence of that story—Philomel's tongue is cut off, but her hands remain; one rapist is baked in a pie, not two—is, as Titus himself tells us, extended in his own tale. This is a frequently noted point, but an examination of *Titus Andronicus* alongside Ovid's presentation of the tale in the *Metamorphoses* would take the issue beyond common observation and into the territory of a fascinatingly rich essay.

Next, it is vital to note Lavinia's role in this passage and to locate the seeds of an essay on her character. Note that her role here is passive: She holds the bowl to collect the blood, incapable of speech as she has been for much of the play. Lavinia has become an important focal point for gender critics looking to explore Shakespeare's representation of women and his incorporation of Renaissance ideals of femininity (chaste, obedient, and silent). While it is not clear that Lavinia is physically capable of playing a more active role in the revenge, there is something stereotypically domestic about holding the bowl and collecting the terrible ingredients (though it is Titus who will play cook). Notice at this point in the play how removed she seems from this key moment of action, a serving maid to her own revenge.

Note also how Lavinia is not the only one silenced in this scene. Critics have worked broadly with the theme of silence in the play. In such a theatrical, bombastic work, it is fascinating to note the frequent instances of forced silence, of not being able to perform and speak lines, or—in Lavinia's case—to have silence forced on her to the extent that even writing becomes a great physical challenge. The brothers' noticeable inability to respond, to speak, is in direct contrast to Titus, who assumes the right to speak for all involved in the passage, to perform the role of avenger uninterrupted by victims and villains alike.

TOPICS AND STRATEGIES

Every essay requires a focus; you cannot write about everything in the play at once. In the section on how to write an essay, you will be presented with a number of ways of turning a focus into a thesis, observations into arguments. However, the starting point is nearly always finding an initial point of departure, making first observations. You can then seize on and develop the budding ideas you will have as you make your way through the play. By no means should you feel limited to these topics, however. Instead they can be viewed as triggering suggestions encouraging you to break out into your own critical directions.

Themes

A number of strong themes are on offer in the play. Let us look, for example, at how we might turn the theme of "violence" into an essay. This kind of topic is an effective one (for the less confident writer, especially) because it sets the student a clear and focused pre-writing goal of identifying parts of the text that are marked by acts of violence— and, in *Titus Andronicus,* these are not subtle—and sequencing them in an outline. The trick, of course, is to go from a topic—violence in *Titus Andronicus*—to an argument. After all, it is not enough to say "*Titus Andronicus* is a very violent text." This much is obvious to anyone who has made it past the first scene of the play. So we need to arrive at an idea of the significance of the violence. This is, of course, the tricky part, but it is essential (and not quite as difficult as you might imagine). For example, we have already touched on the porous boundary between comedy and tragic horror in *Titus Andronicus.* Violence and, in particular, the gratuitously camp violence on display in this play, seems to be the chief bridge that connects these two generic tones and emotional responses. This insight could easily be formulated into an essay's thesis statement: The reader of *Titus Andronicus* cannot help but notice the extraordinary amount of brutal violence in the play. Shakespeare appears to use this violence, however, to create a particular species of tragicomedy, one that does not so much mix the forms of tragedy and comedy, the happy and the sad, but rather imbues the tragic with grim laughter and humor.

Alternatively, on the same topic and starting with the same observation, the thesis could recast as The reader of *Titus Andronicus* cannot help but notice the extraordinary amount of brutal violence in the play. Shakespeare appears to use this violence, however, at least in part, as a means of intensifying his treatment of gender in the play through the mutilation of Lavinia and the silence she is forced to assume. The violence of her attackers, the savage and simultaneous destruction of her body and spirit, contrasts sharply with Lavinia's enforced passivity after, creating an intense and extreme vision of the pathetic in order to illuminate the gender discourses Shakespeare wants his audience to explore. Notice that both these models of a thesis statement begin with the same observation and the same move to explain and substantiate why violence is featured so prominently in the play. For the first essay on violence, you would certainly want to explore 1.1 in considerable detail, as the two deaths in this sequence are vital to understanding the structure of the play and Titus's character, among other things. The violence against Lavinia as it appears in 2.4 would also, of course, be important. The chopping off of Titus's own hand is also representative—notice how the episode is a practical joke played by the devious Aaron and that he then assumes our role of audience member, laughing at the terrible excesses unraveling onstage (3.1). A more nuanced moment of violence is the "fly" scene (possibly useful if you want to escape the violent set pieces for a moment and work with a more low-key episode in the text [3.2]), while the extreme revenge of 5.2 provides yet another large and dramatic moment of violence.

Sample Topics:

1. **Rape:** In what ways can we suggest the rape of Lavinia is the central episode of *Titus Andronicus?* In what ways can we see the rape as a grotesque emblem of everyday female disenfranchisement?

You may wish to begin an essay on rape and female agency (or lack thereof) with some analysis of the action from 1.1. The word *rape* is actually used in the exchanges surrounding Saturninus's initial claim to Lavinia's hand in marriage, in fact. How does this first episode with Lavinia foreshadow the literal rape to come? You may want to include some consideration of 2.1 in which Chiron, Demetrius, and Aaron plot the crime. How do they talk about Lavinia? How is the female body imagined in this conversation? Another interesting exchange can be witnessed between Tamora and Lavinia in 2.3. How are issues of female chastity and sexuality treated in this exchange between two fundamentally different models of womanhood?

Of course, a major scene for the writer here will be 2.4, with Marcus's speech providing an interesting contrast to the terrible sight of poor Lavinia. If you choose to extend your essay out into the aftermath of the rape and its consequences for Lavinia, you will certainly be able to use the remarkable set-piece scene in which Lavinia, using a copy of Ovid's *Metamorphoses* and some creative writing strategies, articulates the crime that has befallen her and the vicious culprits responsible. You may also want to tie in the killing of Lavinia by her own father, a final act of male brutality against the suffering Lavinia. The rape is obviously a central moment in the play leaving many readers or audience members speechless after encountering the second act. They back away from the play and from class discussion, repulsed and disoriented by what they have read. As you write, do not lose sight of the enormously disturbing power of this scene. Why in the world does Shakespeare go to such extremes?

2. **Silence:** In what ways does *Titus Andronicus* contrast silence with performance?

As we have already seen with violence, it is relatively straight-forward to spot a noticeable pattern put forward by a text. However, the more difficult next step must be to apply mean-ing and importance to such an observation. We can certainly see numerous examples of silence in the text, but how could we theorize this motif? Well, we could focus on the issues of silence attached to Lavinia's position as a woman in a patriar-chal society. But there are enough examples of silence in the play that we could certainly extend the essay beyond Lavinia. We could suggest that in such a theatrical play, silence is set against performance and loud action—the mute juxtaposed with the raucous and chaotic. In addition to many of the moments discussed in the "rape" section above that witness a silent Lavinia (though notice, importantly, that at least one such moment of silence occurs in 1.1 before the rape), you could examine and include a variety of moments, from minor episodes of silencing (2.3.300, 5.2.165–204, for example) to more memorable ones such as Aaron's final punishment—the man who has done so much harm through his words is to be ignored by all as he slowly dies. Against all of this, are moments of extreme drama, excesses of speech and hyper-bolic action. As a writer, if you can explore this jarring rela-tionship between the hypervocal and the silent, you will likely articulate some powerful insights into the play.

Characters

The characters in *Titus Andronicus* are a little more developed and well rounded than in the earliest of Shakespeare's comedies, plays written at roughly the same stage in his career. In his first comedies Shakespeare tends to make his characters emblems of some problem or ideological position. Valentine and Proteus of *The Two Gentlemen of Verona* are shallow vessels that help to depict the inconstancies of men in love. Similarly, the Antipholi of *The Comedy of Errors* are simply bodies on the stage used by Shakespeare to explore the fragility of human iden-tity and self-consciousness. Shakespeare uses characters a little differ-ently here in his first tragedy. While Lavinia is essentially an emblem of idealized but horrifically persecuted femininity, and a character study of her would feature many if not all of the moments outlined in the preceding "Themes" section, she nonetheless resonates as a suffering individual in a way that the respective twins in *The Comedy of Errors*, for example, do not. Aaron, moreover, may be a caricature of evil, but his peculiar idiosyncrasies and racial identity make him far more interesting than the closely related figure of Don John in *Much Ado about Nothing* (and put him in the same league as later tragic villains Edmund from *King Lear* and Iago of *Othello*). With this in mind, then, although the behavior of these characters may sometimes make little sense (this is especially true, as we will see, for Titus), you should nonetheless approach them with the same eye for motivation and transformation as you would the shifting, multidimensional characters you will find in the later tragedies.

Sample Topics:

1. **Tamora:** If Lavinia represents the chaste and silent model of early modern womanhood, how does Tamora function within the symbolic framework of *Titus?*

A reasonable, though somewhat simplistic approach to this topic might frame a discussion of Tamora as the "bad woman" alongside Lavinia's "good woman." This is clearly inherent in the text, as we can see clearly in the exchange between the two women in 2.3. Again, think in terms of how the key Renaissance virtue of female chastity is discussed in this scene. In addition, through scenes in which Tamora forcefully and effectively speaks (such as 4.4.94), you can clearly contrast her with the mute Lavinia. You may see similarity or difference in the cleverness of the two women. Lavinia is resourceful when she communicates the details of the crime against her, while perhaps we might talk differently about the kind of cleverness we see from Tamora at moments such as 1.1.431–55. And, as a number of critics have done, you may wish to talk about Tamora as mother, particularly in 1.1. Here, perhaps, the good/bad dichotomy is complicated somewhat. After all, as has been observed often, the play essentially spins on a mother's love for her lost child and the revenge she pledges in his name. Surely something must be made of the fact that it is Tamora who literally personifies the figure of revenge as this revenge tragedy finally spirals out of (her) control.

2. **Aaron:** How important is Aaron's racial identity to understanding his character?

For modern audiences, Aaron is probably Shakespeare's most regrettable sketch of a minority character. The dramatist's portrait of Shylock the Jew in *The Merchant of Venice* is deeply rooted in centuries of stereotyping and anti-Semitism, and yet Shakespeare takes the trouble to invest him with some humanity and sympathetic hues. Othello, as we have seen in this volume, may be stereotypically naïve and prone to passionate violence, but the play amounts to a remarkably sophisticated examination of the complexities of racism and its effects on a character of color. Aaron has, of course, few redeeming features. He more resembles Christopher Marlowe's Ithamore from *The Jew of Malta,* a vicious African slave who competes with a vicious Jew to outdo each other in sadistic acts of villainy, than one of Shakespeare's infinitely more nuanced portraits of "otherness" later in his career.

Yet, again, the essay writer must reach for complexity where she apparently, at first glance, finds little. Just as we have seen Tamora's role as mother may complicate an essay on gender in the play, there are several aspects of Aaron's character that, though they by no means redeem him, make him far more interesting than the two dimensional sketch of evil he seems to be.

First, you may want to identify some of the more predictable aspects of his character. We see his ambition (2.1.10–25, for example) and the way in which his evil nature is linked directly to his racial identity by himself and others (2.3.72 and 3.1.200, for example). But some critics have suggested that Aaron's treatment of his own child is in stark contrast to Titus's killing of Mutius in 1.1. How does Aaron's devotion to his son fit into the play's thematic structure as a whole? Does it require us to view Aaron differently than we would without this detail in the play?

Next, although many of the things that Aaron himself says, and that others say about him, are noxiously racist, there are flashes of a kind of racial pride in Aaron that suggests the play's discourse on race may be a little more complicated than we first think. In particular, look at the passage 4.2.95–104, and the implications of Aaron's "Coal-black is better than another hue" (4.2.98). Moreover, and perhaps most compellingly, think about the ways in which Aaron represents both Shakespeare and us, the audience, in the play. He is a kind of trickster figure, but one determined to enjoy himself and, frankly, have a good laugh as he partially directs the proceedings of the play. The moment where Aaron is hidden from sight enjoying the bloody spectacle of Titus lopping off his own arm forces us to identify with him as a fellow voyeur and the engineer of our entertainment.

3. **Titus:** To what extent do we sympathize with our revenge hero?

The discussion of revenge tragedy found in the "Form and Genre" section that follows will also be of use to you here. However, start by asking yourself whether you sympathize with Titus or whether you find him from the beginning a fatally flawed creation. Many writers have convincingly suggested that Titus is designed to be an exaggeration of Roman honor and virtue, and that his unyielding devotion to the letter of Roman moral conduct is unpardonable after just the first scene. His conduct in 1.1, then, will deserve extended treatment, and you might even suggest that his murder of Lavinia in 5.3 tells us that Titus has learned nothing and made no progression during the bloody action of this play.

You may also want to consider Titus's view of himself as avenger and his treatment of Lavinia throughout the play, even during moments when he appears to be dedicated to her care and vengeance. The lines 3.1.218–32, for example, will be especially helpful and worth some detailed close reading.

Form and Genre

Typically, Shakespeare's career is loosely talked about as having two halves: the first ten years can be broadly characterized as devoted to comedies and histories, while the second half is focused on tragedies and, finally, the romances. *Titus Andronicus*, then, in some ways is thematically and generically out of place so early in Shakespeare's canon. In fact, it is quite out of place in Shakespeare's canon period. For me, it shows the early Shakespeare under the influence of bombastic older playwrights such as Thomas Kyd and Christopher Marlowe, emulating popular styles more than being faithful to his own nascent aesthetics. Shakespeare's writing of this play could have been commercially motivated, just as today we see Hollywood stars earning paychecks with big blockbusters and then working to maintain artistic credibility by working on more independently-minded films. None of this is intended to denigrate *Titus Andronicus*, but rather to stress simply that it is quite different from anything else Shakespeare has done before or will do after. There are two quite striking generic components to the play that would both make solid foundations for an essay. First, the play is clearly an example of a popular genre on the English stage called revenge tragedy. Related to generic issues surrounding revenge tragedy, we may want to give more attention to the incongruous power of comedy in *Titus Andronicus* too.

Sample Topics:

1. **Revenge tragedy:** In what ways does Shakespeare play with the conventions of revenge tragedy?

Playfulness in early modern English revenge tragedy is an expansive topic. The issues of self-awareness, of the role of satire, irony, and comedy, or of how conventions are being distorted and why are key questions to ask about all plays in this genre, not least of which *Titus Andronicus*. For example, we are told that later examples of the genre, such as Thomas Middleton's *The Revenger's Tragedy*, are ironic and aware of their own excesses, taking to absurd extremes a genre that even in its mildest form is usually a bloody burlesque of violence and sex. And yet, when we look at the first example of this genre on the English stage, Thomas Kyd's *The Spanish Tragedy,* many of the elements that are later talked about as pastiche and irony are already very much present. It may be all about degrees of excess, then, rather than degrees of "seriousness," and, as is routinely noted by critics, *Titus Andronicus* is nothing if not a meditation on excess and camp grotesqueries. So perhaps *Titus Andronicus* can be viewed as a parody of revenge tragedy, but this may be difficult to do without adequate reading in the genre. Nonetheless, it is vital to be aware that Shakespeare is writing here in a form that is popular, highly theatrical and notoriously devoted to shock value. It also has a common set of narrative conventions too. These conventions include a hero who is wronged, usually by someone in power (such as a duke or a king). The high status of the villain means that the wronged avenger cannot seek redress at court and must take matters into his own hands. At this point, some variation of a moral problem emerges. The avenger steps over the line and does more than he needs to do, kills more, hurts more, and, suddenly, we find that we cannot support him any longer. He has become "part of the problem," part of the corrupt society he had set out to cleanse. With this in mind, the avenger himself must almost always die, and there is traditionally a last-minute effort on the part of the play to suggest that, rid of hero and villain, a new, improved order can be established in the state.

To do convincing comparative work within the genre, you will need to do some additional reading (the two plays cited are particularly important examples of the genre). Still, you can do compelling genre work by staying simply within *Titus Andronicus* and asking questions about how the concept and ideology of revenge function in the play. For example, as is often observed, notice that the first pledge of vengeance comes not from the titular hero, but from Tamora—and thus the first "crime" of the play is committed by Titus himself. How does this influence our understanding of the revenge motif in the play? Consider how it is often said about this play that apparent opposites, on more sustained inspection, frequently collapse into each other. This appears to be true of the theme of revenge too. After all, Tamora believes that she is the avenger righting a wrong against her, while Titus refuses to acknowledge his killing of Tamora's son as a crime and therefore sees himself as the wronged party and thus Tamora's claims to vengeance do not register with him. It seems to be a matter of perception. Evaluate, then, how both sides of the revenge battle feel themselves to be "in the right" (though this is a particularly inappropriate term, given the monstrosities committed by each side, of course). In what other ways do these "sides" collapse into each other, and "good guys" and "bad guys" resemble one another?

Also, you may want to evaluate the kind of revenge hero Titus turns out to be. Review the section of characters for suggestions that may also be helpful in an essay here too. Think, also, about the role of the dramatist figure in this play. It is often the case in revenge tragedy that we find a figure representing the dramatist and/or the audience, designing or authoring the action of the play onstage and reveling in the ingenuity of the devices on display and the bloody outcomes of the plots deployed. Aaron is potentially one such figure in the play, but Titus is certainly another. In what ways does he fulfill this role? How effective is he as author? How much do you enjoy his script?

2. **Comedy:** What emerges from the grim juxtaposition of comedy and tragedy in the play?

Dark humor is nearly always a component of early-modern revenge tragedy, particularly the kind employed in *Titus Andronicus.* So while this may well be one aspect of a broader essay on revenge tragedy and the form of the play, the grim humor at work here could also be talked about more independently as part of the play's generic structure—it tries to get laughs at absolutely the most inappropriate of moments. I have made suggestions throughout as to the effect of comedy on the play. For example, when Aaron laughs at his sick joke on Titus, we too may guiltily chuckle as Titus, Marcus, and Lucius each argue for the right to chop off his own hand (though we likely stop laughing when Titus lops off his own hand—the joke has gone too far, and we possibly feel confused or even guilty). The use of laughter heightens our pleasure in the text and allies us with the villains of the piece. Other ways in which comedy could be used in an essay might be to explore how the absurd undercuts or challenges certain ideological norms. For example, the pathetic figure of Lavinia after the rape and the repeated jokes at the expense of her "stumps" potentially help the audience to see the absurdity of a patriarchal society that arbitrarily privileges men over women and sentences women to symbolically have their tongues and hands cut off to prevent speech and action.

Compare and Contrast Essays

Titus Andronicus is structured in a way that seems to demand attention to the compare and contrast options available. There are numerous parallels in the text, apparently deliberately employed to encourage questions about each component of the comparison. For example, as already noted, numerous critics have spent time on the opposition in the play between Romans and barbarians, but what emerges most strikingly from this mirroring is the similarities rather than differences between the Goths and their imperial enemy. Tamora could be effectively used in a compare and contrast essay with either Lavinia or Titus, while Aaron could likewise be placed in a paper alongside Titus. There are numerous more pairings for you to discover as you brainstorm in the prewriting stage.

Among other plays by Shakespeare, unexpected connections could be made between several early comedies. The use of a lurid style of farce in *Titus Andronicus*, for example, connects the play with *The Comedy of Errors* or perhaps even *The Merry Wives of Windsor*—both plays incorporate violence and excessive slapstick action, just as *Titus Andronicus* does. Perhaps an easier task lies in comparing our play to *The Taming of the Shrew*, a comedy that essentially foreshadows Shakespeare's portrait of

Lavinia through the abused and tortured figure of Kate. In that play, Kate is traded between husband to be and father, just as Lavinia is between Titus and Saturninus in *Titus Andronicus,* then physically abused by Petruccio in scenes that creep in the direction of Lavinia's mutilation, and finally symbolically silenced by her husband when her "shrewish" voice is replaced by one of subjugation and compliance. So, these two women cut similar figures, but, with this connection as a starting point, you could still choose to stress differences over similarities. For example, is it worth making something of the fact that Kate is abused by her husband rather than by two virtual strangers? With this line of thinking, you could emphasize the role of Titus here, too, as a man in her life who should be protecting her but is eventually an enemy. Perhaps most promisingly, however, you might craft your essay around issues of resistance. For example, though Lavinia begins her play far more passively than Kate, can we argue that the former is in the end the more active woman? Alternatively, another natural pairing to explore juxtaposes *Titus Andronicus* with *Hamlet.*

Sample Topics:

1. **Comparing *Titus Andronicus* to *Hamlet:*** How is revenge treated in these two plays? What do these apparently very different plays have in common?

   Both plays fall within the genre of revenge tragedy, so it will be helpful to look over the preceding "Form and Genre" section on the subgenre before outlining your essay. In many ways, these plays are at opposite ends of the spectrum of revenge tragedy, so a natural point of departure would be an essay focusing on differences. *Hamlet,* after all, is notoriously a revenge tragedy that cannot quite bring itself to be so for most of the play, while the multiplicity of revenges and crimes in *Titus Andronicus* means that blood is being spilled almost continuously from act 1 on. The two "heroes" of the plays seem like fundamentally different creations even though they are set much the same task: revenge. Alternatively, or as part of a more nuanced reflection on the relationship between the two texts, you could focus on potential areas of overlap. For example, it is often observed that Titus, before decisively cooking-up his final act of vengeance, experiences a period of delay in which he performs a number of strange and apparently quite ineffective acts of menace. The episode that leads to the execution of the innocent and hapless clown figure has caused particular puzzlement. There are similarities between the two central figure's perceived madness, too, and you may want to explore these echoes. Moreover, arguably, *Hamlet* finally seems to reject revenge as a viable means of justice. Can we say the same for *Titus Andronicus?*

2. **Comparing the play to Julie Taymor's 1999 film,** *Titus:* How does Taymor's film use *Titus Andronicus* to comment on late twentieth-century culture?

First, a warning. Taymor's film can to some be a disturbing adaptation of a disturbing play. If you are even somewhat sensitive to violent or graphic images, perhaps it is best to skip this film and essay topic altogether.

While the film contains extreme potentially startling representations of violence (the visual image of Lavinia after her rape and mutilation is straight out of modern horror cinematography), it is nonetheless an interesting response to an obscure Shakespearean work. One way of approaching the film *Titus* might be to view it as a commentary on contemporary culture, particularly its penchant for virtual violence through film, video games, music, and other media. Look, for example, at the role of the boy who eventually becomes young Lucius. In the opening scene, we watch him playing bloody war games on his kitchen table with ketchup and toy soldiers. After he is transported to the film's postmodern Rome, you may want to trace his movements and actions, thinking about ways in which he potentially becomes a surrogate of the audience. Think about the use of anachronistic details such as guns and motorbikes or the evocation of modern political imagery. Consider, as well, how the film evokes the techniques and commonplaces of numerous cinematic genres, from the Roman epic to the horror movie. If Rome is barbaric, does postmodern Western culture offer more difference or continuity?

Bibliography for *"Titus Andronicus"*

Antonucci, Barbara. "Romans versus Barbarians: Speaking the Language of the Empire in *Titus Andronicus." Identity, Otherness and Empire in Shakespeare's Rome*. Maria Del Sapio Garbero, ed. Surrey, England: Ashgate, 2009: 119–30.

Barker, Francis. "A Wilderness of Tigers: *Titus Andronicus,* Anthropology, and the Occlusion of Violence." *The Culture of Violence: Tragedy and History*. Chicago: Chicago University Press, 1993: 143–206.

Dickson, Lisa. "'High' Art and 'Low' Blows: *Titus Andronicus* and the Critical Language of Pain." *Shakespeare Bulletin: A Journal of Performance Criticism and Scholarship,* 26, 2008: 1–22.

Kahn, Coppélia. *The Roman Shakespeare: Warriors, Wounds, and Women*. New York: Routledge, 1997.

Robinson, Elaine L. *Shakespeare Attacks Bigotry: A Close Reading of Six Plays*. Jefferson, NC: McFarland, 2009.

Thompson, Ayanna. *Performing Race and Torture on the Early Modern Stage*. New York, NY: Routledge, 2008.

INDEX